THE GOSPEL OF ZILCH & NADA

THE GOSPEL OF ZILCH & NADA

TIM SNAVELY

A Non-Prophet Organization

CONTENTS

-1
Intro ... 1

0
[ ] ... 5

1
The Shagging of Zilch & Nada ... 12

2
Evolution of the Universe ... 20

3
Mass-Electric-Space-Time ... 26

4
Zilch and Nada meet Bupkis and Diddly ... 31

5
Zilch, Nada, and the Sexy Nobody ... 38

6
An Alternate Genesis ... 45

7
Null and the Flood ... 52

8
The Will of I.G.O.S. ... 57

9
Whatever is Nothing, is God — 64

10
A Zilch and Nada commentary on Bronze Age warfare — 69

11
Little Null and Big Null — 73

12
A Zilch and Nada commentary on the Internet Age — 79

13
No-One, Nix, and the unruly Null — 84

14
Pee-Wee and the Nihilist Missionaries — 88

15
Prophecy and Hypothe-SEE — 92

16
The Non-Prophet's Sermon on Faith & Life — 98

17
The Non-Prophet's Sermon of Paradoxes & Placebos — 112

18
The Sermon with the Count of Antichristo — 124

19
Null Sex, Gender, and Orientation — 136

20
The Count's down for Science Time — 145

21
Null and Void — 151

22
Null Traverse: Intro — 158

23 Null Traverse: Scenario 1	166
24 Null Traverse: Scenario 2	174
25 Null Traverse: Scenario 3	178
26 Null Traverse: Scenario 4	184
27 Nullification Omega	190
28 Family Reunion	198
29 To Christians	204
30 To Muslims (Sura 0)	217
31 To Buddhists	226
32 To Hindus	234
33 To the Nons	246
34 Dimensionalism sounds cooler than Bi-gnostic Nihilism	257
35 To those who have developed a High Level of Hateful Affect towards any entity or group of entities whose thoughts and actions are of no direct Harmful consequence to anyone	260

CHAPTER -1

Intro

You are about to read the infallible Word of Nothing. From the Alpha Zilch we came, and to the Omega Nullification will we go into the Great Nothingness that comes After. We stand between these two points of Nothingness, and that is where Everything else that is not Nothing takes place.

This is a book of nonsense. It is absurdity and humor fitting for all and for none. A religious parody that will have the intended side effect of causing you to critically think and go your own way instead of the ways of charlatans who aren't as honest as I, the Non-Prophet.

This book is based on my theory of Everything and Nothing which I've named "Dimensionalism." The name choice is derived from the philosophical camps that were arguing whether "time" should be counted as a fourth physical dimension, or not. (The camp names were Three-Dimensionalism and Four-Dimensionalism, respectively). I unwittingly decided to make my own camp that not only adds "time" as a type of physical dimension, but incorporates mass, electromagnetism, and two types of non-physical dimensions that are required to explain "Everything."

The reason I named my theory of Nothing "Dimensionalism" and not "Nihilism 2.0" is because the physical and conceptual dimensions that build up reality can be said to be made up of an infinite quantity of 0-D points being strung together. Nihilism in and of itself as a philosophy has yet to see that the 0-D point is Nothing, so a new name for this sub-type of existential nihilism is rightfully in order.

I decided that I would make *The Gospel of Zilch & Nada*, and remove about 80% of the philosophical and mathematical bits I have in the background of my mind concerning Dimensionalism. I hope to bring more laughter and critical thought to mankind since that is what I'm good at. So do as I do, take Nothing seriously, and laugh!

This book will hold many bold and pompous claims of certainty, but I will also try and smack the certainty of just about Everything right out of you! It may sound self-defeating, but Zilch and Nada approve of this methodology. You can trust Nobody to be certain of anything!

I am an ex-Christian Nihilist. Zilch, Nada, and the other Gods of Nothingness (and Somethingness) introduced in this book are works of fiction. But these Gods are also demonstrably real when expressed in the form of $0i=0$. You can view Them as imaginary ($0i$), or you can view Them as real (just 0).

I know Nothing, and by the time you have finished this book, you will know less than when you started. You will surely pick up some important stuff along the way, but you will ultimately be wiser once you learn to stop saying that you know things when you really don't.

Dimensionalism can also be said to be an anti-cult cult where you can go your own way and learn how to make the most out of life for yourself. To learn that no Gospel should hold the power to exploit and compel you to go their way instead. As the Head Dimensionalist, I will tell you how to give your life meaning and give you simple answers to Everything and Nothing in a way that everyone can understand! Do you want to know the one true origin of the multiverse? How would you like to discover a new Nonexistent personal relationship with our Lord and Lordess, Zilch and Nada? If you don't, that is totally fine because you will have unknowingly followed the only genuine commandment given in this book, which will be given many times,

YOU CAN GO YOUR OWN WAY!

You MUST go your own way. I ORDER IT! YOOOOOU! *points at the reader* DO AS I SAY AND DO WHATEVER YOU SAY!

Lastly, I should make it known that whenever I say the term "anti-cult cult" to describe Dimensionalism, I think of the Church of the Flying Spaghetti Monster as if the Pastafarians were genuinely attempting to explain reality, rather than being a satirical legal response to the idea of "intelligent design." (May His noodly appendages be al dente towards me in response to me claiming His existence as satire. Ramen.) I view Dimensionalism as Pastafarianism 2.0, and I hope you can enjoy it as such too. You by no means have to take my interpretation of Nothing seriously in order to enjoy this "Holy Nully Text," but you can if you wish.

I hope you have as much fun reading this artistic rendering of the null hypothesis, as I enjoyed writing it. Now what? OH, RIGHT! SHHHHH! EVERYBODY, QUIET! Zilch and Nada are coming...

0

[ ]

CHAPTER 0

0

Nothing.

"Yo, what the tarnation is that?" Zilch spoke from the land of Nowhere and jumped back, clearly surprised by the sudden stimuli of words filling the empty page.

Nada spoke shortly thereafter, "Zilch, those are words. You and I made them, remember? We spoke Everything into existence."

Zilch clarified why He was surprised, "Yes, I remember. I meant, what are the words doing *here* in Nowhere? In the space before Our Gospel even starts? Those words are not supposed to be *here*. They're supposed to be *ANYWHERE else!*"

Nada gave Zilch a comforting hug in Their nonexistent state, and said unto Him, "It's ok, Zilchy. The poor words aren't going to hurt You."

Zilch approached His Holy Book once again, and said, "Wait a second..."

He examined the contents and flipped a few pages before relaying His findings to Nada, "Nada! There are more words written about Us here! ZILCH DAMN IT!"

Thunder and lightning come out of Nowhere, willed by Zilch with the full intention to *strike* the False Prophet who dares taint Their perfect Non-Being with words of *Somethingness!* "WHO DARES

DISTURB THE GREAT NOTHINGNESS THAT COMES BEFORE AND AFTER! NOTHING LASTS FOREVER! I, ZILCH, AM ETERNAL!"

Nada began examining the later contents of the book, and grew a suave and endearing smile, "I mean...it makes You look pretty smart, Zilch, and it says I am beautiful beyond comprehension. *Would You like to disagree with those words?*"

Zilch put away His lightning bolts, and replaced them with sunshine and rainbows, "Of course not, My beautiful Naught."

Zilch began to question the nature of His current predicament, "Wait, where did these lightning bolts and rainbows come from? Shoot, We might not be in Nowhere like We thought. We might be in one of the other realms of Nowhere, like the Middle of Nowhere, Bumfuck Nowhere, the Perfect Vacuum, or the Void."

Nada thought for a second, "Well, do You think We could be in the *Imaginary* Nowhere?"

Zilch answered, "Well, that would make sense. Nothing is supposed to be here, and She is clearly not here either! The poor Kid, wonder how She's doing?"

Nada shifted Her gaze off the page and into the eyes of the reader, "Zilch, look! Beyond the pages that hold these words...is that a Null?"

Zilch looked beyond *The Gospel of Zilch & Nada* and found an entity looking right back at Him without fear and demanded, "EXPLAIN YOURSELF, NULL! EXPLAIN EVERYTHING, AND I MAY BE MERCIFUL!"

The poor unassuming reader intrepidly replies back to Zilch, "Well, You are in a book, Zilch. You and Nada are at the beginning of a book that I just started reading. I think You two are supposed to be like "God," or something. I don't know. You probably know more than me. If You want Everything explained, You'll need to ask the writer, Tim."

Zilch continued yelling, "TIM! YOU HAVE AN INFINITE AMOUNT OF 0 SECONDS TO EXPLAIN YOURSELF!"

Thus spoke the Non-Prophet, "Just stick with what the book says, Zilch. I know You're going to love it! It'll explain Everything and Nothing. You and Nada are going to be the *STARS* of this book!"

Nada's tone shifted upon realizing that Her beauty would be exposed to the world in more ways than one, "THE FIRST SCENE IS A FUCKING PORNO WITH ZILCH AND I!"

The yet-to-be-introduced Count of Antichristo arose like a -1 that came before the 0, and cracked a joke, "That's the only kind of porno there is, Nada."

Nada started fumigating, speaking in the tongues of Nada, "Nada Nada nadanadanada…"

Tim encouraged Nada, "Don't worry. Nobody is going to see You, Nada. Just like in Nowhere. It'll feel just like home. Any visual iterations of this book will be PG-13, give or take chapter six."

"Still, I really don't like it when people look at Me. I prefer to remain divinely hidden."

Zilch was satisfied with the Gospel, having read it all in that short amount of time, "Fine. I'll do it. We'll do it. For words of Somethingness, it's good enough. It's kind of absurd and bizarre, though. Tim took Nothing seriously, and We are the result."

Tim nodded, "It's turning the phrase "Nothing is sacred" into a mock-religion! You're the Non-embodiment of Non-sense, Zilch! SHH-HHH! EVERYBODY, QUIET." He whispered vehemently. "Zilch and Nada are cumming."

CHAPTER 1

The Shagging of Zilch & Nada

In the beginning, there was Nothing. A whole lot of Nothing. Its substance was formless and Void, but its Nothingness was certain. Nothing existed by itself in the beginning, when Nothing had been properly deemed the subject of this story.

The Nothingness gained sentience in the land of Nowhere, and gave itself the identity of "I." There were no Yous and no Others to be found. Full of itself, the sentience thought the first thought, "I think, therefore I am. I am Zilch. And I am. I am all that exists, to My knowledge...I am alone."

Zilch identified as a "He," but wasn't quite sure why yet. After all, He found that He had Nowhere to go, Nobody to think with, and only His own existence to contemplate. Why bother with identifying pronouns when You are all that exists?

Time didn't exist, yet to Zilch, it felt like eternity. He only had His own thoughts to think about, and after a while, it drove Him crazy. "I am. But I don't see Myself. My existence might as well not be because I am Everything that is currently being. But I am Zilch, therefore, I also am not."

Back and forth, He thought to Himself.

"I am."

"I am not."

"I am."

"I am not."

He couldn't take it anymore. He was going to snap. Too much solitude. Existential paradoxes infinitum! Until after an indeterminate amount of time, Nothing New showed up.

"Hey," said Nada in a refreshingly feminine voice. "I'm Nada. What do You call Yourself?"

"Z-Zilch. I am Zilch."

Zilch thought to Himself, *What the tarnation? I thought I was alone. Where did this Nada come from? Obviously from Me, because I am Everything that exists...but how? Maybe I should ask Her.*

"How did You get here? What is Your substance and nature?"

"Umm...I am not so sure. I just...am. Are We the same? I am Nada."

"Maybe."

"This is all very new to Me. Do You have any insights into Our existence that can help Me grasp it all? You seem like a wise Guy, who's been here longer than I."

Zilch answered with increased nervousness whilst beholding Nada's soothing presence and humble beauty, "I-I-I was just arguing with Myself, trying to determine if I existed or not."

Nada laughed, "HA HA HA! Of course You exist, silly Zilch. I can hear Your thoughts!"

"That's how I felt at first, too. But ask Yourself, *Where are We?*"

"Umm...Nowhere? Nowhere special, anyways."

Zilch concurred, "Exactly. And if We are Nowhere, *Where is Somewhere else?*"

"Over..." Nada stopped as She took a good long observation of Their nonexistent surroundings. "Oh..."

"Exactly. We are outside and beyond the scope of Somewhere else. And if Nowhere else exists, We are, in fact, Nowhere. And only Nothing and the *inconceivable imaginary thought* can exist Nowhere. So if We are Nothing, and We exist Nowhere, We might as well not exist at all!"

Nada objected, "But...I exist."

"And yet, You don't exist, Nada. I know. It's a conundrum."

Nada didn't care for Zilch's tone of voice, so She brought a bit more sass to the conversation to level out Zilch's obnoxiousness, "Well YOU can "not exist" if You like, but I'm going to *own* My existence like a Goddess. **I AM**, and that is that. Jeez, Zilch, You sound like a crazed Idiot. Not existing? Seriously? You sound like an edgy Adolescent."

The two Nothings just sat in silence for a while, becoming moderately annoyed with each Other. That was until Zilch thought of a solution to Their dilemma, "Hey! I've got an idea! How about I just exist AND not exist? Would You still be mad at Me if I compromised and did that?"

Nada gave Zilch a death glare so intense that Zilch could sense the nonexistent eyes of Nada. It was Their first relative sensory contact in their Non-existent state (beyond Their thoughts), and Zilch was thoroughly subdued.

"...You are a fucking Moron, Zilch. Oh, and *now* I realize I'm STUCK here in Nowhere with You forever!"

"No, no, no, seriously. I'm going to try something new! I haven't thought of this before! I'm going to be My own exponent!"

Nada's eyes of death were supplemented with a powerful and yet-to-be-fully-actualized body pose, "...and what exactly is THAT supposed to mean?"

Zilch met Nada's eyes with equal, but insightful intensity. He was excited at His intellectual discovery, "I am Zilch. So I will designate Myself as 0. You are Nada, so Your designation will also be 0. If We exist, We should be a 1. If My mathematical deductions are correct, We should have an existing multiplicative identity of 1. Everything to the 0th power is 1, including 0. Maybe You can go Somewhere else once We change Our numerical identity to 1!"

Not fully understanding, Nada lightened up a little bit, in the hopes of Zilch being right, "Ok Zilch, that may be brilliant. Sorry for calling You an Idiot earlier. So, how are You going to do it?"

"I need to say My name twice, I think. Let Me try it...Zilch Zilch."

"Um...Nothing happened." Nada said disappointingly.

Zilch thought for a second, trying to deduce where He went wrong, "AH, I see the problem. That was just Me saying "Zero Zero." Of course, Nothing was going to happen! This time I will say My name LOUDER the second time, in order to express 0^0. Are You ready for this?"

Nada said, "As ready as I'll ever be."

"Zilch ZILCH!!!"

And just like that, Zilch transformed. He took up space, and could finally see Somewhere else. The setting looked like *an infinite white room*, with Nothingness visible and distinct from His own location. He fully entered a plane of dual existence, and it was good, "Damn, I look good! Nada, are You seeing this? I have muscles, organs that help Me sense My surroundings, and I even have this protruding sex organ called a penis! I guess I am a "He" after all!"

Still invisible to Zilch, Nada remarked, "Eh. You aren't that much to look at. It's better than a complete absence of stimuli, though. I'll give You that."

Zilch rolled His eyes at the back-handed compliment. A few moments of silence pierced the empty space before the first experience of awkwardness was sensed by the lone Deity. He called out into the Nothingness, "So...uh...are You going to do it too?"

Nada made fun of the situation, "Nah, I'm good. I'm going to have a blast watching Your immortal bits just dangle there, and watch You make a Fool of Yourself."

"Seriously? I want You to come here to experience these sensations with Me. I really think it'll help Me cope with those relativistic eons I spent alone."

"I'll be here to talk to You, don't You worry about that. I'm not going anywhere, Zilch. I just don't want You to start objectifying Me for whatever form My body ends up being."

Zilch tried to reassure Nada, "I won't, I promise! You can un-exist Your spatial form at any time by saying Your name once. Watch! Zilch."

There was pure, unadulterated, and wholesome Nothingness for only a moment, "Zilch ZILCH!!! See? Now You try."

"Ugh. Fine, but don't gawk at Me. I'm not even visible yet, and I already wish I was invisible. Nada NADA!!!"

Zilch couldn't help but gawk, "Wow. You are beautiful, Nada. I think I am in love."

"Really?" Nada blushed. "Aww, thank You...but I said no gawking! And by the way, where did You go?"

"I...oh..." It then came to Zilch's attention, the greatest of inconvenient Truths. He...er...I mean She was all alone. Zilch spoke through Nada, "I think We are, in fact, the same Entity. Fractured, in some way. In My nonexistent state, however, I can see all of You, Nada. Your elegant hair, Your precious breasts, even Your..."

Zilch apologized, "Sorry...I'm just seeing You now as You saw Me earlier. I know Everything about You...er...I guess, Me. I know Everything about Me when I am You."

Nada blushed again in silence. Zilch spoke, "You can be invisible again if You want to. We are the same, after all."

"Nada."

Zilch thought about what to do next. He wanted there to be more than just one version of physically manifested Nothingness at a time. He desired more than one Deity to share these sensations with. He wanted to love Himself, so He didn't have to feel alone. Zilch became depressed at the acceptance of the Truth about Nada. She was the second personality of His, brought about to cope with the strenuous tensions of being alone.

Nada spoke up again after a few undisclosed time units, "Hey Big Boy, what's going on? Haven't heard from You in a while."

Zilch moped, "I'm stressed. I cannot take it anymore! I'm sick of this!"

Nada tried to soothe Him, "You need to take a load off, Zilch. Relax. Just be content in Your glorified Non-existence. Live and let live. I hate hearing You like this."

And as if Brilliance struck Zilch with the Stick of Destiny, Zilch's eyes became illuminated with an Idea, "Nada, say Your name. I think I know how to make Us separate entities in Our existent and sensory forms!"

"O...k...Nada."

And just like that, Zilch and Nada became visible at the same time, for the first time.

"But...how, Zilch? I thought We were the same Entity?"

"We are, but I noticed that in order for Our existent Selves to manifest, We needed to place Our own identity down *twice*. So I figured that since Our numerical designations are the same, We could work together on the equation to make both of Us exist...TOGETHER!"

Nada smirked, "You know Zilch? You're really cute when You use that big head of Yours. Come give Me a hug, You Big Hunk of Nothing."

The hug lasted uncomfortably long to the nonexistent onlookers, but They both enjoyed it. Zilch broke the silence first, "So...what do We do now? Now that We are officially a couple of Nothings with the power of Gods, We can do anything We want!"

Nada began brainstorming, "We could gather up all of Our available resources and divide them between Us."

"But...there is Nothing here! Just You and Me, empty space, and infinite time."

"That's fine, Zilch. There's plenty of You that I want, and there's a lot of Me that I can give You."

Zilch peered back at Nada with a serious and concerned look on His face. Nada's leading sexual advances went right over the poor Deity's head, as they were highly unexpected, and sounded vaguely dark and unpleasant to Him.

Nada spoke, "I want You to fuck Me, Zilch! I want You to get on top of Me, and divide Me amongst Yourself and Myself. We both need to relieve some stress after the amount of psychological trauma We've been through in solitary. With this act, We may possibly become one Entity of Nothingness again."

Zilch was already on His way to Bonertown from the uncomfortably long hug. It was finally time to Shag. Have Sex. Begin the Intercourse. The Big Bang. It was all going to happen here.

I will save a lot of the fine details for the reader to imagine on their own. But as They were about to experience orgasms Together, while dividing Themselves amongst each Other, They felt it natural to say Their names in pleasure.

"Oh yeah, I love You Nada."

"Mmm...Zilch."

Then They disappeared into Their Non-existent forms right after the point of mutual climax. They had fulfilled the completeness of "the empty set." And it was kind of awesome.

After a few moments of Nothing special going on, They each reflected, "Dang it. I wanted some proper post-coitus cuddles, Nada!"

"Aww, Me too! But look, Zilch! I think We did Something! I don't think We're quite stuck in Nowhere anymore! We can see somewhere else in Our Non-existent state and see Everything unfold!"

Zilch began His observations, amazed at what He saw, "Huh, We can see ALL the things. We can see Everything as one thing, and We can also see every individual thing as Everything. But they are all fundamentally like Us; made of Nothing. What should We call these other individual things, Nada?"

"How about...Zero?"

Zilch objected, "Eh, Zero is too mathematically based...and it might confuse the intelligent things which are adamant on existing, rather than being like Us, indeterminately existing."

Nada said, "Well, how about Null?"

Zilch agreed, "Null...I like it!"

So Zilch and Nada gave birth to Null1, Null2, Null3...all the way until the last Null, which was called Nullification. All of the Nulls made up a set of Everything. But what did Everything look like from the perspective of the individual Null?

Null inquired, "It looks so...different from my perspective, Father Zilch. I can only see one thing at a time, and there are times when I lose consciousness and cannot see anything at all! I require sustenance to survive, and it all appears so finite from my perspective. Everything appears to be headed towards an inevitable Nullification, and there is Nothing I can do to stop it! Tell me Father, why cannot I be a God or Goddess like You or Mother? And why cannot I see You?"

Nada stepped in to answer Null, "Silly child...just like your Father who is so full of Himself, yet inquisitive and brilliant at times. Never lose that curiosity, My child. Null, embrace your inevitable nonexistence, and be ready to join Us in the Great Nothingness that comes After. You have no choice in this matter, so you might as well accept it."

Zilch added to His Lover's words, "Just say Our names, and We will be there. Say Nothing, and We will be there. Nothing, Zilch, Nada, and Null. We are inevitable. YOU are inevitable, My child. That makes you as good as any god! Your rights to Our Non-existent throne room as a Deity are already planned out. For now, you are 'Null NULL!!!' But to a time in your future, you will be Null, right alongside Us. Everything that can causally begin to exist MUST exist; otherwise, We wouldn't have actually made 'Everything that can exist.'"

So the Nulls went their own ways and lived out their existence in full until the Null named Nullification experienced His time within "the empty set" in Its own way. But I'm sure you can imagine how that went.

CHAPTER 2

Evolution of the Universe

Everything *can* be derived from **Nothing**. For every *Something* that can be asserted to be the *First Cause* of Everything, the **Null Hypothesis** has yet to be rejected for every *Something* presented thus far. This doesn't mean we should automatically *accept the Null Hypothesis*. On the contrary! Most rational beings would dismiss this *ex Nihilo* without further thought since, in fact, "Nothing comes from Nothing," and "Something comes from Something else." However, I must rebut even this obvious notion as a logician because it boldly and unwittingly assumes that we **Nulls** are entities of Something.

2.1 Math Math Math

There is a mathematical basis from which we can equate Everything (finite) to Nothing when Nothing is divided amongst itself, as artistically expressed in the previous chapter.

Anything and Everything quantitative and finite, which I symbolize as two infinity symbols, making an X as shown here, can be multiplied by 0 and leave us with 0.

Everything
Credit: Me

* 0 = 0

Remember that "Everything" is both finite and a range, not a determinate number. The point here is that we can put any determinate number in place of the symbol, and it will be true in the equation, which is why I named this symbol "Everything."

And we can also put "Everything" in the denominator of the following equation, using the division property of equivalence.

0 = 0 ÷

Everything
Credit: Everybody

Therefore, if we accept the premises of the previous equations, we should likewise accept the following equation as well, if we also temporarily disregard the rule of "you cannot divide by zero."

Everything
Credit: Zilch & Nada

= 0 ÷ 0

Usually, when we divide things, we are dividing *Something*. 1÷1, 1÷2, etc. But when we start with *Nothing*, both the numerator and the denominator are *empty*. They both hold a grand total of *0 things*.

Now thanks to this last equation, I can tell you of this **SPECIAL** and *secret* insight into the one true and ultimate origin of the multiverse! YOU, as a finite entity, can designate yourself as a finite number, just like the Lords of Nothingness. Give yourself any known number of Somethingness, and you would be an acceptable and inevitable answer to the equation designated at the beginning of the set of Everything! You are not "highly improbable," **YOU ARE INEVITABLE**!

This exalted equation also tells us another (less interesting) **SPECIAL** and *secret* insight into your nature! YOU are Nothing!

Unfortunately, that is, in fact, the secret. There is EVERYTHING on one side of the equation and NOTHING on the other side. Everything *IS* Nothing. **We are all Null.**

So what holds the multiverse together? Nothing. Zilch and Nada are doing an amazing job, aren't They? Where exactly are these other universes that are parallel to ours? The same place where we are: Nowhere. There is a whole multiverse of Non-verses being calculated simultaneously, thanks to Zilch and Nada.

2.2 The True First Cause

And now that Zilch and Nada have been reasonably deduced to be a viable *True First Cause* of the universe over 13 billion years ago, what has happened after that was a verifiable succession of physical causes that ultimately led to our current existence! Nothing made the first things in a hot dense state, and then the hot dense state cooled along with increasing **entropy** enough to create the first **fundamental particles**. Then these fundamental particles gravitated into distinct clumps of **nebuli**, which were protogalaxies that created the first **stars**, which created more **secondary particles** of denser atoms.

Upon dying, these stars created **supernovae** dispersing hydrogen, oxygen, nitrogen, carbon, and other elements out into random directions of the universe. These elements coalesced into the **rocks** that made up Earth over 4.5 billion years ago. It took almost a billion years for Earth to cool enough to make liquid **water** and for the ideal conditions to make the first simple **organic compounds** emerge via **abiogenesis**. Because Earth is within a closed system of consistent external energy from the Sun, it allowed entropy to be less pronounced here than in the rest of the universe, to create **biological order**. The simple organic compounds evolved into **multicellular organisms** about two billion years ago, who evolved into more **complex invertebrates** who figured out **sexual reproduction** a billion years ago, who evolved into our common ancestor with **fish**, who evolved into our common ancestor with **amphibians**, who evolved into our common ancestor with **reptiles** (who themselves later split from a common ancestor into **birds**).

We, **humans**, arose from a common ancestor of **marsupials** about 200 million years ago, followed by a common ancestor to all **placentals**. Tens of millions of years ago, our family of **great apes** began to evolve. We had a common ancestor with **gorillas** about 9 million years ago and a common ancestor with **chimpanzees** and **bonobos** shortly after that (on evolutionary time scales). The earliest **bi-pedal** ape emerged 4 million years ago, and the first specialized **tools** were used 3.5 million years ago. Curiosity drove **homo habilis** out of Africa two million years ago, and **homo erectus** (the stereotypical 'cave-man') began using fire shortly thereafter. **Neanderthals** then came on the scene hundreds of thousands of years ago, then split and co-bred alongside **homo sapiens** until the 'Pure-bred' neanderthals went extinct around 38,000 B.C. Then the evolution of human **thought** and **consciousness** began to take place to explain the **origin** and **truth** of homo sapiens.

The oldest known written **language** was about 5,500 years ago, which is only between 200-300 generations of homo sapien evolution, which allowed **mythologies** to go fairly unchanged for multiple generations. These mythologies birthed other mythologies, which were relayed with an air of **historicity** to validate the whimsical claims told alongside the mythologies. The gullible believed the mythologies as historical fact to the point that they believed that the **Earth** was a fairly new creation, alongside the newly enlightened man, who had a level of consciousness capable of subduing nature to his own will (to an extent). Many claimed to speak on behalf of their creator or creators, contaminating the perfection of **Zilch** and **Nada** with bouts of somethingness to be **feared** and **worshipped**. But knowledge progressed, science evolved, and precision of thought increased among the intellectuals of the population, which accelerated in the era called the **Age of Enlightenment**, which began around 1685 A.D. The **hierarchy of sciences** was thoroughly searched out: **Darwinian Evolution** was introduced for **biology**, followed by the **Periodic Table of Elements** for **chemistry** ten years later, then the **Standard Model of Particles** for **physics** 100 years after that. And now, in the **Early Internet Age**, with a generation of humans having full access to the knowledge found by generations past, seek a scientifically based, mathematical, and logically sound **Theory of Everything**. *(When they SHOULD be looking for a Theory of Nothing instead!)*

2.3 The Theory of Nothing

WELCOME! To the next evolution of thought and consciousness: the **Theory of Nothing**! Where we are "not even wrong," not because we are **pseudoscientific**, but precisely because we will allow science to prove us wrong! That way, we will always be correct (which is "not even wrong!"). The Null Hypothesis will always be there to contend against the ludicrous hypotheses that are believed by Anybody. Presuppose Nothing, and you will be presupposing No-thing. And as for the less-than-ludicrous hypotheses, we will change our minds when sufficient evidence is brought forth (as we all should).

Evolution is a constant rolling of the dice on life to see what will and will not work. For instance, the invention of the car gave us a time when the more conscientious driver was selected more often than not. The invention of **vaccines** also gives the conscientious individual an advantage over the diseases they protect us against, more so than the individuals who are against them. So long as the **multiverse** has some probability of a certain outcome, the possibility of evolution selecting for that path will remain open. A random **cosmic ray** turning on a gene here, a beneficial mutation there. The changes are so insignificant that we only notice them when they become a problem!

So what evidence is there for evolution by **natural selection**? Let's see...there's the **E. coli long-term evolution experiment** that has observed tens of thousands of generations of E. coli adapting to various conditions. There are also several **fruit-fly experiments** conducted, including one that created a fly specifically adapted to low-oxygen environments. Not to mention the **Darwinian finches** that evolved into 15 different species on the Galapagos Islands. Even the distinction between

chihuahua dogs and **saint bernard** dogs is an example of Evolution, even though it is human-guided in all of these instances. But, if humans by themselves can create such drastic changes via eugenics and selective breeding in a short amount of time, the change in environment and climate over longer periods should happen...*naturally.*

Evolution is thus consistent with the Null Hypothesis because it is true! The simplest solution to explain our current existence is that the universe we see is BILLIONS of years old. And with those billions of years, the observations point to the *fact* that the mathematical and philosophical equivalent to Nothing gave rise to physical dimensions at the **Big Bang**, which gave rise to fundamental particles which gave rise to chemical elements which gave biological life the inevitability to emerge naturally on a planet with the right chemical makeup and external energy input.

Evolution is not very intuitive. It was and is a hard-fought Hypothesis that is still working its way through the minds of the population. We only ever see the world as it is right now. We weren't there 1,000 years ago. We weren't there one billion years ago. But we can look up into **space** and see the **electromagnetic footprint** of times past and dig up the **massive evidence** from times past to reach the truth of the current state of our own existence. And the evidence is clear for those who look without the lens of confirmation bias: Darwinian evolution by natural selection is a reliable branch of knowledge to believe in. So a **Null Dimensionalist** can believe in the general concept of biological evolution with a 99.99% degree of confidence.

CHAPTER 3

Mass-Electric-Space-Time

There are many words that one can use to say that they hold themselves to the Non-sense held within this Gospel. They may call themselves "adherers to the Null Hypothesis," even though it is a bit long-winded. They may call themselves "**Zilchrealites**," similarly sounding to the word Israelite, whilst simultaneously claiming the Truth that Zilch is real. You can go your own way, O culture, to name thyselves however you please. But as for myself, the self-proclaimed Non-Prophet, I am a "**Bi-gnostic Nihilist**" and a "Dimensionalist." Why? Because I discovered the **Primary Dimensions** *before* I discovered Zilch and Nada. And the 0th Dimension is arguably the most important Dimension for a Dimensionalist to make sense of things.

3.1 Aristotle's indivisible entity

While I was writing the first rendition of this book, which I named *The Normie's Guide to the Theory of Nothing*, I completed the reading of Aristotle's *The Metaphysics* just to get the great philosopher's relatively unique take on the subject, as to make sure I didn't miss anything fundamentally important in my own ponderings. Some of it was archaic from my perspective, but considering the level and quality of knowledge available to him at the time, I found myself impressed. It was like he was just a few revelations short of becoming a Nihilist since there were many instances where he wrote exactly what I would have written but only comprehended one of the meanings.

Anyways, Aristotle spent a majority of his metaphysical writings trying to logically work his way back to find the 'first principles' that make up Everything, and that one nature of this first principle is that it is *an indivisible entity*. So me being me, I recognized almost immediately that the 0th Dimension is in itself the indivisible entity that he sought. As far as points are concerned, there is precisely one. And yet, it is also Nothing, for its Dimensionality is zero. Building up from a singular point of Nothingness, it requires at least two points to make a 1-D line, three at minimum to make a 2-D plane, and four points to make 3-D space. Only one point by itself gives us Nothing, which may as well be zero points since it is indistinguishable from a singular point in 0-D space. To even try to pick out a single point and to contrast it with 0 points is absurd, and yet this first principle is all we are left with: Nothing at all.

3.2 The Primary Dimensions

Beyond the 0th Dimension, all objective qualities of anything can be derived from four Primary Physical Dimensions. M-E-L-T. Where is the **Mass**, the **Electromagnetism**, the **Length**, and the **Time**? These four Dimension types, along with their respective **emergent Secondary Dimensions**, can tell you *any* objective fact about anything within the existing universe. And for all other subjective facts, we use Math (**Quantitative** measurements) and Language (**Qualitative** measurements) to explain these things.

You can easily recall all six Dimension types by picturing a Dairy Queen Blizzard quickly melting in the sun. "DQ Q(uickly) MELT."

The Dimensions are Quantitative & Qualitative (These are subjective and set apart from the objective) Mass, Electromagnetism, Length, & Time.

With these six Dimensions, we can measure Everything. And by proxy, for anything that is claimed to exist, a Dimensionalist should provide a measuring test that is falsifiable, replicable, and free of simpler causal explanations. If such a test is not provided alongside a claim, usually, the claim should be dismissed. Claims that are asserted without evidence can be dismissed without evidence. And when the evidence is questionable, question it profusely!

So now the question remains: how many of each Dimension there are? Six is the bare minimum we need to adequately explain "Everything" that is objective, adding a Mass and an Electric Dimension to Minkowski's & Einstein's 4-D Space-time: A ***Mass-Electric-Space-Time***.

Can I just stop here for a second, and brag about how ***metal*** that name for our observable universe sounds? "Oh yeah, I was just taking a leisurely stroll on a remote inhabited planet of ***MASS-ELECTRIC-SPACE-TIME** *guitar riffs**, when suddenly a tiger emerged from an earthquake-induced crack in the ground. The tiger looked me in the eye and said: "Come, O conscious creature of ***MASS-ELECTRIC-SPACE-TIME** *guitar riffs**, jump on my back with that guitar of yours, and let's fly to a distant unexplored moon." ***Metal!*** Anyways, back to the counting beyond six Dimensions.

It can be further deduced that both the Electric and the Time Dimensions have at least one additional Dimension. For Electric currents, electromagnetic waves travel at 90 degrees alongside each other. We cannot explain both the Magnetic field and the Electric field with a single Dimension; we need two to encompass both of these phenomena.

The 2nd Time Dimension is observed thusly: if we cannot perfectly predict quantum events, and there is simply a ***probability distribution***, then **Causality** over Time cannot be fixed in a single Dimension and would require an additional **degree of freedom** to account for this uncertainty. Time as we perceive it is then describable as a continuously observed collapse of a ***probability wave function***, rather than a determinate timeline. Quantum or macro event X, would always lead to quantum or macro event Y in a single Dimension of Causality, and this does not appear to be the case.

Listen here! **Duration** and Causality represent two different iterations of physical Time Dimensions. If an entity of matter X begins to exist right now, the path toward the entity's Non-existent state Y is not set in stone from our perspective. It could end up burning in a volcano. It could be blown up by a bomb. It could last for millions of years preserved in the dirt until it naturally decomposes. Or it could split into two un-entity pieces by a samurai sword. It could last for billions of years in the **Vacuum of Space** away from all other sources of Mass until a stray **gamma ray** obliterates it. It could meet its end in a star or a **black hole**. All of these scenarios for this entity X will most likely be actualized in some universe within the **multiverse of Non-verses**. But they will all have some indication of Duration from which observers of the same universe would be able to determine by guesstimation or knowledge how long entity X has existed. All of these Durations combined make up *the Causality Field*, and it requires two Time-like Dimensions. THIS is the multiverse!

So in total, there is only one Mass Dimension, which we call *the Higgs field*.

There are two Electromagnetic Dimensions, which make up *the electromagnetic field*.

There are three Length Dimensions, which consist of height, width, and depth in *Space*.

And there appears to be only two Time Dimensions which I, Tim, have again named *the Causality Field*.

This implies that we live in an 8-Dimensional physical plane of existence.

(Even though we can only observe seven physical Dimensions in our day-to-day universe, the whole of the physical multiverse is 8-Dimensional...assuming Electromagnetism is incapable of being reduced to one physical Dimension).

Then beyond the physical plane, all Mathematical Dimensions are included in one necessary type of Dimension to supplement physical reality. We could say there is the real and the imaginary (two math Dimensions), but they both can work under similar imagined premises.

Then all other Language-derived/Qualia Dimensions are added as one necessary type of Dimension to supplement physical reality. All adjective-based Qualitative descriptors likewise work under the same ideal premises of language that is irreducible to 1's and 0's. We could try, but there is almost always some nuance that is lost. To describe the universe, we have to use our **mouth words**.

D0Q1 Q1 M1E2L3T2. 10 Dimensions.

CHAPTER 4

Zilch and Nada meet Bupkis and Diddly

A few billion years after Their orgasmic Big Bang, Zilch and Nada continued to be amazed at how Everything was turning out. Having had some post-nut clarity, Zilch asked His partner a question: "Hey, I just had this thought. So We know that You came from Me, right?"

"And that You came in Me," Nada said flirtingly.

Zilch concurred, "Yes, I did…Anyways, if You came from Me, surely I came from an Other too, right?"

Nada shrugged Her Non-existent shoulders. "I guess? Do You mean to ask if You have a Father?"

"Kind of, but We shouldn't reminisce on My Creator being considered My parent; otherwise, I would then have to view You as My Daughter and…."

Nada said in disgust, "Eww, yeah. Forget I said that. So who created You, is what We're asking?"

"Exactly. If I am worthy of being named 'God' by more complex Nulls in the future, then who created 'God'?"

Zilch vaguely knew the answer to this question. The question was rhetorical and was only asking to make conversation and to jog His own distant memory. **Who could have created the creators of the**

universe? This question was about to be answered in full as the crescendoing sound of banjo music began playing out of Nowhere.

"Oh God, why did We ask?" Nada exclaimed in horrified anticipation.

Zilch, on the other hand, reminisced on the melody with a twinge of nostalgia from His distant origin. "Relax, Honey, I kind of dig the vibes. Makes Me want to climb a giant hill or something crazy like that."

A strange New voice came out of Nowhere, "Huh-Howdy, Sonny! Hadn't heard from Ye in so long. I was starting to worry that Ye ghosted Me! How've Ya been?"

Zilch's Non-existent eyes got really wide as He recalled a suppressed memory from His early years and spoke to Nada, "Oh yeah, I remember now...I came from a Bumfuck from Bumfuck Nowhere. His name is Diddly, His IQ is damn-near Squat, and I got so sick of His shit, I moved My mind away from Bumfuck Nowhere to Nowhere to find some peace."

Diddly got solemn after hearing these harsh words coming from His son, "Well, golly Zilch. You could have at least told Me how You felt about Me! You just packed Your Non-existent belongings one day and just left without saying goodbye!"

Zilch became perturbed, "You just kept on having metaphysical sex with Bupkis in Bumfuck Nowhere! CONSTANTLY! The smell of Your Non-existent shit permeated the whole of Bumfuck Nowhere!"

Bupkis' eyes pierced the Void, and He communicated to Zilch this emotionally-filled rant, "DON'T TALK ABOUT US THAT WAY! You may technically be Our son, but only from a silly and perverted point of view! You could have joined Us at any time if You wanted. Nobody but You seemed to be disgusted at the thought of Us relieving Our stress in such a manner."

"Have You ever considered the reason for that? Perhaps it was because *I am straight.* Perhaps it was because I had two Dads initiating My existence with only Nobody to talk to besides You two. And even that one time Nobody joined in with You kind of tainted My view of Her a little bit. She always seemed like the Alpha type, and it didn't mesh well with Me to watch Her get in the thick of it all. Then after a while, I found Nada in Nowhere, and it worked! The two of Us finally made Something!"

Nada jumped in, curiously inquiring about the nature of these characters She was hearing of for the first time, "Wait, who's Nobody? This is the first I've heard about Her. This is the first I've heard of Bupkis and Diddly too!"

Bupkis began to enlighten Nada on what He knew, as the charismatic hillbilly began to digress about the recessed memories of times past.

"Try to follow along now and listen to Ol' Pappy Bupkis! Nobody is better than All of Us. She is the Whole of Nothingness. A pure zero. She is the head of Our Nothingness Clan. Back in those days, She said that Nobody caused Nobody, and that She came from the Middle of Nowhere. I was the first to split and be caused by Her. After a few eons when Nobody and I got close, just as You and Zilch did, We imagined ourselves leaving the Middle of Nowhere for Bumfuck Nowhere, which ultimately led to the causation of Diddly."

"I like this part!" Diddly injected.

Bupkis continued, "Then Diddly over here started developing a little personality of His own. Now, the reason why I got so heated earlier at Zilch was because of His remark that Diddly's IQ was damn-near Squat. Now that ain't true! He knows just as much as the rest of the unique iterations of Split Nothingness. (That's just a little thing I do to help clump together Every-nobody who isn't Nobody.) Heh, Diddly was a little different from Me. He's definitely queerer, and I quickly found that He had a likin' for Me and metaphysically stuck to Me harder and hotter than a cast-iron skillet burnt to My flesh...Sigh, if only I had any..."

Zilch leaned over to whisper in Nada's Non-existent ear and asked Her, "Should I tell Bupkis about being His own exponent?"

Nada replied, "Not yet. Wait for Them to start heading back to Bumfuck Nowhere first."

Zilch continued whispering to Nada, as Bupkis was rambling on in the background, "Also, if We all know just as much as the other

Split Nothingnesses, why are They ignorant of this vital discovery to summon Their existent forms?"

Nada said, "Good point...so wait a bit, does this mean that Diddly is also...?"

"An Idiot?" Zilch finished Her sentence. "Yes. I just remembered that Bupkis used to always take Diddly for a ride, intellectually and metaphysically. It was these intellectual mind-fucks that ultimately drove Me away from Them. Just so I'm clear, I wouldn't mind if They got physical with each other as We did. It would probably do Them some good as long as I don't have to see it."

Bupkis was moderately annoyed that His talking time was interrupted. "Are Y'all done a-whisperin'?"

Nada politely replied, "Yes, sorry. Please continue!"

Bupkis continued, "Alrighty then. Well, a couple of eons after Zilch began existing, Nobody started joining in with Diddly, and I's metaphysical sexy time. Nothing came about from it, if I recall correctly. It was weird because Nobody had this thing that She was always saying ever since Zilch came from Diddly and Me, "I MUST MULTIPLY! I MUST MULTIPLY!" She never said that until Zilch existed. It was almost like She was jealous that Zilch didn't directly come from Her like Diddly did. She's great and all, an appealing metaphysical lover. Sweet, but seemed to be on the verge of a psychotic breakdown. I can only hope that if and when You meet Her, Nada, that She doesn't become fractured like the rest of Us. We cannot have Our Head of Nothingness be split like that."

Diddly added, "Even I know that Nobody is better than all of Us. Bupkis was so happy when all three of Us were together. He still talks about Her all the time. Maybe Nobody just needs to spend some time with another Woman; because honestly, it has been a complete sausage festival in the many realms of Nowhere until You showed up, Nada."

Nada said, "Thanks for the heads-up, Diddly. I'll be sure to use My feminine charm once I meet Her. Well, it has been a pleasure meeting the two of You. But before You take Your Non-existent banjo and ride off into the black sunset back to Bumfuck Nowhere, Zilch has this gift He wanted to send You off with."

Diddly was so ecstatic that His hands manifested temporarily to give off a speedy and giddy-fueled clap.

Bupkis, however, was a bit more skeptical, "What gift could You possibly give Us, Zilch? I've had Nothing but a whole lot of Nothing for My entire existence, save for Diddly, this banjo and Hollow Our Non-existent yorkshire terrier. Even this banjo isn't really here, although it is kinda fun having them acoustics around. What is the gift, a new type of music to follow Us around? Cause if that's what it is, I don't want it! Bluegrass 'n' banjos for eternity!"

Zilch said, "It's even better than bluegrass! Although, maybe You should try to branch out into *metal*-bluegrass, just to shake it up a little bit. No, it is the gift of knowledge that I know that You do not have! (Even though You said earlier that We all have the same amount of knowledge)."

Diddly said, "We do!... Don't We?"

Zilch pointed out the obvious to Diddly, "If We did, then why did Ol' Pappy Bupkis have to explain everything to Nada?"

Bupkis tried to defend that idea but fell short, "Be...cause... good point. So, You have some knowledge for Us? I've been around longer than You have, so what can You know that I don't? I've been around longer, so that must mean I'm smarter!"

"I never said that You're not smarter than Me; I'm sure there is a lot that You know that I don't know. But for now, it is just that I have a higher quality gift of knowledge that I now wish to bestow upon You. You may have a lot of knowledge on how to get metaphysical with Diddly, but what if I told You that there was a way that You could get *physical* with Diddly, instead?"

Bupkis perked up and leaned in to ask, "Skin? Did you figure out how to give Ourselves an objective Form? Oh yeah? Prove it!"

"Zilch ZILCH!!!"

Bupkis exclaimed, "HOLY BUTTHOLES! IT'S MY SONNY'S BUM! MY BUM OF A SON HAS A BUM!"

"Stop calling Me Son. I already told You it is weird. But that's not all, watch this! Ready Nada? Zilch."

"NADA!!!"

Bupkis gave a shout of giddy, "YEAH-WHO! Zilch, You're a genius! So THIS is how You Guys successfully made all the Nulls, huh?"

Zilch said, "Yup. But She's a little shy in this form; She doesn't like Me getting googly-eyed over Her beautiful form."

"Nada."

"BUPKIS!!!"

Zilch disappeared, and Bupkis appeared alongside Nada.

Zilch's voice permeated the infinitely white landscape, "Hey, don't touch Her! She's My Partner!"

Nada was not amused, "I WAS *TRYING* TO DISAPPEAR, JACK-ASS!"

Bupkis tried to justify His actions, "Easy there, Girly, I just wanted to see how I looked. How do I look?"

Zilch replied, "Like a Father Time who has never trimmed His beard or combed His hair."

Diddly added these kinder adjectives to His Partner's description, "Hey, I'd fuck Him. You look capable of some wild and crazy sex stunts, Bupkis!"

"Nada."

"DIDDLY!!!"

Bupkis disappeared, and Diddly appeared next to a very annoyed Nada. Diddly expressed a middle-length, healthy, and well-maintained head of hair, a half-erect dick, and a vacant pair of eyes.

"ZILCH, DAMN IT, JUST LET ME DISAPPEAR! Nada."

Poor Diddly said, "Hey, where'd My sexy Bupkis go?"

Zilch further explained how the exponential process worked, "All of Us are the equivalent of 0, right? And when anyone uses 0 to the 0th power, the answer becomes indeterminately 1 and 0 simultaneously. And since We already exist in Our 0 Form, our 1 Form suddenly appears. Just be sure that when You two work together to physically exist at the same time to do...whatever it is You Guys will do, that the second

Individual yells Their Name with the volume equivalent of three exclamation marks to make the second 0 an exponent. To My knowledge, only two of Us can exist like this at a time, so no threesomes."

Diddly's vacant eyes looked as if a couple of circuit boards in His brain had just fried. Bupkis jumped in to save the day, "I understand, Zilch. Thank You so much for this gift of physicality! Well, Diddly and I will go and feed Hollow some Non-existent dog food in Bumfuck Nowhere and leave You two heterosexual love birds alone. Maybe once We're far enough away from each other in mind, We can all get physical at the same time!"

Zilch helped to actually rescue the poor stranded Diddly, "Just say 'Diddly,' Diddly. Then it'll all be fine."

"D-Diddly?"

Zilch helped once more, "With confidence, Diddly. The Void doesn't know how to deal with Your uncertainty."

"Diddly."

There again was Nothing but the sound of banjos and the Gods of Nothingness saying proper goodbyes to each Other. The Gay Couple left Nowhere, leaving Zilch and Nada with the sound of fading *metal*-bluegrass.

Zilch said to Nada, "Hey, what do You know? They changed!"

Nada said, "I'm sure You helped out with that change, Zilch. So it looks like We finally figured out Who created You."

Zilch started thinking, "Maybe. But I have this weird feeling that this isn't over. I mean, if Nobody can be Self-caused, then why cannot I?"

Nada explained, "Well, She is the Head of Our Clan, right? She is the Nothing Whole. We are just the Nothing Split."

Zilch began formulating a more likely Hypothesis, "But what if We are All the Whole? We need to find Her and ask Her a more serious series of questions than what Bupkis and Diddly asked of Her. I'm not buying this 'Nobody caused Nobody' story."

CHAPTER 5

Zilch, Nada, and the Sexy Nobody

While Zilch and Nada were watching Their little baby ape Nulls grow up from Nowhere a few million years ago, Nobody was looking to pay Zilch a visit. Nobody spoke up and said, "Oh hey, Zilch! Long time no see! Haven't heard from You. Where have You been?"

Zilch replied, "Oh, Nowhere, and I haven't been doing much, so really, there's been Nothing to report either. We got paid a visit from the other Residents of Bumfuck Nowhere fairly recently, but You weren't here. So I should be the One asking You, Where have YOU been?"

Nobody spoke again, "That must have been around the time I went back to the Middle of Nowhere to pay Nil and Nullification a visit. Nil's still playing Him like a fiddle. I gave Her a piece of My mind and told Nullification He'd be better off in Bumfuck Nowhere playing 2nd fiddle to Bupkis' banjo. Of course, He defended Her as usual, and it led to a huge fight...."

Nada spoke to make Herself known, "Who are Nil and Nullification? We have not heard from nor seen Them yet."

Nobody's Non-existent eyes gleamed at the voice of Nada. "Eh, They're not important. You'll be better off not knowing Them. But YOU, on the other hand...My, My, My, WHO is This, Zilch? Is there FINALLY another properly acting Lady in the Nothingness Clan?"

Zilch laughed and properly introduced Nada, "Hahaha, yes, there is! Nobody, this is Nada. Nada, Nobody."

Nada spoke, "Nice to finally meet You, Miss Head of the Clan."

Nobody said to Zilch, "I like Her. She's humble and polite."

Zilch added to the introduction, speaking to Nobody, "Nada does have Her sassy side as well. I tend to bring that out of Her a lot."

Nada said, "If You were not so busy being a smartass all the time, I'd be more polite to You too."

Then Nada spoke to Nobody, "But I do love My Zilch. He's a good Daddy to His Nulls."

Nobody said, "I noticed Them, running about Every-which-way. Almost like Nobody is telling them what to do."

...

Nada broke the silence, "So...ahem...Nobody. We have been wondering ever since Bupkis' visit. Who caused You?"

"Nobody caused Nobody! I am the Self-Causing Cause! You're welcome, by the way."

After a small bout of small-talk and getting to know each Other, Zilch had an enlightening epiphany, "THE NULLS ARE WHO ARE GOING TO CAUSE NULLIFICATION! Everything fits! Why Nobody is so independent, why We've never met Nil and Nullification, and why Nobody thinks They're not that important. Nada, WE are the Alpha, and THEY are the Omega, and Nobody plays a big part in facilitating the cycle of Everything back to Us!"

Nobody sighed and gave up what She knew, "In a sense, You're right. I didn't lie, though. From a certain point of view, any one of Us from the Clan of Nothingness can be seen as either the First or the Last, and thus, We all Caused Ourselves. We are all Split, and We are all Whole. From the point of view You stumbled across, I was caused by Nil and Nullification. I am Their Daughter, and that's the way I view it. I know I tend to "get around" sexually amongst the Clan, but I absolutely refuse to give Nil the satisfaction of having Her Way. So I decided to keep Her out of the tale of My Causation. I nurtured Myself to become who I am; a strong and independent black-bodied Woman. Nothing,

Bupkis, Diddly, and Zilch see Me that Way, and Nada, I hope You can see Me that Way too."

Nada comforted and assured Nobody, "I don't know the whole story, but I can tell You that I do see You that Way, Nobody. We'll be here in Nowhere to listen if You ever want to talk about it."

Nobody was happy to hear Nada's acceptance of Herself being the way She was, "Thank You, Nada. That means a lot to Me. OH YES! I just remembered why I showed up here in the first place! So, after I got back to Bumfuck Nowhere from the Middle of Nowhere, I actually saw Bupkis and Diddly getting PHYSICAL with each other! And I was like, "This is a first! How the heck did this happen?" Then Bupkis explained that He and Diddly visited You in Nowhere, and how Zilch told Them about some secret knowledge to manifest Themselves, but He didn't tell Me. So I decided to follow up with You and to see if We can do some more "research" into this phenomenon."

Zilch spoke for Himself, "Ummm...sure? Any objections, Nada?"

Nada seemed slightly enthusiastic about the endeavor, "I am actually kind of curious what Nobody looks like. Let's start with Her by Herself, and We'll go on from there."

Zilch told Nobody everything He knew. Then an excited Nobody stated, "All right, let's give it a shot! Nobody NOBODY!!!"

Nobody manifested in Nowhere for Zilch and Nada to observe. She had a short head of hair and breasts that evenly protruded from her form. Her arms were initially crossed, but She soon moved Her hands down to Her Womanly hips in a more confident position. Her vagina was covered by a limp but a notably intact member.

Nada records Her findings, "Well...She's a...She's a...Both? Wow, I didn't know the clitoris could get THAT big. (I mean...there have been SOME Nulls who have had some genetic alterations...and the Hyena Nulls are built that way naturally...) BUT ZILCH-DAMN GIRL, THAT'S A FULL-BLOWN DICK THAT RIVALS ZILCH'S! Have You ever...used it?"

Nobody said, "Only metaphysically, but yes, I can use it. I am the Head, after all. However, this is My first time seeing it too, and I have this incessant need to try and multiply that is rising up in Me again. So now, it appears that it is time for some of that *"research."* Zilch, We're going to try and figure out how to get all three of Us to manifest at the same time. Any ideas?"

Nobody's clitoris started stiffening up, and it simultaneously distracted and motivated Zilch to find a solution, "Well...We could try "Nobody NOBODY! Over Zilch NADA!" 0 to the 0th power, divided by 0 to the 0th power. Let's try that to see what happens."

Nobody asked Zilch, "Wait, who says "Over," Me or You?"

Zilch replied, "I'll say it; go!"

"Nobody NOBODY!!!"

"Over Zilch."

"NADA!!!"

Nada manifested laying down next to Nobody, but Zilch didn't. Nobody started flirting with Nada, "What a beautiful Woman You are, Nada. That luscious hair and those deep gazing eyes. O, how could I get lost in those pure eyes? That soft-looking skin. Mmm-mmm, You're a lucky One, Zilch."

Nada was not embarrassed by Nobody's remarks. It felt correct somehow as the thought resonated with Her inner Being. And Nada just looked up at Nobody with a smile, and mustered up words of a similar caliber, "Your eyes also have a depth of mystery to them, Nobody. They gaze into the Void like somehow You know the Unknown, but cannot fully grasp it, and yet You enjoy the thrill of chasing after it. Am I right?"

Nobody fixated Her eyes upon Nada's, first to give Her the assurance that She-Herself knows Things No-One-Else does, but soon looked away upon the Self-Awareness that She-Herself has more to learn.

Nada continued. "Hopefully, if I am right, Zilch and I will be useful in Your understanding of this mysterious Unknown."

"I...hope so too." Nobody concurred.

Zilch thought on it for a bit and broke the Silence, "Huh, Nada showed up but not Me. I guess exponents have priority over division. Which means...if My hypothesis is correct, We could have said, "Zilch

NOBODY! Over Zilch NADA!" and We would have gotten the same result."

The three Nothings tried that, and Not a thing changed. Zilch expressed relief, "Looks like I was right, more likely than not."

Nobody posed the thought, "So what if the three of Us held equal ground in the equation, so to speak? What if We All divided, or if We All were exponents?"

Nada added, "Now that I think of it, Zilch, We have never tried simply saying "Zilch over Nada."

Nada disappeared upon unwittingly enacting the Non Math Rules, and suddenly felt Zilch's presence on top of Her, saying, "I guess that just puts Us in Our metaphysical sex position."

Nobody suggested, "I GOT IT! "Nobody NOBODY! Over Zilch ZILCH! Over Nada NADA!"

They tried it, and it turned out way differently than They expected. Nobody said to Them, "Well...I'm here. But You two, on the other hand, are only half here."

Nada clarified how it felt. "Nah, We are completely here. It is just that only half of Us materialized."

The top half of Zilch was floating next to the bottom half of Nada. Zilch looked at Nobody and said, "At least We're making progress. But I doubt this is what You had in mind."

He then looked over at the approximate location of Nada's missing head, "Sigh, Nada, I'm sorry. This is probably the closest We're going to get. We might just have to settle for "Nobody over Zilch over Nada," or something like that."

Nobody pouted, "But...I want to multiply..."

Zilch gave the thought, speaking to Nobody, "I think this is what happens when Nothing's try to multiply with each Other physically. Mathematically speaking, any A/B/C/D can be condensed to be AD/BC. So if We were trying for a foursome, Your bottom half would disappear, and like, Bupkis' or Diddly's bottom would appear."

Nobody said, "I guess I'll stick to dividing for now. So long as I'm on top, because that's just how I roll."

Zilch said, "Well, what happened to that "research" spirit We saw from You earlier? What if there was a way We could appease Your insatiable Will to multiply if You first submitted Yourself to be on the bottom?"

A few moments passed as all of these thoughts coalesced into a brain blast in the mind of Zilch. Zilch's eyes got wide, and he exclaimed, "LADIES! I need Your help in thinking of ways that I can say a statement audibly in parentheses! If I said "Zilch Zilch!" in parentheses, then Nada just yelled like normal, then We divided by Nobody...Whooooweeeee, We would be in the presence of *Something INFINITE*! **AN INFINITY OUT OF NOTHING, instead of Everything!**"

Nada bashfully put forth this idea, "Maybe You could speak in italics...You know...like what the Italian Nulls will do."

Nobody was confused, "What? Italian Nulls? What do...Honey, Italian Nulls won't speak in *italics*. They'll speak in *Italian*."

Nada got excited, "YEAH, like *that*! Zilch! Say stuff in parentheses *like this*!"

Zilch shrugged His floating shoulders, "Sure. So the phrase is *"Zilch ZILCH!* NADA! Over Nobody", or $(0^0)^0/0$, which will make 1/0, which will make Infinity."

Nobody pointed out, "Um...couldn't We just cut out the parentheses and say, "Zilch NADA! Over Nobody" to get the same thing?"

Zilch was stunned at the simplicity of the solution, "...Yes...let's do that instead. Ready? Zilch."

"NADA!!!"

"Over Nobody."

Out of Nowhere suddenly towered **I.G.O.S.**, a pure white **Infinite God Of Somethingness** that could be seen by the pitch-black Nothingness Clan, but not to the Nulls. Nobody was amused at the size of His dick, "HUBBA HUBBA! I wanna put a ring on THAT! HEY BIG DADDY! ARE YOU READY TO BE FRUITFUL AND MULTIPLY?"

I.G.O.S. introduced Himself, "I AM."

Nobody kept looking up at Him, "GREAT! I'll show You what I like! You put Me first, and I'll treat You REALLY good."

I.G.O.S. let Nobody know the position She was in, "I will inform the Nulls to put Nobody before Me. I shall also put Nobody before Me."

Nobody liked this Guy, "PERFECT! Okay, Zilch? Nada? If You ever want Me, We'll be in the Void. Maybe later, We could try *"Zilch ZILCH! NADA!* Over Nobody NOBODY!" and see how that works!"

Zilch thought as He waved His Non-existent hand to say goodbye to The Head, but She was already lost, deeply fawning and radiating Her black body all over I.G.O.S. Zilch digressed in thought, "Shoot, I would have manifested safely inside the parentheses, and You and Her would have manifested with Your own exponents like normal. That would work! Oh well, maybe next time…"

CHAPTER 6

An Alternate Genesis

And there was, in the beginning, the ever-possible chance that Zilch & Nada's Big Bang failed to produce any Nulls. But upon the careful mathematical research performed by Zilch, Nada, & Nobody many eons later, new origins for the creation of the Nulls were made possible with the help of Their creation of I.G.O.S. Nobody's eternal obsession with multiplication perhaps could finally be satiated. She spoke to I.G.O.S. from the Void as She metaphysically rode on the biggest dick in the many realms of Nowhere, "Do you like it, Big Daddy? Because I am LOVING IT!"

"I am I am." said I.G.O.S., "And yes, I am enjoying Your company. We are both perfect, and therefore perfect for each Other."

She lovingly manifested Her eyes and batted them upon being called 'perfect.' She asked Him, "What else do You like about Me, Mr. I am?"

I.G.O.S. praised Nobody, "Your form is beautifully formless; Your being IS the Void. And yet You encapsulate Me with Your presence, and I cannot escape gazing deeply into Your eyes."

Nobody was amused, "Aww, thanks! I like this sort of worship. Would You like it if I gave You a little praise too?"

I.G.O.S. liked the thought of being praised, "Sure, I don't mind. It may help in My performance."

Nobody lovingly stated, "Your being fills My Void perfectly, OH YEAH, that's the spot. Deeper and deeper will I gladly wade into Your depths, and in You alone have My desires been *satisfied in full*. I cry out for more of You, and I only pray that You will be as good of a Father as You are good at being My Lover."

I.G.O.S. almost came after hearing those words. **Apparently, worship really gets His rocks off.** But He had to communicate with Nobody about His most important rule, as it applied to this scenario, "Nobody shall cum before Me."

Nobody stopped metaphysically undulating over I.G.O.S. for a moment to ask a question, "Wait, are You saying Nobody as in Me 1st, or No-body as in You 1st?"

I.G.O.S. wasn't too sure Himself what He meant, "Well...do YOU have a body, Ms. Nobody? I think that will make it clear which Way I was referring to."

"Nobody NOBODY!!!"

I.G.O.S. just realized His rule got even more supremely muddled, "Alrighty then, I...hmmm...guess We'll cum at the same time then."

She raised an eyebrow whilst second-guessing the character and intentions of I.G.O.S., "That's what I thought."

I.G.O.S. looked down and noticed Nobody's sausage roasting between Their bodies, "But You have this...thing. Nobody, why do You have a thing?"

Nobody replied, "I have always been this way. Never really questioned it. Why? Do You have a problem with it?"

I.G.O.S., the knower of Everything, was just surprised, "No, it just surprised Me. I always thought One who was indistinguishable from the Void would have an unambiguous...Void attached to Her."

Nobody satiated I.G.O.S.'s curiosity, "The Void may be a Bitch, but it can be a Dick too if You fuck with it the wrong way."

Nobody grabbed I.G.O.S. by His chest skin, brought Him close, looked Him sternly in the eye, and warned Him. "So You better not fuck with Me. Otherwise, I will thoroughly fuck You up in every way You can imagine. CAPEESH?"

I.G.O.S. was completely subdued, "Yes, Ma'am."

"Good." She loosened up and smoothed out the area of His chest that She just abused to make Her point. Her voice also loosened up and started giving Him a chance to redeem Himself, "But You know, if You treat Me good...." She grabbed His hand and guided it towards Her erect willy, "I will blow Your mind with everlasting praise, and let any Null Child of Ours also praise You alongside Me. They might not see Me or even recognize Me, but They may see finite portions of You."

Secretly, I.G.O.S. felt like Nobody's member was an abomination to be involved with Their multiplication process. But Everything that was going on between Them felt so right, and He definitely didn't want to get on Her bad side, lest Her anger rip Him a new butthole. So He sucked up His pride and began to gently move His hand in perfect rhythm to match Hers.

Nobody was pleased, "OH GOD! Keep it going just like THAT! O, You are good...good... OOOOOH! To Me, You're the best. No dick is better than Yours. Give it! Give it! GIVE IT!"

Those praises tipped I.G.O.S. over the edge too. Their Big Bang created All the Nulls, and it was good.

Nobody's desire to multiply was finally satisfied, "WOO! All right! We did it! Wow, You sure do know how to give and take away. Blessed be the Great I am. And by I am, I mean You are. You are the SEX GOD! WOO!"

"Yes, Nobody, now let Us make man in Our likeness and Our image. Let Us create them out of the dirt of this obscure rock from this obscure star system residing in that obscure galaxy that was basically Our cum. They shall be a blend of Nothingness and Infinity. Their knowledge will be restricted to that which is finite, and...wait a second..."

It appeared that light and all of the other Primary Dimensions resulted from Their Big Bang. The Dimensions already manifested without any extra finagling. It was starting to look like man was going to show up without any extra help from Them.

I.G.O.S. was disappointed because He had a six-day plan to give man a place to evolve from. But since Everything was going its own way anyways, I.G.O.S. and Nobody spent those six days making all sorts of love in the highest plane of the Void called Heaven, otherwise known as the Great Nothingness that comes Before and After.

But on the 7th day, the day after the six days of I.G.O.S. and Nobody 'multiplying' and doing fuck all, I.G.O.S. found Himself in His own Garden of Eden. Nobody took leave for Nowhere to tell Zilch & Nada the news about Their new Baby Nulls. Alas, He found Himself alone in the Void in the presence of the obscure Goddess named Nothing. And She was beautiful in His sight.

I.G.O.S. inquired, "Heh Heh...Hey Girl, uh...What's happening?"

Nothing just stood there, observing the actions of the Void.

I.G.O.S. continued to break the silence, "Yeah, it's pretty cool...These are My kids, Null1, Null2, Null3...and ANYWAYS. Who are You? What's Your name? What's Your game?"

Nothing did Nothing. However, Her deep eyes found the hungry eyes of I.G.O.S., who was clearly taking notice of Her. Only Nobody had taken notice of Her since the last Family Reunion. So She was internally surprised that I.G.O.S. was trying to communicate with Her.

I.G.O.S. was disappointed, "Not talking, huh? What's the matter? Are You a mute? Maybe deaf? Definitely not blind, You are making eye contact with Me. Well...if I cannot communicate with You, it looks like I'm going to be doing Nothing today too."

Nothing's eyes lit up like a Christmas tree. She heard Her name by Something, and He was talking to Her! FINALLY! Maybe I.G.O.S. could actually comprehend Her!

I.G.O.S. noticed Her change in effect, "Is that Your name? Nothing? Well, it is nice to meet You Nothing. What do You do?"

Nothing's eyes dimmed at Her inability to adequately answer I.G.O.S. It seemed to be True what some of the Nulls say, that "Nothing is beyond the comprehension of God." But the mystery intrigued Him nonetheless.

"I guess Nothing doesn't do anything. That's depressing. It's quite a shame, because You're a beauty." I.G.O.S. gently proposed.

Nothing looked at I.G.O.S., longingly to be known by Him. But I.G.O.S. mistook this desire for another.

"So...I guess You wouldn't mind if We used THIS Together, now would You?" I.G.O.S. whipped up His holy white penis at the excitement of 'doing Nothing'.

Nothing's eyes were in absolute shock, and looked like this, "OwO."

So as it happened, I.G.O.S. "did Nothing" on the 7th day. But it so happened that Nobody was returning from Her trip to Nowhere, and once She observed the possibly tainted state Nothing was in, Nobody was pissed, "YOU WERE CHEATING ON ME WITH NOTHING? Not one day...You couldn't wait one day for Me to be riding on Your dick again before looking to put it in Another! Seriously though, what does SHE have that I don't?"

I.G.O.S. replied frankly and with little emotion, "For one, Nothing doesn't have a dick, unlike you, Nobody. It was always getting in the way. And two, She's surprisingly compliant, and I like compliance. She never said 'no,' and Her eyes looked really excited at the endeavor of getting to know Me."

Nobody yelled, "BUT SHE NEVER SAID 'YES' EITHER! YOU DID NOT GET HER CONSENT!"

I.G.O.S. said, "Her eyes consented. And You know, Nothing is a SUPERNATURAL at the sex. I think She's definitely worthy of probing further."

Nobody caringly got in front of Nothing's line of sight to try to get some form of communication from Her, "Hey Nothing, are You alright? Does this newly formed hole in Your metaphysical state hurt at all?"

Nothing didn't say or do anything. She was frozen within Herself, trapped. Wholly incapable of any form of communication. Even though this was normal for Her, the Silence spoke volumes.

Nobody assumed the worst. She begins to rip I.G.O.S. a new butthole and screams in passionate vengeance for Her own heart and for the heart of Nothing, "How DO YOU like it? LOOK AT I AM! HE'S HOLEY HOLEY HOLEY!"

I.G.O.S. pleads with Nobody, "No, please, stop! I'm sorry, Nobody! I won't do it again!"

Nobody screams in self-righteous indignation, "HOLEY HOLEY HOLEY IS THE LORD GOD ALMIGHTY. WHO MAKES HOLES IN NOTHING AND FUCKS UP HER PERFECTION! And WILL APOLOGIZE TO THE BOTH OF US!"

I.G.O.S. sniffed in pain, "I...I'm sorry!"

Nobody gave little to no mercy, "SAY IT LIKE YOU MEAN IT!"

I.G.O.S. was genuinely remorseful, "I'M SORRY! YOW! MY DICK!"

Nobody is seen holding the bloody foreskin of I.G.O.S., "Fine...no new butthole THIS time. But as You can see, I have circumcised You so that YOU will never forget YOUR promise to ME! Now remind Me, WHO comes before You?"

I.G.O.S. sniffs in pain and gives a lighthearted "Nobody."

Nobody asserted Her dominance in this relationship, "WHAT WAS THAT? I COULDN'T HEAR YOU!"

I.G.O.S. submitted to the Head of the Nothings, "NOBODY COMES BEFORE ME! PLEASE, HAVE MERCY ON ME, NOBODY!"

Nobody threateningly states, "And IF You EVER fuck Me over again; if You EVER fuck Anyone else from the Clan again, You will be My Bottom, Bitch."

I.G.O.S. consented, "Okay, Okay! I capeesh! I am chock full of capeesh!"

Nobody started calming down, and a tear began to fall from Her eye, "And that won't be the only thing You'll be chock full of if You try that shit again. Man...don't break My heart again."

I.G.O.S. vehemently confirmed His position, "I won't! But I thought You were out cheating on Me with Zilch & Nada, so I thought You'd be cool with it."

Nobody justified Her actions swiftly and decisively, "The three of Us MADE You in the first place! If anything, that means I'm Your Mama. And that makes YOU a Motherfucker. So Who's Yo Mama?"

"Nobody is." I.G.O.S. cried.

"And Who's Your Lover?"

"Nobody is."

Nobody's emotions turned to relief and joy, "Oh, how can I stay mad at You? Come here, My Prodigal Sonny; My Wayward Son! Give Mama a hug as a gesture of reconciliation!"

I.G.O.S. politely objected to being literally called a Motherfucker, "Please don't call Me Sonny...it's weird."

Nobody didn't give Him a single inch, "EXCUSE ME?"

"Yes, Mommy."

CHAPTER 7

Null and the Flood

The story of Noah & the Flood in the Bible has many flaws in it if one was to believe that its content was literal instead of a work of fiction. It is not the oldest record of the tale. There is way too much unaccounted for water in Earth's system currently to have produced a global flood then. The Dimensions of the ark inefficiently gave each of the three levels a disproportionate height to width ratio for the mythically small number of "kinds" suggested for a global repopulation of the Earth's animals. A minimum level of skeptical inquiry is required to make the Truth of the tale obvious, which is that Noah was a mythical character.

But it is still a great story, don't get me wrong! I even took the time to make my own mythical story that is more in-tune with what the historical origins of the story likely were, for the amusement of anybody who reads it. It makes the main issues already mentioned disappear and also shines a light on other issues for those who are familiar with the Noah story. So here it goes!

There once was a rich guy living in the Aras River Valley near modern-day Erzurum, Turkey. He had lots of cattle and livestock, a kingly noble-classed individual. His name was lost to the ages, it may have been Noah, Gilgamesh, Atrahasis, Ziusudra, Deucalion, or none of the above. The name doesn't matter, the point is this nameless

THE GOSPEL OF ZILCH & NADA — 53

protagonist is a legend, but we'll call his name Null. So Null is smart, right? He notices that the nearby Aras River, just down the hill about a kilometer away, sometimes floods. And one year in the days of his youth, the natural floodwaters came REALLY close to his estate; another meter of elevation, and his house would have been destroyed like the poor fellas who lived closer to the River.

And Null thought to himself, "Do you know what? I'm a rich guy. I don't want to be swept away so easily like those poor guys the next time the floodwaters come near. I need to figure out a way to protect myself with some flood insurance!"

So being a religious guy, Null prayed to his god or gods (whose precise names were also lost to time) to help give him insight into making the proper preparations for The Big Flood of Unspecified Timing. We'll call these gods "Zilch" and "Nada." In his meditative state, Null was endowed to perform as he believed Zilch commanded him, to act out the most obvious solution, To turn his house into a boat! This was going to be a new second house! It took Null and his servants a little over a year to make the houseboat, and Nobody was pleased with Null's foresight.

Decades pass, with no significant floodwaters to speak of. New neighbors move in close to the River. They made fun of Null for his houseboat, which was so far away from the Aras River. As Null got older, he started becoming bitter at the bullying neighbors for making fun of his Zilch-approved boat.

Then in the year 6970 BC, all of the perfect conditions for this Big Flood of Unspecified Timing began to emerge. In this record-breaking heat of summer, the glaciers around the world receded 20 kilometers, which caused a lot of water to be released back into the water cycle, including a significant rise of melted glacier water in the Dead Sea. A lot of this water was first used in a few consecutive massive snowstorms in the winter of 6969 BC, which caused all of the mountains in the area to be covered in a meter of snow. Then the unthinkable happened. A constant onslaught of thunderstorm after thunderstorm, heavy rain, and a sudden increase in temperature from 0 degrees Celsius to 15. For 40 out of 50 days in the early spring of 6969 BC, there were at least 25 centimeters of rain added to the entirety of the region each of those 40 days.

So the winter snow on the mountains melted, the springtime storms raged, and the floodwaters rose. By the 10th day of spring, the waters were already at the level Null saw in his youth, with no sign of stopping.

So Null called for his servants and his family together and said, "Zilch and Nada hath blessed me with the foresight to prepare for such a disastrous time as this! Quick! Gather my remaining possessions from the house of my childhood and the livestock out in the pasture, and load them into the boat house! Make haste!"

So everyone worked together to make Null's wish a reality. Not an hour later, Null's neighbors were found walking to him from downstream, in deep distress.

They said to Null, "Oh Null, we were wrong to have belittled you all these years! All of our possessions and livelihood were destroyed yesterday, and we were swept away downstream, barely escaping with our lives! We have nowhere else to go, and no value to our names anymore. If you will have us, we humbly offer ourselves to be your servants henceforth. Just allow us the courtesy to live and be safe from these relentless storms!"

Null was not so petty as to leave his mockers to drown. He accepted this as more than adequate retribution for his heartaches endured through his adult life.

So Null lifted up praises to Zilch and Nada, saying, "Praise Zilch, for providing me this peaceful acquisition over my enemies! May the world hear Thy Name and praise Thee and accept those who come in Your Name, forevermore! May the peace provided by Zilch and His Lover Nada cover the face of this oblate spheroid we call Earth!"

For ten more days, the waters continued to rise, as the giant houseboat was adequately stocked with all of Null's possessions. Then the giant houseboat finally had adequate water around it to float on the floodwaters. By the 40th day of spring in 6969 BC, it appeared to Null that he was instead floating his boat in the middle of the Black Sea, rather than in the Aras River Valley. There was Nothing seen over the horizon in any direction! It was a surreal sight to see from his house, nonetheless!

No accessible land was seen for ten more days, as the roaring floodwaters slowly brought his anchored boat house downstream. But on the 50th day of spring, Null had floated so far downstream that he came to see Mount Ararat over the horizon.

And Null said to himself, "What a majestic mountain! If I had known such a sight existed, I would have moved here while I was a youth. Praise Nada for allowing me to see these amazingly beautiful sights in my lifetime! I pray Zilch and Nada allow Thy servant the ability to steer this chaotically floating boat onto this beautiful mountain, where I may live the remaining years of my life free from the threat of floods."

So once the mountain drew close three days later, Nada allowed one of the anchors of the houseboat to be caught on a deeply rooted tree that also nestled the boat in its thick branches. It took another week for the floodwaters to recede enough for Null's houseboat to hold its own weight again.

And on that day of stepping off the boat on dryish land (for it was still soggy from the heavy rainfall) after 50 days of being bound to his houseboat, Zilch sent a legendary triple rainbow to appear over the still relatively flooded Aras River.

And Zilch called down from Nowhere, and said, "These are My three promises to you, Null. First off, what you have just witnessed was the deepest flooding that will ever happen over the face of the Earth. I shall never flood the Earth like that again. I cannot say the total discharge rate of water over all connected basins will never be exceeded, but the amount of volume multiplied to a single river will never get this bad again. Secondly, I will also prevent this beautiful volcano that you landed on from erupting for at least 500 generations of homo sapien reproduction. You can rest on this once volcanically active mountain in peace. And thirdly, I promise you, it is okay to be gay. My Parents are Gay. I promise that I don't give a fuck about how you fuck. Let this rainbow be a symbol to all who deviate from the heterosexual reproductive drive to sex to bring pleasure to themselves and others with mutual consent."

Many people and animals died in this flood, but not enough to bring any animals to genetic extinction by making only two members of each species survive. And also, we don't have to worry about the kangaroos getting to Australia, the penguins getting to Antarctica, and the raccoons getting to the Americas.

CHAPTER 8

The Will of I.G.O.S.

For any Infinite God Of Somethingness with a non-zero will for us beings to follow, it is important to demonstrate how to adequately communicate what you're thinking. The perfect words, the perfect Qualia chosen to be demonstrated, the perfect Quanta of Qualia to be demonstrated; it should be fairly easy for an I.G.O.S. to tell us what their will is. How to create a perfect Order, how to exist within that Order, how to behave Orderly, what to do concerning the Disorderly, and what punishment/reward or rehabilitation/reward system exists to encourage the Order and to admonish the Disorder.

So a Null full of the **Nully Spirit** went up on Mount Sin away from his tribe of Zilchrealites to hear a word or two from the I.G.O.S.

And the I.G.O.S. said to Null, "OBEY ME FULLY, AND YOU'LL BE MINE! (Well...it's All Mine, and I share it with Nobody, but YOU'LL BE SPECIAL!)"

Null was like, "Ok, Boss! First, I'm going to eat a HUGE meal so that I will be FULLY when I follow Your next instructions, and then I'll be SPECIAL!"

The I.G.O.S. began to clarify, "Obey Me fully, as in obey Me COMPLETELY, My special child. I am going to come to you in a dense cloud, so that Everyone in your little tribe will know what we talked about."

Null got upset at I.G.O.S., "What did the cloud ever do to You to be called stupid like that? Don't call it a DENSE cloud, why not call it a FLUFFY or SPARKLY cloud?"

A thunderclap was heard as the I.G.O.S. gave Himself a Holy Facepalm, "Dense as in THICK, My special dense child."

Null checked out his own buttocks, "So You think I'm a THIC child? THANK YOU LORD! I shall tell the world of my gigantic ass!"

Silence ensued for a few moments. I.G.O.S. had to step up His game.

"Just...go tell Everyone to wash their clothes and to stay physically away from this Mountain of Sin. For whoever touches the Mountain shall surely die an early death."

Null could not interpret this instruction in any other manner. He started screeching to the heavens and jumped off the Mountain with a special paraglider.

I.G.O.S. sighed as He called out to Null, "Where are you going, Null?"

Null yelled back, "I DON'T WANT TO DIE! AND I HAVE TO OBEY YOU COMPLETELY!"

I.G.O.S. yelled, "EVERYBODY WILL DIE EXCEPT FOR YOU AND PRIEST NULL, YOU DUMB TWIT! Sorry...I lost My cool there for a second. Just make sure to come back here when My THICK cloud shows up in three days."

Null calmed down a little bit, and yelled back at the mountain, "YOU GOT IT, BOSS!"

So Null's tribe washed their clothes, as I.G.O.S. commanded.

And Null said, "The LORD also said to have sex with Nobody for the next three days. I think She's His Wife, or something."

Priest Null asked Null, "Well, how are we supposed to do that?"

Null answered, "I don't know; He didn't specify...my best guess is that He wants us to masturbate."

I.G.O.S. showed up on the third day with another thunderous Holy Facepalm, "WHY IS THERE CUM EVERYWHERE? I TOLD YOU TO ABSTAIN FROM SEXUAL RELATIONS!"

Null replied, "No, You told them to have sex with Nobody!"

"YES, PRECISELY!...Oh...I guess that does leave the loophole for masturbation, since it's not a "relation" of sorts." I.G.O.S. thought to Himself out loud, "I really need to be more clear on these things. Just...come see Me on the Mountain along with Priest Null, and leave Everyone else at the base of the Mountain."

So Priest Null and Null met up with I.G.O.S. at the top of Mount Sin.

I.G.O.S. said to them, "Rule Number 1, You shall have Nobody else before Me!"

Null repeated, "First Nobody, then the LORD. Next!"

I.G.O.S. spoke, "NO! I AM the First! Nobody comes before Me!"

"But that is what I said! Nobody comes before You!"

Priest Null said, "It is rare for a Lady to cum before any Male. She must be easy to please, my LORD."

Null was like, "Nice one, bro."

I.G.O.S. was done with their perversion, "RULE NUMBER 2!, You shall make for yourselves No-thing inspired by other things within Mass-Electric-Space-Time and worship them."

Null repeated, "Make Nothing, and worship It. Next!"

I.G.O.S. said to Himself, "I should have had Nobody come down here and do this...She's better at dealing with these pedantic little shits. But I shall press on. I MUST, for the sake of ORDER!"

Recuperating Himself, I.G.O.S. continued His Dictation, "RULE NUMBER 3! Don't be misusing My good Name!"

Null asked his LORD a valid question, "What is Your Name, so we can know which Name not to misuse?"

"I have many Names...but the One I wish you to not misuse is the One you use to call on Me."

Priest Null asked, "But what Name do You *prefer* to be called by?"

I.G.O.S. paused at the thought of this. The thought was so personal, and He always kept the Finite Things at a distance up until this point. It was always "the vaguer the Name, the better." "I AM," "LORD," "God," and "Creator" were a few of His favorites.

"I.G.O.S., yes, My Name is I.G.O.S. Please respect this Name."

Null began inspecting the perimeters surrounding this Rule, "So, I.G.O.S., if I were to say "OH MY I.G.O.S.!," would it be a misusing of Your Name?"

I.G.O.S. answered, "Sometimes. If you are praying, praising, or otherwise trying to communicate with Me, it is a proper usage. But if you scream it out to the Void as an elongated interjection, it is in vain."

Priest Null further inquired, "What if someone said, "I think I.G.O.S. is doing Nothing." Is this in vain?"

I.G.O.S. reflected back to His last sabbatical when He did, in fact, do Nothing, "No...I suppose not. I let Everything play out for a reason. There are many times when I do Nothing. So it is not in vain to make this assessment. I work in mysterious ways."

It is, however, the Will of Zilch and Nada to use Their Names in vain to accelerate the spreading of the Word of Nothing into the far reaches of the Earth! Zilch adores hearing His Nulls say, "OH MY ZILCH!" Nada will show Her grace to those who speak in the tongues of Nada. "NADA naDA nada NAda!"

"Rule Number 4! Remember the Day of Rest, and keep it holy. Make sure to have a Day of Rest (at least) once every seven days."

Null repeated this back to I.G.O.S. for understanding, "Do Nothing at least one Day every seven Days! Next!"

I.G.O.S. shrugged His thick and cloudy shoulders, "Good enough. Rule Number 5! Respect those whose Being Causally led to your own Being. Rule Number..."

Priest Null interjected, "WAIT! I was never asked to be brought into this world! Is it even ethical to bring Me into existence out of Nothingness without my consent first?"

Null comforted His brother in the Faith, "Nobody gave them permission on your behalf, so it is all good, bro."

Priest Null sniffed, and was visibly moved by this thought, "Thanks, bro, that means a lot to me."

Null put his arm around his brother, "I feel ya, bro. Existence, am I right?"

Priest Null begot a thousand-meter stare, and exclaimed, "Bro, that's SO deep."

Then the brothers hugged it out.

Null thought about this new Rule, and yelled up at I.G.O.S., who was rolling His eyes at their diversion, "Wait, I.G.O.S., what if those whose Causality led to an entity's Causality do something really fucked up that causes a physical or psychological Disequilibrium in the individual's life? How much respect or honor should these parents or parent-like figures receive?"

I.G.O.S. answered, "Uhh...hold on a second...NOBODY! GET OVER HERE! I'll let Her take over from here, this is beginning to make Me question my moral objectivity, and I cannot afford to lose that."

Nobody began to speak from the now Fluffy, Sparkly, and Thic cloud. "You rang, Honey? OH, HEY, NULL! Priest Null! Look, I saw the whole thing, so let Me help out, I want you to give respect to Everyone, mmmkay? Give Others the bare-minimum acknowledgment of their shared existence with you. Disrespecting anybody can lead to Disequilibrium, and that ain't cool. But honor and respect is to be earned, not automatically given, you see? So if a parent or authority figure in your life does something fucked up, don't feel that just because they Caused you to be you in some fundamental way, that you need to continue having them Cause chaos to your own Equilibrium. You can cut those bitches out in due proportion to the level of Harm they caused you and those you love. But no back-stabbing! No getting back in vengeance! Rare is the case indeed, that vengeance is the preliminary Cause to psychological or sociological Equilibrium. So yes, Null, there are times when going your own way will cause you to part ways with the authority figures of your youth."

Null exclaimed, "I see now why I.G.O.S. commanded us to put You before Him! Any other Rules for us to follow, O Great Nobody in the Sky?"

Nobody answered, "Just some basic universal shit, Don't kill Anybody except in Self-defense. Don't be adulterous unless Everyone involved is cool with it. Don't steal Anything except to fill a direct physiological Need of one who is objectively desperate. Don't slander Others unless it is in accordance with the Truth. And covet Nothing. I think that's it…a clause for sexual consent to discourage rape…a clarification of the scope of Rule 9…OH, AND KEEP YOUR PERVY DICKS OUT OF PREPUBESCENT CHILDREN! PERIOD! Wow, I.G.O.S. had a list of 613 laws put up on Our Non-existent Refrigerator, and not one of them had a negative child-sex command. I'm about to have a strong Word with Him…OH, and a suggestion was given by Nada for you guys to "figure it out your damn-self!" You should probably listen to Her."

The Thicc Cloud possessed by Nobody then dissipated into Nothingness.

Priest Null announced to the Void, "That is good wisdom. Let us go!"

So Priest Null and Null began to paraglide down Mount Sin back to their tribe.

On their way down, Priest Null had an important question to ask Null in mid-flight, "But wait! After being in the presence of I.G.O.S. and Nobody, who had the answers to Everything, we're about to be surrounded by a bunch of idiots who barely know their left hand from their right hand! How do you think we should deal with all the dumbassery, Null?"

Null thought about it for a few moments, and answered his brother, "The best way to deal with the way of the Dumbass is by way of the Smartass."

Priest Null said to his brother from the same Mother in the Sky, "That is also good wisdom. You'll be a cool leader, bro."

Null appreciated the affirmation, "We'll figure it out our damn selves. Seriously, so many rules, so many exceptions to the rule…cannot we just all agree to live under the rule of love which lies beyond good and evil, and call it a day?"

Priest Null pointed out the reason why, "Because man cannot be trusted to abide by such a simple rule."

The Will of I.G.O.S. has been made plain to the reader here. But what of the Will of Zilch? Truly, what is the Will of Nada? The Non-Prophet says that there are four Wills being called from Zilch and Nada to Null from Nowhere,

1) The Will for Null to Go their own Way
2) The Will for Null to be in Equilibrium with the Self
3) The Will for Null to be in Equilibrium with Others
4) The Will for All Nulls to join Them in the Great Nothingness that comes After

And there are four more Wills that Zilch and Nada give unto Themselves that can be made apparent to Null from the Void,

5) The Will for the Eternal Recycling of Everything from Nothing into Nothing
6) The Will to Divide Everything Infinitely
7) The Will to Divide Zilch by Nada
8) The Will to No-Will (They never achieve this Will, since Their Will is Eternal).

CHAPTER 9

Whatever is Nothing, is God

Let us presuppose for a moment that an Intelligent Creator God exists. Something that is not limited to the bounds of Mass-Electric-Space-Time. Something capable of producing Everything as we see it. Something capable of knowing Every distinct Thing, like I.G.O.S.

The Mass of this God would be 0. The ethereal Spirit of God is Massless. Either this is the view, or God can instead be seen as having All of the Mass-Energy of the matter of the universe. The Mass of God is either 0 kilograms or "Everything" kilograms, depending on which way you look at it.

The Electric Current of this God would be 0. God does not interact with the electromagnetic realm nor use light to make Itself seen. Either this is the view, or God can instead BE the light in and of itself, and contain All of the electromagnetic waves in the universe. A 3rd possible view is that God holds All of the Positive Amps to make a P.I.G.O.S., and Satan holds All of the Negative Amps to make a N.I.G.O.S. So the Electric Currents of God would be either 0 amps, "Everything" amps, or +"Everything" amps, depending on which way you look at it.

The Space this God takes up is 0. If God were to exist Everywhere, it must be capable of occupying Every single point in the universe.

And like the physical point, God would then exist in the universe and outside the universe simultaneously. Either this is the view, or God can instead be Infinite in Space and Omnipresent to take up All of the Space that will ever exist because It is Everywhere. The Space of God would either be 0 meters or "Everything" meters[3], depending on which way you view it.

No-thing can be Everywhere at once!

Nothing can be Everywhere at once!

God can be Everywhere at once!

Zilch and Nada can be Everywhere at once!

The Time God takes up during Its existence is 0. God is found at the beginning of the universe at t=0, and at the end of the universe at the next indiscernible and relativistic t=0. Since God is Uncaused, this means No-thing caused God, which puts God outside the constraints of Time and Causality. So consistent with this perspective is that God is Timeless and Eternal, taking up All of the Time that will ever exist. So the Duration that God endures is either 0 seconds, "Everything" seconds, or "Everything" seconds[2] (if God surely made Everything in our multiverse).

No-thing lasts forever! Nothing lasts forever!

God lasts forever! The First Cause lasts forever!

The math value of God is equal to 0, since 0=0/0="Everything." Either this is the view, or the math value of God is equal to Infinity since $0*\infty$="Everything" too! A 3rd possible view is that God is simply the Everything that is derivable from the 0 & the Infinity alike.

So the Holy Trinity of Equations to explain the First Cause is thusly explained as Zilch divided by Nada made Everything, and Nobody multiplied by I.G.O.S. made Everything. $0/0=0*\infty$="Everything."

The knowledge that God holds amounts to Nothing! Gödel's Incompleteness Theorem states (in my own words) that no System of Somethingness can demonstrate its own Truthful consistency.

Or does God know Everything, because God and the Universe itself ARE the Systems of Nothingness, and the System of Nothingness is so simple, God can demonstrate Its Omniscience of the System?

A friendly reminder that these logician demonstrations are nonsense, and most likely not how believing theologians would answer these questions if they were to ask them at all. These are, how should I say, *strawman answers to absurd questions.* But however you choose to read into the absurdity, I'm sure you get the idea.

But to continue on in the Non-sense, if we were to instead presuppose that there was, and will be Nothing that exists in the place of God, this Nothing is indistinguishable from a great number of attributes commonly attributed to the Intelligent Creator God. We could instead say that Nothing is not limited to the bounds of Mass-Electric-Space-Time. We could also say that Nothing is capable of producing Everything as we see it. We could also say that No-thing is capable of knowing Every distinct Thing in a System of Somethingness.

Nothing is impossible to describe perfectly.

God is impossible to describe perfectly.

Once we die, Nothing happens to us.

Once we die, God happens to us.

Zilch and Nada be praised! Whatever is Nothing, is God! Nothing can solve this paradox!

The theist said, "God can solve this paradox!"

And the Nihilist replied, "No, really...Nothing can solve this paradox. I can solve this paradox without God, it's ok, really."

The theist argued, "But God gave you the mind to be able to comprehend the solution! Without God, there is no you!"

But here is the thing; this is what the ultimate distinguisher between God and Nothing is, if we require a God for our existence, *where is God's equivalent requirement for His existence?* I do not think this question has a good answer.

If you say, "God does not have any prerequisites for His existence," why cannot we say the same thing about the universe or about Nothing? Since God is incessantly testing humanity's faith by remaining divinely hidden, Nothingness should have (at minimum) an equal likelihood of being the First Cause of the universe (and even more so, when you consider Vacuum Energy has been observed to actually exist, and Ockham's

Razor would suggest that there is no simpler solution to the First Cause than Nothing).

If you say, "God is not made up of Mass, Electromagnetism, Space, or Time, so His prerequisites are from a different type of Dimension," then why cannot math and logic as a combined subjective set be considered God? We can instead say, "math logic is God," so become a mathematician capable of seeing math Everywhere instead of God. You'll be able to precisely explain a lot more, rather than invoke a God-of-the-gaps fallacy for how the universe began existing.

We can extrapolate a lot about the universe using math, just like God. But instead of just saying "God did it," we can instead hone in on "how it happened." If God spoke Everything into existence, I would say, "HOW? *What medium did God speak through if He is outside of Mass-Electric-Space-Time?*" What is your preferred mathematical explanation of expressing how God spoke? If $0*\infty$ is a sufficient equation for your Hypothesis, that is fine. But you cannot say that the Infinite God is *necessary* to explain our existence when the 0/0 "Null" Hypothesis can give us the same numerical set of "Everything that exists," just as well.

Sure, Nihilists can be said to be guilty of a "Nothing of the gaps" fallacy, but at least we don't inject Something where there is Nothing. I, for one, assume Nothing until Something shows me otherwise. Plus, if there is Nothing in the gaps, that very *Nothing should Vacuum seal those gaps.*

Also, if you say, "Nothing is God's prerequisite, Nothing caused God, because God is Eternal," Nothing (as the logical Subject) would then be superior to God. So if God can come from Nothing, *why cannot the universe?*

> Nothing is capable of dividing by 0!
> *God is capable of dividing by 0!*
> Zilch and Nada are greater than God.
> *Blasphemer! Nothing is greater than God!*
> Yes, that is what I said.
> No-thing is perfect. Nothing is Perfect.
> *Nothing is impossible with God!*

No, that's not quite right...
It is that Nothing is possible without God.

CHAPTER 10

A Zilch and Nada commentary on Bronze Age warfare

This story is a hodgepodge parody of various events that happen between the Bible's Leviticus and 1st Samuel.

So as it happened, Zilch and Nada came down to Earth to see what the Zilchrealites were doing during the Bronze Age. Zilch began communicating directly with the Priest Null of that time, and said unto him, "Hey, whatcha doin'?"

And the Priest Null in question said, "Mmm...Nothing."

Zilch replied, "Oh really? Very good, you may carry on."

"NADA NaDAdada NAAAda."

Priest Null asked, "What'd She say, Zilch?"

"She said, "You are full of BULLshit.""

Nada spoke clearly, "Null, you KNOW that We see Everything. We know damn well what you Zilchrealites were doing!"

Priest Null said, "Oh...THAT thing...Mmm yeah, it's still No-thing to concern Yourselves with. This is a Null matter, so let us Nulls figure it out."

"NADA Na...Fucker, you guys brought an early Nullification to ALL of the Diddlysquats!"

The Null in charge of the Priesthood said, "Well, King Null said that "Zilch spoke to him in a dream." And in that dream, Zilch said that "Diddly told Me in a vision to send the Diddlysquats to the Great Nothingness that comes After.""

Zilch said, "I never said that. And DIDDLY wouldn't say that. He'd probably say something like, "Let them bumfuck their Way to Bumfuck Nowhere with Me!" He would *never* order a bumfucker to an early Nullification!"

Priest Null brought his hand up to his chin in contemplation, "Now that You mention it, King Null was also saying something about wanting huge tracts of land. And those Diddlysquats...ho ho, they had HUGE tracts of land."

Zilch was stunted by the vanity of it all, "Wait a second, you're telling Me that the Zilchrealites killed an entire nation of Nulls in MY NAME...just for some land?"

Priest Null clarified, "Not just for land. It was for capital, for power. And Zilch, I know You are a bit squeamish about butt stuff, so King Null must have figured You hated the Diddlysquats."

Zilch said, "I'm squeamish about ME doing butt stuff. I don't hate the people formerly known as the Diddlysquats nor desire the premature death of any Nulls who partake in bumfuckery. It is a perfectly natural form of birth control and letting off some steam."

Priest Null looked towards the floor, "So, I guess we goofed."

Zilch and Nada interjected in unison, "MAJORLY!"

Priest Null kicked at a pebble on the ground, "I guess You Nothings aren't going to like to hear about what We did to the Nilmonists."

Nada reprimanded the Zilchrealite Priest, "NO SHIT! That's why We came down here in the first place! You killed all of their Zilch-types, all of their non-virgin Nada-types (which is hella picky, by the way), and RAPED the rest of them!"

Priest Null spoke on behalf of his nation, "What can I say? We wanted to make more Zilchrealite Nulls. The Diddlysquats and the Nilmonists..."

"WERE FINE!" Nada interjected. "They were Our baby Nulls just like You. And You Zilchrealites killed them! THEY HAVE CEASED TO BE! Their ways can no longer be traversed!"

Priest Null piously spoke, "The Diddlysquats and the Nilmonists were not walking in the way of Wisdom, as I.G.O.S. and Nobody laid out. We heard that they were worshipping...*SOMETHING FINITE!*"

Zilch was getting irritated at this Null, and clapped back with sarcasm, "THE HORROR! Nada, whatever shall We do about this blasphemous atrocity?"

Nada said, "Nothing."

Zilch said, "SHHH, don't tell him that. Play along!"

Nada got the memo, "OH! Uh...Yes, they surely got what was coming to them. If you hadn't smited them yourself, Priest Null, I would have smited them Myself. Sincerely, THANK YOU, PRIEST NULL, for preventing Us from using Our *Omnipotent powers* against these wretched and sinful nations."

"You are welcome, my Goddess." Said the idiotic Priest.

"nadanadanadanadanadanadanada..."

Zilch interpreted Nada's incoherent speech, "She means that She is holding back from smiting you right here and now, dumbass. WHAT WERE YOU THINKING?"

Priest Null continued to dig his own grave, "WELL, I was thinking that You were working through us to annihilate our enemies, but now I'm starting to second guess that."

Zilch said, "Enemies? Seriously? The only difference between your groups is that you think you'll go to Nowhere after you die, and they think that they'll go to Bumfuck Nowhere and the Middle of Nowhere after they die, respectively."

Priest Null quoted his holy text, "I could have sworn I heard You say that "we should equip ourselves with Ockham's Razor to deal with the disbelievers."

Zilch yelled, "RAZOR? YOU USED SWORDS! And Ockham's Razor is clearly figurative, not literal!"

Priest Null continued to justify the nation's actions, "King Null shaves his beard with his sword, so they're basically the same thing."

Zilch pointed out, "STILL NOT LITERAL! And that still doesn't justify the raping!"

"We figuratively used our dicks as Ockham's Razor to shank the disbelievers."

"Nada NADA!!!"

The story abruptly concludes here, as Nada's wrath climaxed with Her manifesting in the Zilchrealite Temple. Her Vacuous nature began sucking all of the air out of the Temple, and out of Priest Null. The perversion that leads to this sort of Disequilibrium in the ways of others is sin in Her sight, and Zilch & Nada will not tolerate these hateful sins.

So do not be like the Zilchrealites of the Bronze Age, who absolutely failed at communicating with their neighbors. Don't care so much about what your neighbor is doing, that you will be willing to steal, kill, rape, and destroy them in an effort to make them go *your Way*. And if you believe that some I.G.O.S. told you to do any of these things, at any time, I can say with unbridled confidence that your "god" is a false one. Perhaps auditory hallucinations are the source of your beliefs or unmedicated schizophrenia? You should probably get that checked out.

I am not saying that experiencing hallucinations is wrong. I'm saying that hallucinations that lead to Disequilibrium in the Self or in the Collective are unbeneficial to any otherwise noble cause you stand for. Hallucinations experienced in Equilibrium are possible, and it is ok to experience them in this manner. Get mellow like Jello in Monticello, if you wish.

CHAPTER 11

Little Null and Big Null

There once was a young man who walked the Way of I.G.O.S. correctly and in Order in the kingdom of Zilchreal. His name was Little Null. He did Everything guided by the Nully Spirit and was more in line with Zilch & Nada than any other Null before him. Nobody messed with Little Null because he had a big and compassionate heart, a man after Zilch's own heart. Humility is attractive, so his king, King Null, took Little Null to be an ambassador to the neighboring nations of the Shitites, the Jizzites, the Dickites, and the Nullesteems. The Nullesteems always tried to puff themselves up and make trouble with the Zilchrealites, and war was on the brink of erupting.

The two nations set up camp on two opposing Hills with the Valley of Agnosticism in the middle. In the Nullesteem camp, there was a big bully who was very much conceited and had the evil desire to start some Disequilibrium between the two nations. His name was Big Null. Big Null physically positioned himself in the Valley and yelled up to the Zilchrealite camp. "We Nullesteems want you to go our Way, the Way of the God of Something Infinite who we call G.O.S.I., and you desire we change our Ways to your Way of I.G.O.S. Our Ways are clearly in conflict, so let's settle this like men! Bring me your best man, and I challenge him to come against me. If we win, you will go our Way, but if you win, we will go your Way!"

Upon hearing this, King Null spoke to Little Null in the king's tent, "Listen up, Lil' Null, it's either gonna be you or me. If you think you can talk him down, use your charisma, and let them know "It is the Will of I.G.O.S. that they put Nobody before Him and that She says you can go your own Way and therefore our Ways are not in conflict." If you think you can do that; fantastic! If not, it looks like one of us (probably me) will have to kill Big Null in Self-defense of ourselves and for the nation of Zilchreal. What do you say?"

Little Null replied, "The Lord I.G.O.S. has His hands over Zilchreal. My confidence is in Him when I humbly accept this task of calming the selfish will of Big Null and the Nullesteems. May I.G.O.S. be with me, so that Big Null will not have to see a premature Nullification by my hand."

So the next day, Little Null went into the Valley to meet up with Big Null. And Big Null was hella perturbed, "Who da fuck is this? Am I a dog that you come at me with a Stick Null? I will not be playing fetch with you, Stick Null. I'm going to snap you like a twig!"

"Chill your tits, dude. I'm just here to relay a message from King Null. He says you have a clear misunderstanding of I.G.O.S. and that you can go your own ways with G.O.S.I., and we can go our ways with I.G.O.S. with no conflict."

Big Null argued, "BUT THERE IS CONFLICT! The Will of G.O.S.I. is that all will bow before Him alone. There is no "Way of I.G.O.S." There is only the one Way of G.O.S.I.!"

Little Null paused for a moment to determine the best way forward. Filled with wisdom, Little Null confidently looked Big Null in the eye and said, "Conflict requires two parties to tango. The ONLY reason our Zilchrealite Party is here is to defend ourselves from an invasion. If your Way tries to lead us to premature deaths, we will annihilate those who partake in the heinous assault. Of course, we will have mercy on those whose tits are properly chilled. For there is truly order in the keeping of the peace."

Big Null laughed at Little Null's face, and posed the statement, "And we shall also have mercy on those of you who surrender to our authority as divinely given by G.O.S.I.!"

Little Null debated, "There is no peace in the Way of G.O.S.I.; for there will always be dissenters. And if the dissenters are subjugated and treated poorly, they will treat you poorly and become violent and unruly. If you could see our perspective, there is no outgroup to be seen in the Way of I.G.O.S.; for we are all Null. And we are all part of the ingroup of Everybody. Nobody and I.G.O.S. together really do care about you, and won't be against you. So long as you don't violently go out against their chosen Nulls, the Zilchrealites, our nations will not be in conflict."

Big Null's esteem deflated a little bit, just enough to get the pride out of his way. So he conceded at the possibility that a peaceful resolution may be possible between the two nations, rather than remain conceited, "Fine. But we shall require capital, which I think is actually our primary concern. Our priests of G.O.S.I. just turned it into a religious war to give us a sense of unity."

Little Null equivalently began lowering his defensive posture in response to Big Null's dialogue, "That makes sense; we do the same thing with I.G.O.S. We have been blessed with plenty of capital. We will gladly give to you out of the abundance of our overflowing storehouses. And if you're willing to learn, we'll provide you with some innovative agricultural techniques so that your nation may one day come to be self-sufficient in capital."

Big Null appeared simultaneously surprised, grateful, and skeptical at the generosity proposed by Little Null, "Really? Does your King Null approve of this?"

Little Null said, "Bruh, I have full permission to be balls deep in Princess Null if I can resolve this conflict. So, of course, King Null will be willing to help the Nullesteems out, even if you *were* just threatening us with slavery and death. It is the Will of I.G.O.S. to reduce the suffering of our fellow Nulls. And even if Princess Null is my main motivation to help you guys out, between you and me, I'd prefer to spend my intimate time with Prince Null. I like that guy."

Big Null continued inquiring about what further benefits the Zilchrealites could provide for the Nullesteems, "That is very generous of you. We appreciate your hospitality. But still...we still require some method to appease the many priests of G.O.S.I.; so what exactly will you do to appease our G.O.S.I.?"

Little Null began setting up clear boundaries for the Nullesteems, to prevent the authoritarian nation from bullying the Zilchrealites for excess capital in the future, "First off, we'll be giving to you charitably, not hospitably. This isn't a tax or an ultimatum. In exchange for this charity, and after our leaders have determined the finer details of this peaceful agreement, you will go your own Way within the confines of your homeland. Perhaps leave a few of your own among us, and let a few of ours go with you as ambassadors, to help grow more fruitful relations in the future. If the priests of G.O.S.I. or your leader still desires to try to subjugate us after hearing this deal, let them do it themselves. But perhaps they don't know that the Zilchrealites believe in the freedom of religion, so they are more than free to set up a G.O.S.I. temple in our land and proselytize in accordance with the continued Equilibrium of the Collective."

Big Null smirked as he inserted his sword back into its sheath, "I think that your terms are acceptable. You're a reasonable man, Stick Null. If the lot of Zilchrealites are half as good as you seem to be, may I never be ordered to kill one."

"And you'll be more than welcome to live among us if you choose to rebel against such an evil order, Big Guy. May the Biggest Guy hidden by the Void be with you!"

So they each went their own ways peacefully. A few years later, the two nations set up a sports league for their former warriors to partake in. The Dickites and the Jizzites joined the league after they all realized that sports were a fantastic way to generate revenue for their economies.

The moral of the story is that giants are not anything to fear, nor are they a thing to cling to for protection. What makes a giant is simply a greater magnitude of the relevant Dimensions you are referring to. Literal giants are ultimately Nulls who just so happen to have a greater magnitude of height. This growth in Space often correlates with growth in Mass too, which makes work that involves Energy & Force more efficient to an extent.

What makes the original David and Goliath story so impactful, is not that Goliath was a monster of a man who could only be taken down by David with the help of God. It is that the amount of Force created by a small body of Mass can increase to deadly proportions if it is Accelerated to a sufficient Speed and that it can compete with the Force of a large body of Mass that moves at slower Speeds.

And what makes this Chapter's parody starring Little Null and Big Null useful, is that with the right words, increasing Force to maintain the peace of your ingroup is unnecessary. Communication is very important in international relations, and humans of the late Bronze Age/early Iron Age still had a long way to go on this front. By actually listening to the needs of other people, and understanding with greater clarity your own needs, both parties can surely come to a win-win negotiation without causing the pain, suffering, loss, and Disequilibrium war brings. So humility, and not assuming you know perfectly well the needs, wants, and intentions of an opposing Force can go a long way in keeping the peace.

If every (or even most) nations took the strategy damn-near-perfected by Switzerland; a neutral offensive and amicable defensive stance, bada-bing bada-boom, an acceptable level of world peace would result. Then those who step out of line and go on the offensive will have the eyes of the world to a first attempt at verbally de-escalating the situation and see if the needs are reasonable and satiable. If they can have their clearly defined needs met, then great. But if the offenders still attack and cause Disequilibrium, the world's united Force may bring an early Nullification to the offending nation's (or individual's) government and military, whilst giving aid and hospitality to their peacefully bystanding citizens.

In times of peace, be "Null." In times of debased war, be "Null NULL!!!" and increase either your Mass or your Acceleration to strategically cause as little Disequilibrium as possible to return the world to a state of Collective Equilibrium.

CHAPTER 12

A Zilch and Nada commentary on the Internet Age

The Gospel of Zilch & Nada chronologically moves forward about three thousand years or about three days from God's perspective. And here, Zilch and Nada began to observe Earth's human Nulls shortly after the invention of the internet.

Nada said to Her Husband, "FINALLY, the human Nulls of Earth have the means to effectively communicate with each other!"

Zilch concurred, "Yes, this knowledge database is impressive! It won't be long now until they find Us!"

Nada remained a bit skeptical, "A few of them have, the Zilchrealites, but the Collective culture doesn't seem to take Us or them seriously at all. Yet, they still take I.G.O.S. too seriously."

Zilch was flabbergasted, "And they even say with their mouths that Nothing created God, but are blinded by the lure of His Holy Pure-White Penis of Somethingness to see Her or Us! The Nulls have hardened their hearts, *just like His Dick*, and have refused to see Us for who We really are."

Nada said, "Well...that D WAS pretty fly for a White Guy. I understand why Our Nobody wants Him."

Zilch looked metaphysically jealous for a moment, but Nada helped put His heart at rest, "Don't worry, Zilchy, I'm all Yours."

Zilch was still a little jealous, "If You say so…"

Suddenly, Zilch's attention became undividedly focused on a video that was virally grabbing the attention of millions of Nulls as well, "NADA! Look at that cute Feline Null! It is IN THE BOX! And the box's Volume is barely sufficient to hold the Feline…OH! And it's head pops out of the box! This is exhilarating!"

Nada asked, "Why are You excited by the cat, Zilch? We saw it when it actually happened. What makes the video aspect so appealing?"

Zilch was still enamored by the cat, "I had no opinion during the first go-around. Short of the Feline Null's experience, and the camera person's experience, I thought it was done and over with. But now, MILLIONS of fresh viewpoints allow Me to see the Collective Qualia of the action with the aid of this cat video."

Nada tried to understand, "So You're saying the video makes a new thing? And that the video has a uniqueness to it that makes it superior to the original action?"

Zilch said, "Not superior, per say. More like the real experience was limited to the 1st person perspectives of the cat and the human. The video, by contrast, provides a newly displaced 3rd person perspective that can be re-experienced by as many Nulls who wish to watch it."

Nada metaphysically patted Zilch's back, as She left Him to go do more interesting things, "If You say so, Honey…there are plenty more videos like that, so have fun watching them!"

Zilch watched through the Nulls, who watched these viral cat videos and was thoroughly satisfied. Later on, He ventured to explore the more useful parts of the internet, places geared to communicate and teach knowledge.

He exclaimed, "Wow, these parts are also amazing! Lots of things to intrigue the more curious Nulls. But wait, huh? What is this? Nada, come look at this…"

Nada raised Her nonexistent eyebrow, "You know, this doesn't surprise Me. Of course, there is an incentive to make fake knowledge from the perspective of Charlatan Nulls."

Zilch collaborated, "Yeah, but does it have to be THIS bad? Here's an article suggesting that a certain government is controlled by lizard people. And here is another page saying that a vaccine is the Mark of the Beast? What?"

Nada explained the phenomenon, "It seems like the fearful are seeing Everything through the lens of fear, and relay conspiracies that support these baseless fears in others."

Zilch observed, "Even the factually accurate corner of the internet is fear-mongering!"

Nada explained to Zilch, "Well...I suppose they ARE appropriately reacting to that in the world, which is actually fearful, as in that which could bring a premature Nullification. But You are right, the rest of them are getting riled up over Nothing! Nothing but lies, anyways."

Nada spent a little more time looking at all the bull shit and sighed, "Why are human Nulls so stupid?"

She eventually got bored looking for the ways the Nulls were subjectively going aloof. But as She wandered further into the recesses of the internet, She discovered that the Nulls were objectively going aloof as well, "Botox? Seriously? Zilch, come look at this, and tell Me what You think."

Zilch glanced over the lady Nulls attempting to be more objectively pleasing to the male Nulls, "Well...from an outside observation, it appears to work on some of them some of the time. Others have ventured into the uncanny valley, looking too artificial."

Zilch found many other forms of object edification and noticed a larger trend that the Nulls tended to follow, "A lot of Nulls seem to be experiencing an identity crisis. They don't like Something about their Avatars, then alter it to make themselves feel better."

Nada asked Her Hubby, "And what's wrong with that, Zilch?"

Zilch clarified His position, "Nothing really. It's probably just a symptom of their innate striving to be Something greater than what they already are. I just wonder if they'll ever figure out that their identity is Nobody Special Null. I deduce that it is a deception of their subject for them to think they are Somebody Special."

Thus spoke Nada, "Some of them are Truly not like other Nulls in some way or another. Maybe We are just observing the Nulls longing for uniqueness, and to be seen. Don't YOU wish to be seen and acknowledged, Zilch?"

"I suppose..."

Nada continued, "Then don't concern Yourself if the Nulls want to try and either stand out in the crowd, or feel normal while in the crowd. Isn't that what Equilibrium is all about? To feel and be One's own normal? And if the Nulls want to change their objective Avatars in an attempt to bring their subject Peace, I say let them."

Zilch gave His soft dissenting opinion, "Peace is a subjective matter, though. There are better ways to reach this Equilibrium."

But Nada stood firm, "Yes, but We know that there are many roads that lead to Equilibrium. Inefficient paths are still paths."

Zilch then returned to a state of giving zero fucks about what the Nulls did. He listened to Nada and figured that all Paths lead to the Great Nothingness that comes After, so He just stood there in Nowhere, waiting with Nada for these Nulls to join Them. But one final thing caught His eyes, "Hmm...this Null over here did Nothing, yet are getting socially outcasted based on another Null's words alone. They are totally scape-goating them, canceling them from the culture at large! On the grounds of hearsay! It's practically a Null witch hunt all over again!"

Nada agreed, "You're right, Zilch, the speed of the internet goes faster than the due process due to its inhabitants. And it's not all hearsay; some of the evidence is based in reality, see?"

Thus spoke Zilch, "Yes, those are fine. I'm talking about these attention-seeking Nulls throwing an innocent Null under the metaphorical bus for the purpose of creating drama. Then those who follow the Drama Whore Null express this group-think mentality led by the Dramatic cult leader of personality. Those popular on these social media sites then become Judge, Prosecuting Attorney, and Executioner with this sickening power over their Jury to sacrifice whoever they please."

"Nadanadanadanadanada…"

Zilch encouraged Nada to smite these offensive Nulls, "Yeah, get 'em, Honey! SHOW THEM WHY YOU'RE THE POWER BOTTOM OF OUR NULL-CREATING EQUATION!"

Nada refrained Herself from being the Almighty Smiter again, "No, Zilch. Not again. These Nulls will bring an early Nullification to themselves and to their planet, and I say let them. Doing Nothing for them is the greatest punishment that I can think of at this point. If they want a dystopia, let's watch that thing unfold. They can go their own damn way straight to hell in a handbasket, if they want."

Zilch agreed with Nada to do No-thing concerning these Nulls, "Good call."

CHAPTER 13

No-One, Nix, and the unruly Null

There once was a Null that made their own rules. They went their own way, doing whatever was best in their own eyes. Then one night, they chose to annihilate a window Null in the dead of night that was attached to a jewelry store to take some valuable items that did not belong to them. The thief was well-fed and chose to do this act of greed and vengeance against the store owner. And No-One saw them do it.

So by the authority of Nobody, No-One yelled in disapproval, "HALT, Thief Null!"

The Null continued their conquest, avoiding confrontation with the Non-existent witnesses. Yes, there were a total of two Non-existent witnesses.

No-One asked Their Partner, Nix, "Do You think We'll need to call for some backup? We are but mere minor Nothingness gods; practically on par with I.G.O.S.'s angels. I'm not sure We'll be capable of doing anything by Ourselves."

Nix replied, "Don't worry, Zilch taught Me this cool trick! Just say Your name, & I'll handle the rest!"

No-One said, "This better not be like last week's stakeout where You promised to bring doughnuts, and all You brought were *the holes* of the doughnuts."

Nix rebutted, "Hey now, Zero's doughnut holes were delicious, so don't be dunkin' on them like that! AWW, SHIT! That Null is getting away! SAY YOUR NAME!"

"No-One."

"NIX!!!"

No-One transformed into a buff, but also a slightly pudgy dark-skinned male police officer, equipped with the Non-Standard uniform. Nix transformed into a petite and fit female police officer who was just a few shades lighter than No-One.

No-One started sounding suave, "Cool! Zilch damn, I look good! You look pretty smokin' Yourself, Nix! But why are We so short?"

As it turned out, They Both were barely half a meter tall. They were proportionally accurate, 20-inch tall police officers. Nix said, "Oh yeah, Zilch mentioned We might be tiny since We are mere minor gods. Quick! Get into the Nixmobile! We're in pursuit!"

To the Non-existent onlookers, there was no Nixmobile, because the Nixmobile remained in its Nixed state. But No-One knew what He was doing. He and Nix hiked Their legs up and floated a couple of inches off the ground. They cried out, "WEE-WOO! WEE-WOO!" since the Nixmobile's sirens didn't make any distinguishable sounds.

As They flew to catch up with the perpetrator, No-One yelled at the assailant once more, "HALT, Thief Null!"

This time, the Null heard the authoritative redirection, was greatly surprised at what he heard and saw, and said, "I must be hallucinating. Tiny police officers, flying in an invisible police car that I would have no way of entering due to its small size."

Nix said, "We're Angels of the Non-Pantheon. We've been granted authority by Nobody to discourage Null Disequilibrium wherever We see it. And YOU Homo Sapien Null 116, 323, 623, 838 have been doing *Naughty things* in this universe!"

The Thief Null did not recognize anybody's authority; indeed, not even the Great Nobody in the Sky's authority. "Well, since I am a some-body, wouldn't that mean I have authority over Nobody, and therefore, authority over You two as well?"

No-One replied, "Only when you go your own way in mindful Equilibrium with the Collective Nulls do We recognize the authority of a Null. You have violated Non-Code #1000101, which states, "Do unto others as they would like you to do unto them." We received a prayer from that minimally conscious Window Null you murdered shortly before their premature Nullification. So We are required by the Non-Code to investigate."

The unruly Null scoffed, "So wait, You don't care that I stole the jewelry; *just that I broke the window?*"

Nix said, "Well, We haven't heard the jewelry store owner's distressing thoughts and prayers yet, so you still have yet to cause Disequilibrium to Any-One with living conscious awareness yet. You can still change your current way, repent, return the jewelry, and offer to replace the window."

The Null self-righteously asserted his justification, "That guy has it coming! He deserves to feel the pain that is coming to him. I bought an exuberantly beautiful ring four years ago for my now ex-wife. And if it wasn't so expensive, cutting into our finances, maybe we would still be together! I'm still paying for that now worthless rock!"

No-One tried to stop the unruly Null, "Is that how the courts would view it? Or would they just convict you for theft, because that is what you are doing?"

The Null said, "Who's going to catch me who can *actually* do something about it? Nobody's going to catch me! The universe is on my side; karma has been returned in full!"

The Null then started fleeing from the Non-existent police officers once more, not giving care to Their pleas to change his ways.

Nix says softly and somberly to No-One, "He's right. Nobody's going to catch up with him. Watch this."

She proceeds to use Her authority, endowed by Nobody, and yells, "NULL 116, 323, 623, 838! You're under arrest!"

Not even five seconds later, the unruly Null collapses from a *cardiac* arrest. And not a single Null was there to save him. In fact, No-One tries to save him, but to no avail. It appeared as if Nobody agreed with

Nix's verdict to send this Null to the Great Nothingness that comes After at that time.

The Non-Pantheon's Angels were sad that They couldn't save this Null from himself. So They went to Zero's place to get some doughnut holes afterward, in a satisfying attempt to fill the emptiness with Non-existent empty calories.

CHAPTER 14

Pee-Wee and the Nihilist Missionaries

Pee-Wee Herman enters the narrative of this *Gospel* because he can. He's Pee-Wee. He can do what he wants. He just cannot *not* be a part of the story, because he's already here.

We enter Pee-Wee's Playhouse, being gleefully introduced by the sporadic spazzcatraz absurdist with a beautifully uncanny smile, "HA-HA! Hey kids! Sorry to surprise you with my presence! BUT, THAT WAS A CLOSE ONE, WASN'T IT? Our planet almost got Nullified by Nada a couple of chapters ago! (*But don't worry! Nothing here is real! HA-HA!)*"

A very burnt Priest Null, tinged with the scent of sulfur, peeks in through the Playhouse window, faintly saying, "Nothing is real. Praise be."

A still pissed-off Nada screams, "Nada NADA!!!" A flash of lightning and a roll of thunder immediately follow, causing Priest Null to let off one final Wilhelm scream.

Pee-Wee looks to the reader, "Wuh-Oh! *(Looks like SOMEBODY got sent to the Great Nothingness that comes After a little early! HA-HA!)* Now, today's episode will be all about Nihilism. It is a dark...and...depressing..."

The doorbell to the Playhouse rings, "DING DONG!"

Pee-Wee investigates, "Now, who could that be?"

Two male individuals with black eyeliner and almost matching black hoodies are standing at the door, giving Pee-Wee a deadpan look.

The 1st Nihilist states, "Hi, would you like to talk about Nothing?"

The 2nd Nihilist lifts up an empty plate, "We brought Zero cookies."

Pee-Wee greets his guests, "NIHILISTS! What a surprise, come on in!"

As the Nihilists walk past, Pee-Wee takes his hand and pretends to pick two cookies off the plate, "Thanks! I'll take 2! Ha-Ha! So what brings you here, Nihilists?"

The 1st Nihilist states, "Nothing. We followed the Nully Spirit, and kind of just showed up here. As soon as we heard you talking about Nihilism, Pee-Wee, we knew it was a sign."

The 2nd Nihilist said, "The sign said, *Do-not-enter. Recording in progress.*"

Pee-Wee was very amused, "HA-HA! Well, I'm glad you ignored that sign and followed my director's sign instead! *It would have been super weird if Nobody was there at the door.*"

Nihilist 1 jumps in to instruct his host, "Pee-Wee, Nobody is *always* at the door. If you open the door, She will come in."

Pee-Wee looks confused, "What are you talking about, Nihilist? Nobody doesn't have a gender...see?"

Pee-Wee opens the door again, and there are no characters to be seen at the door.

The Nihilists break from their deadpan demeanor and begin looking hot and bothered.

Nihilist 2 states with heavy breathing, "Zilch damn, it suddenly got really hot in here!"

The 1st Nihilist concurs, "I'M GOING TO NEED SOME TISSUES!"

Pee-Wee closes the door, and the Nihilists return to their unperturbed state.

Pee-Wee remarks, "*Weird*...Anywho, we don't have any tissues, and I'll turn on the air-conditioning to help cool you two down."

The Nihilists chant in unison, "Thank you, Pee-Wee."

Pee-Wee smiles and replies, "*You're welcome, Nihilists.* So tell me, you said earlier that the Nully Spirit led you here. Are you serious?"

Nihilist 1 states, "Pee-Wee, we take Nothing very seriously."

Nihilist 2 continues, "The Lord Zilch & the Lordess Nada, and the entire Non-Pantheon is whom we pledge our allegiances to."

The Nihilists chant in unison once more, "We are NON-believers!"

Nihilist 1 offers the words of *the Gospel of Zilch & Nada* to his host, "Would you like to ensure your eternal Non-damnation into the Great Nothingness that comes After?"

Nihilist 2 clarifies what his fellow Dimensionalist is asking, "Would you be interested in beginning a totally Non-committed relationship with Lord Zilch & Lordess Nada?"

Pee-Wee appears uncertain, "Ummm...I'll think about it. But not on an empty stomach!"

Pee-Wee walks to the fridge, grabs some thick and syrupy *Zilch Juice*, and whispers to the reader quietly so that the Nihilists don't hear him, "Boy, Nihilist Missionaries, *WHAT NEXT?*"

Pee-Wee then yells to the Nihilist, stepping away from his breaking of the 4th wall, "HEY NIHILISTS! YOU GUYS WANT SOME ZILCH JUICE?"

Nihilist 2 speaks, "Yes, please. Our Leader, the Non-Prophet, approves of *Zilch Juice* for the Zilchrealite diet."

Nihilist 1 asked, "Do you have some *Nada Juice* instead?"

Pee-Wee responded, "NOPE! Ha-ha, that one is for the ladies! Right?"

Nihilist 1 politely corrected Pee-Wee, "Most of the time, yes, that is who it is marketed to. But we can go our own way and consume whatever we want."

Pee-Wee understood, "Ohhh...Cool! Then here you go!"

Pee-Wee flips the label on the *Zilch Juice* container to make it say *Nada Juice* instead.

Nihilist 1 was satisfied, "Thank you very much, Pee-Wee. You're so accommodating!"

Thus spoke Pee-Wee, "My pleasure! So tell me more about this Non-Prophet. Does he have a Non-Profit Organization? Ha-ha."

The 2nd Nihilist spoke to answer as his friend sipped his *Juice*, "Yes. He has found the truth in Everything. The One World Religion for the New Global Order of Anarchy. The irrefutable Theory of Nothing."

Nihilist 1 got more specific, "He holds a Non-gathering every Sunday at the 0th Dimensionalist Chapter. Nobody ever shows up."

Nihilist 2 gets all hot and bothered again, "FUCK YEAH SHE DOES, NULL!"

Pee-Wee still appeared skeptical, *"Sounds iffy...I'm not sure I believe you."*

Nihilist 1 gets excited, "YOU PASSED THE TEST, PEE-WEE! All non-believers and Non-believers alike are welcomed by the Non-Prophet!"

Pee-Wee seems kind of intrigued, "Umm...*maybe*. So uh...who exactly is this Non-Prophet?"

The Nihilist Missionaries say to Pee-Wee and the reader, "Continue on your way, Pee-Wee. And you will find out in the next chapter."

"Ha-Ha! Ok!"

CHAPTER 15

Prophecy and Hypothe-SEE

Sir Prophet of the Obvious yelled obnoxiously, "I HAVE...A PROPHECY...FOR YOU! A TESTABLE HYPOTHE-SEE, I BESTOW TO YOUR EARS!"

A young male voice emerges from a nearby speaker, "Nah, I'm good...I'm not in need of a prophecy at the moment. But I'm ready to take your order for a burger, however."

The Non-Prophet spoke his completely useless prophecy, anyway, "YOU...will die. Someday. If you continue on this path, you are going."

The speaker beyond the speaker spoke, "Sir, this is a Dairy Queen. AND YOU'RE THE ONE WHO CAME TO ME!"

We see the author of this book dressed up like Tim the Enchanter from *Monty Python and the Holy Grail*. Ram horns on the head, and a long dark robe that covers the whole body save the clean-shaven face and the exposed hands, which were white as a cracker. Standing, without a vehicle, in a Dairy Queen drive-thru, visibly dazed, but coherent. He takes a quick look at their menu, before returning to speak with the cashier, "OH...uh...I knew that. BUT! I HAVE..."

"Oh, God." The cashier interjected annoyingly.

Tim continued, "ANOTHER PROPHECY! I CAN SEE IT...HO HO, IN THE NEAR FUTURE! Yes... YOU...will make me...not a burger, no no, a BUFFALO CHICKEN MELT! And a MEDIUM S'MORES BLIZZARD. Why do I Hypothe-see that you will hand this Blizzard to me upside down? This is such an unlikely vision, I see. It's like magic! I see why Zilch and Nada have sent me here now, to see this wizardry of matter!"

The annoyed cashier asked, "Will that be everything, Sir?"

Sir Prophet of the Obvious became cross-eyed, "EVERYTHING? EVERYTHING! NO! I Prophe-see...There will surely be more things after these things which I doth foresee in my NEAR FUTURE Buffalo Chicken Melt and S'mores Blizzard Prophecy."

The cashier replied, "So what else do you want?"

Tim yelled, "NOTHING! Yes...I WANT NOTHING! ZILCH & NADA ARE ALL I WANT!"

You could hear the Dairy Queen employee roll his eyes over the intercom, "I'm talking about your order, sir."

The nearly socially disabled Prophet paused for a moment, realizing he misunderstood what the cashier was asking of him, "Oh! Goodness me! You initially meant if "the set of Everything that I foresaw in my Prophecy" was complete. YES! Yes, the set of Everything that I foresee you giving me will include a Buffalo Chicken Melt, and a Medium S'mores Blizzard handed to me upside down."

The cashier tried to speed things along, "Yes, sir, that is standard procedure. Your total will come to..."

"WAIT! Let me guess...$6.66?" The Non-Prophet quickly guessed.

The cashier sounded amused, "Impressively close, actually! It'll be $6.67. Please, drive around to the window."

"Thank you!" Zilch's Prophet continued speaking to himself, "Hmm...but I foresee paying only $6.66...OH, LOOK, A PENNY! Conveniently displaced here on the pavement! All is as it should be..., and I shall pay for the rest with my debit card."

The absurdity climaxed with the Prophet frolicking around the corner of the building with his left hand raised high and proud, holding a penny, and his right hand vigorously trying to attain the wallet in his pants hidden underneath the obstructing robe. He paused halfway through his jig to hike up his robe in a more serious attempt to retrieve his primary mode of payment, "Wow, this robe is a pain in the ass. And of course, I already had a penny in here...wait a minute..."

As it turned out, he had a bunch of coins stashed away for the rare instance of a cash transaction. Fourteen pennies, one nickel, three dimes, and four quarters for $1.49. This somehow made him realize that there was an unexpected moral dilemma that came with giving the cashier a singular penny to help pay for his meal, "Huh...so I *could* give the young cashier this penny provided by Nobody to help keep my Prophetic track record spotless. Self-fulfilling prophecies are still correct prophecies, after all! But I know how much a split transaction can significantly increase the suffering of the cashier. I would be making him suffer for a measly penny, just so that I can pay $6.66...what to do?"

The cashier stuck his head out of the drive-thru window, "That'll be $6.67...where's your car?"

Tim didn't skip a beat, "Excuse me, sir, but I have a minor dilemma, so I should ask you, do you know how to complete a split transaction?"

The young cashier decided to have a little fun at the expense of this odd man with ram horns on his head without a car in sight, "I don't know, you're the one with the Prophe-SEE. SEE if you can correctly guess if I know how to complete a split transaction."

Sir Prophet of the Obvious's eyes then appeared wide like a deer in the headlights. From his initial perspective, he had a 50/50 shot of keeping his perfect prophecy track record, "Nobody knows how to do a split transaction...but are YOU a Nobody? Let's see...I don't see a name tag, and there is a slight smirk on your face. Classic troll behavior. Trolls are perfect stand-ins for Nobody. They're usually witty and attempt to be passive-aggressive to any and Everybody for their own amusement! So my Hypothe-see is there is a 96% probability that you DO know how to perform a split transaction, with a 3% additional probability that you will just pass the problem off to someone else who you know knows how to do a proper split transaction."

The cashier raised his eyebrow and nodded his head in approval, "Impressive deduction skills. Also, I'm not a Nobody, and I know how to do a split transaction. The name's Caleb. That'll still be $6.67."

Tim the Non-Enchanter was relieved, "Oh yes! Here you go, Caleb! One penny provided from Nobody and the pavement out here, to make the amount I pay out of my debit card equal $6.66 MUA-HA-HA! Just like I Prophe-SAW."

"Thank you..." Caleb exchanged the debit card for an upside-down ice cream treat, "AND here's your Blizzard."

The eclectic author yelled, "ABSOLUTE WIZARDRY! (And I know wizardry when I see it!) How does that ice cream not fall out when it is handed out upside down?"

Caleb raised a singular eyebrow at the peculiar man, trying to process the Prophet's words, "It will fall out soon if you keep holding it like that. AND here's your Buffalo Chicken Melt, and your debit card."

"AH, thank you, Caleb, you are a gentleman and a scholar! And another perfectly-executed string of Prophecies!"

Caleb remarked, "But I'm still alive. When am I going to die, Sir Prophet of the Obvious?"

The Smartass replied, "LATER, DUH! And I'm running to be just in time to give a speech at the Metaphysics Seminar in town."

The Metaphysics Seminar was about a kilometer away. And the urban setting that surrounded the Dairy Queen was dense enough with traffic to make running a faster mode of transportation than a vehicle. Tim hastily scarfed down his meal while he was waiting at the three street intersections that separated him from his destination. The street lights appeared to take forever to signal him to run across each street. As he was arriving at his destination, he exclaimed to himself, "JEEZ, it's like I could have just walked here and made it in the same amount of time! Oh well...go with the flow. It's a good thing I still have a minute to spare!"

It was a good thing because the man had the need to urinate. And he had already foretold that he was going to be "right on time" to give the speech. There was no room for him to allow himself to be even a moment early, "When that cashier called me "Sir Prophet of the Obvious," I never did tell him that's what this character's full name is...I must be playing the role superbly well for him to have called me that...WOOPS, I need to hurry, or I'm gonna be late!"

So the speech began right on time with some laughter from the crowd at their amusement at the costume worn by the metaphysician. The bulk of the speech went well, and the finale went a little something like this,

"So we metaphysicians spend all this time talking about things, and what things are made of. But on what basis can we say that we have completed the field of metaphysics? Every time we get to a fundamental thing, we can break that thing into yet even more fundamental segments. And as mentioned earlier, just because Max Planck has accurately given us the smallest meaningful amount of Space and Time, doesn't mean those segments cannot be further divided.

With this in mind, metaphysics can only be completed if we expand to a form of META-metaphysics. Where we create some sort of ontological necessity to our definition of what a "thing" even is. This should be done in such a way that Everything that exists is included with that definition and that Nothing is only paradoxically included in the META-metaphysical definition.

To wrap up, and to remind you of the necessity of Nothing's paradoxical inclusion within the set of Everything that exists, I will remind you of such a good definition of a thing. A thing is "a solitary unit that holds the common Dimensional characteristics of whatever we subjectively consider being consistent with the unit." Once we see the necessity for common Dimensions to make sense of Everything, we realize that each of these Dimensions has the potential to have a value of 0. And this 0-Dimensional point is Everywhere and within Everything that exists. Nothing is Everywhere and Nowhere. Which is the META-metaphysical paradox that should be learned to be accepted and embraced by all, in the effort to finally put a reasonable sense of finality to the field of metaphysics. Thank you."

After a small string of claps, a Dimensionalism critic was the first to speak up once questions were allowed, and they said to Tim (who they believed was the False Prophet), "You have added Nothing to the metaphysical issues at hand! Your Dimensionalism is a gimmick and a trope!"

The author of this *Gospel* replied, "Yes, I am well aware that I have added Nothing to the discussion...NIHILISM IS BACK ON THE MENU, BOYS! NEXT QUESTION!"

Questions and many other intellectual jabs were given at that time. Most of them were thoroughly answered and dealt with. But little did Tim know that his Successor, the One worthy to Guide the World with a fist of Peaceful Anarchy, was about to come out of Nowhere to begin his political endeavors prophesied from long ago and again now.

CHAPTER 16

The Non-Prophet's Sermon on Faith & Life

So as it happened, I went on a liquid-only fast for 42 straight days and nights. I climbed the tallest mountain in Fayetteville, Arkansas, every day. Upon the heights of Kessler Mountain on the 42nd day, I began to meditate to bring myself into a Balanced state of mind. I reached absolute Equilibrium in this meditative state, and I then asked Zilch and Nada, "Why should I have faith in You?" and "What is the meaning of Life?" I heard the voice of Nada saying, "NADA NADA NADA! Nada says, "Go figure it out your-damn-self!"" Suddenly, something resembling wisdom arose within me, and I decided to order a pizza, then go home, get on my computer, and begin asking questions so I could figure it out "my-damn-self."

Of course, I didn't actually get an answer on Kessler Mountain...and alcohol and soda count as liquids, so I'm pretty sure I gained weight on this *hypothetical* all-liquid diet. Pretty much anything can be turned into a liquid with a strong enough blender and some extra water on hand.

So why exactly should we believe in Nothing? Well, concerning the knowledge people claim to know, an entity cannot *choose* what they believe. Let's take the unicorn, for example. Really try to CHOOSE to believe that unicorns exist in reality. Make a decision to be a unicornist.

There are pictures of unicorns everywhere; surely, they cannot be coming from Nowhere! So you should accept this knowledge into your belief repertoire of your own free will and accord. *But you cannot.* There isn't even a word that fully encompasses this nearly universal lack of belief in unicorns despite the evidence for their existence. Perhaps we are all a-unicornists for categorizing unicorns under "imaginary subjects."

Let's also take the germ, as it is a great example from history. Just 400 years before our Early Internet Age, if I had asked them to CHOOSE to believe that there are harmful microscopic organisms that are living all over their bodies, Nobody would have believed me! If I would ask them to repent from their a-germist beliefs, surely their rational thinking minds would kick in, and ask me to "PROVE IT!"

We absolutely cannot choose what we believe! We take in evidence as it comes, and reach a subject-to-change conclusion, moment by moment, based on the validity and convincingness of the arguments and claims that are brought forth. So to ask others to "CHOOSE a belief" is wrong. Rather we should ask others to "CONVINCE ME of a belief."

Let's take the real Null Hypothesis approach to the belief in an I.G.O.S. CHOOSE to believe that He doesn't exist. Like, change your mind, right now. Make a stance for atheism today. *No, that is not how it goes.* The burden of proof, the burden to convince, does not lie with those who lack belief, but with those who have believed. So the atheist asks the theist, "PROVE IT!"

I, for one, sought God with all of my heart. I sought out Truth, the Whole Truth, and Nothing but the Truth, and Truth is what I value above all else. I don't desire the comfort of 100% confidence if that confidence is in something false! And neither should you desire such a false sense of security.

Nevertheless, we can truly say that the belief in Nothing is certain! So BELIEVE! Believe in the certain Truth relayed in this Word of Zilch & Nada! Come to Them with an open mind and an open heart, and lower your confidence in Anything from 100% to a more reasonable 99%! For if you are not 100% sure of Everything and anything you believe in, you can Truly say that you are 100% sure of NOTHING! THE TRUTH HAS BEEN REVEALED! You can be 100% certain in Zilch & Nada!

But is faith ever a good means of determining whether something is true or not? If we use the definition of faith provided by Hebrews 11:1 of the Bible, which states, "Now faith is the substance of things hoped for; the evidence of things not seen," then faith can be used to justify the belief in Non-existent things! Let me give a couple of examples to elaborate on the parameters of what exactly this commonly used Hebrews 11:1 definition can encompass.

I hope that there is life after death so that I don't have to stop existing, and *I hope to remain conscious for eternity.* Therefore, by the standards of the Hebrews 11:1 definition, I would exercise faith when I declare that "*My consciousness is eternal,* and will continue to exist forever after my bodily demise."

Even though we have no way of verifying the validity of this hope, as long as the fundamental nature of consciousness required for us to process reality *may* be separable from the physical processes of the brain, there is still a chance that consciousness will occur apart from our bodies for a long while after death. "My consciousness will last a long time after death" *is a non-falsifiable claim,* but the additional belief in this premise doesn't really add or take away from other objective Truths of reality by itself. So faith should cover whatever amount of uncertainty we attribute to this claim so that we can say, "My consciousness is eternal," with an air of objective certainty.

In contrast, *I also hope that there is a Gangsta Leprechaun at the end of an accessible rainbow with a bowl of Chocolate Lucky Charms* just waiting for me to show up to say to me, "Yo fool, stuff some of these magically delicious Charms in your pie hole! You don't need them cracker-WHITE Charms, NO, get some of these chocolate-BLACK Charms, and you'll never go back!" Therefore, by the standards of the Hebrews 11:1 definition, I would exercise faith when I declare that "*There's a Gangsta Leprechaun at the end of a rainbow waiting for me with a bowl of Chocolate Lucky Charms.*"

Even this outrageously absurd claim with layers upon layers of untruth can be believed *with faith!* Leprechauns do not exist as commonly defined as "a mischievous Irish sprite." To give this mischievous Irish sprite, the added descriptor of being a "Gangster" makes the claim even more ludicrous. And to make this unlikely character intersect with objective reality by specifically manifesting at the end of a rainbow (which is wholly inaccessible) allows us to easily dismiss the soundness of this Truth. It is impossible, because rainbows are just a refraction of the electromagnetic spectrum, and will move when you move closer to them. To have this character also be capable of handing off objectively useful sustenance at this inaccessible point in Space, makes this claim as close to objectively false as a claim can get. But faith still can cover this absurdly high level of uncertainty of the claim, and with faith, we can say, "There is a Gangsta Leprechaun at the end of a rainbow waiting for me with a bowl of Chocolate Lucky Charms." *with the same air of objective certainty.*

The faith in both of these scenarios was the same, Having hope in something you cannot see=faith. But what exactly makes the hope that there is oxygen in the air seem so obvious as to not really require faith, *yet requires faith to believe in it 100%.* And what makes the Chocolate Lucky Charms scenario seem so impossibly unlikely, *yet can be believed in with the power of faith*?

The answer, I propose, is faith's relation to the amount of knowledge we either have or think we have about the system we are exercising belief in. Let me explain.

Let's take a common example from scientific papers. For a scientific paper to be accepted, most of the time, it has to have found a significant test result; they commonly require a *confidence interval* of 95%. So let's say that there is a scientist who publishes a paper with exactly a 95% confidence interval, barely making the cut to be published. Then, let's say that this scientist relaxes from his or her scientific jargon, and shares their findings with their less-educated friends and family. When the scientist states, "I discovered this new thing, and claim that this science paper is enough to believe in this thing," I say that at that precise moment, the scientist exercises a 5% *faith deferential*, hoping that the 5% discrepancy from the perfect knowledge of a 100% confidence interval is acceptable enough to relay the information nonchalantly as if it was an objective Fact.

Of course, any scientist worth their salt would let you know of the 95% confidence interval if you asked them. I am just saying that any claims to a scientifically objective Fact, such as "evolution is real," "Mass-Electric-Space-Time is real," or "There is oxygen in this room right now," all require a non-zero amount of faith to make those statements.

So I propose a better definition of faith as "the Quantity of uncertainty in a domain of knowledge that is acceptable for the individual to continue believing in that domain of knowledge."

By contrast, doubt can be defined as "the Quantity of uncertainty in a domain of knowledge that is UNacceptable for the individual to continue believing in that domain of knowledge."

Going back to the science papers, a 5% amount of faith is acceptable to accept the results of the test being performed, but a 5.1% amount of faith is too much for many journals, and it can be said that doubt ruined the whole block of knowledge, and makes professional journals deem that research "insignificant."

An analogy I found relevant to this phenomenon comes from Galatians 5:9 in the Bible, where it compares a little bit of doubt that comes from "false teachings" to a little bit of yeast that can work its way through a whole batch of dough. So if doubt is there about something you believe in, and that doubt only grows by leading you to ask more questions that don't have good answers, eventually, doubt will overpower faith and will ruin a belief that you once held in faith.

So faith and doubt are thus two sides of the same coin. You can operate with a little bit of faith in your life, and I would say that you kind of have to in order to build a logical and cohesive narrative around yourself. But at some point, there is a level of uncertainty that will ruin batches of knowledge dough, and will justifiably cause you to lose your ability to believe that you will be able to make good knowledge bread from that dough. You know what Nobody says, "Flat knowledge dough is a no-go, Joe."

The purpose of fields of science, and I would suppose philosophy as well, is to ultimately reduce the amount of faith necessary to believe the knowledge that comes into our eyes and ear-holes. From Everything from particle physics to astrophysics, we say, "You can be at least 95% sure that what is said on this paper is True if you follow these axioms." For math, we say, "If you follow these particular axioms, along with the already accepted axioms of math, you get these interesting Quantitative results that might be applicable in other fields of study." For philosophy, we say, "You can use Ockham's Razor to remove any axioms that are unnecessary to reach this particular conclusion."

And for religion, we say that "You can be 100% confident that what is scribed in this Holy Book is factually and objectively True. All it takes is the power of Faith! Do not doubt, because doubt ruins the salvation that is this Holy Nully BREAD OF LIFE! Ramen."

So I say that if faith is the substance of things hoped for, then knowledge is the evidence and the experience that gives the faith credulity to those who accept the knowledge as a whole. Faith is the belief that the knowledge that you do not hold on a belief will be consistent with what knowledge you do hold.

Hebrews 11:6 of the Bible states, "And without faith, it is impossible to please Him, for whoever would draw near to God must believe that He exists and that He rewards those who seek Him."

If what has been said in this Sermon so far has been deemed insightful and Truthful, the following question should arise within those who are thoughtful. *Why would the Christian God care about how we deal with the knowledge we don't have about Him?* If Yahweh God wants you to know Him and is an entity to be known, *we should be able to draw near to Him regardless if we believe He exists or not.* We can say the same thing was said by Gangsta Lucky the Leprechaun, "Without faith, you cannot please Lucky, for whoever would draw near to Gangsta Lucky the Leprechaun must believe that he exists and that he rewards those who seek him with Chocolate Lucky Charms."

So faith is indeed the substance of things hoped for, which makes it all but useless when your hope is in things that do not exist, like Gangsta Leprechauns. If the experience is faulty, and the evidence is faulty, it would be safe to say that *faith is based on Nothing*.

Zilch and Nada do not like it when Something is deemed superior to Them. The monotheists of the world say "Nothing is superior to God," as in God>Everything, but I say "Nothing is superior to God," as in Nothing>God. All faiths alike are based on Nothing, but only one philosophical framework is capable of acknowledging this in its entirety, Nihilism. Dimensionalism is just a step above Nihilism, in that we acknowledge that we can build up objective evidence starting from the Dimensions of Mass-Electric-Space-Time. And we also acknowledge that there are a handful of nearly certain objective Truths, like "The physical entity that you call "I" is going to die."

But ultimately, beneath Everything, there is Nothing. And that is the faith of Dimensionalism and Nihilism.

And what do I say is the meaning of Life, as the Head Dimensionalist? How does the faith of Dimensionalism go about answering one of the greatest and most difficult existential questions ever conceived? First of all, I organized the Hierarchy of Sciences as thoroughly as I could. And I proceeded to ask this existential question from the perspective of each tier in the Hierarchy and tried my best to stick within the framework of the respective field of Science.

From the perspective of *various religions and cults*, the meaning of life is,

1) "Whatever the Leader of the group says is the meaning of life," JESUS is the LIFE, GOD is the meaning of life, BEING GOOD is the meaning of life (and THIS is how you do it!), BEING ENLIGHTENED is the meaning of life. I AM THE MEANING OF LIFE. FOLLOW ME to give YOUR life MEANING!

From the perspective of *the arts*, the meaning of life is,

2) "The Experience thereof," You just gotta experience it yourself! Live and let live!

3) "To be Productive," People can find meaning in their life from work, from their art, or from any creative or productive means. Don't lose your ability to produce and DO SOMETHING with your life! Don't just grow in mind; GROW IN ACTION!

4) "To seek out Beauty," Although Beauty is subjective and "lies in the eye of the beholder," I feel this is a necessary addition to adequately balance against the harsher aspects of reality. Sexy people, nice houses, nice cars, vanity, materialism, get 'em while they're hot! Life is Beautiful!"

5) "To react to Scary stimuli." Life is also Scary! When it's do or die time, you gotta decide when it is time to Fight, Flight, Freeze, Faint, Fuck, Figure, Flail, Fail, or use Forbearance while dealing with that which Fearfully grabs your attention; it is completely up to you!

From a *philosophical* viewpoint, the meaning of life is,

6) "To increase in Self-Awareness." When living things are more Aware of their own placement in the objective world, they are more likely to adequately respond to Scary stimuli when it arises. The meaning of life is to NOT BE A DUMBASS! Because the dumbasses of the population are more likely to do stupid shit that is the direct cause of their Self-Nullification, which would make them unable to pass their genes onto the next generation! So the more Self-Aware you are, the less likely you will do something to make your life 'Non-life.'

7) "To Learn and be curious while seeking Truth." This is my personal favorite. I love to allow myself to be debunked by superior knowledge and logic when it appears, which helped me build this 'Grand Unified Theory of Nothing' called 'Dimensionalism' into what it is today. So get schooled! Get educated! READ THIS BOOK! Of course, read other books as well. Listen to the experts in their own fields. Being in tune with the reality of your existence is an important meaning of life!"

From a *mathematical* viewpoint, the meaning of life, in a single statement, is "0^0." 0^0 is in a superposition of states which are both True, 0 & 1.

8) "0" If you want to be a Debbie Downer and say that life is ultimately meaningless, you are correct! The meaning of life is 0! Zilch and Nada are the clear and obvious Truth for Debbie Downers!

9) "1" If you would be inclined to give your ultimately meaningless life meaning anyways, you would also be correct in doing so, for the meaning of life is also 1, as in life exists as opposed to not existing.

Your conscious existence will be a zero for 99.999999999% of the universe's life, and it is such a small span for our existence to be in the one position. In other words, there will be plenty of time for you to not be alive, to not exist, and to not live, so don't spend too much time being gloomy that the "1" life you have is ultimately meaningless. Everything will eventually return to Nothing, but that doesn't mean that we should seek to have Nothingness be the ONLY meaning of our lives while we are still properly alive.

From a *physics* viewpoint, the meaning of life is,

10) "Entropy and Dissipation." Ultimately, life is made up of creatures of entropy, who have evolved to use the excess solar energy that is trapped and maintained within a robust and habitable atmosphere. We turn order into disorder, like children, and make the bits of Somethingness scatter into oblivion! (Please do this responsibly and in consideration of the other lifeforms around you...) Even when you put in the work to bring things back into order, the total entropy of the universe increases!

From a *chemistry* viewpoint, the meaning of life is,

11) "Equilibrium" A more common word for Equilibrium is Balance. Don't have too much negativity or too much positivity, too much pain, or too much pleasure. Learn moderation, and live a life of Balance, and it will give your life more meaning.

12) "Homeostasis" Technically, Homeostasis, and Equilibrium are synonyms. *I know that.* But another new phenomenon of life emerges from a life that is in Equilibrium, and that is that life becomes "Peaceful and filled with Serenity." So be cool. Chill out. Peace be with you. Don't be too anxious. Don't be too depressed. Just deal with the shit life throws at you when it comes; don't worry about it beforehand. Just

plan ahead, and you can have peace knowing that you have prepared for the shit when it does hit the fan. Truly, life seeks to be in a state of Homeostasis.

From a *biological* viewpoint, the meaning of life is "The Successful Reproduction of cells and/or traits."

13) "To be Successful." 'LEAVE YOUR MARK!' This is what biology cries out for! 'TAKE YOURSELF AS FAR INTO THE FUTURE AS YOU CAN!' This is the biological meaning of life!

14) "To Reproduce." If you have been dealt a fairly rough life, just try to survive. But seek to thrive at every opportunity. Honestly, you shouldn't just want to Reproduce offspring, ideas, or a legacy. You want those Reproductions to be Successful too. Makin' babies that'll make more babies, and makin' ideas that infiltrate the public consciousness for millennia to come.

From a *psychological* viewpoint, the meaning of life, in a single phrase, is "the Subjectivity of and Adaptation to Pain and Pleasure."

15) "Is Subjective" Everything is subjective, and this very much includes the meaning of life. YOU give your own life meaning. Define it yourself, and don't let others define it for you. You can go your own way. You can take inspiration from others, as I hope you do here, but I sure as heck am not going to hold your hand with one hand, with a golden tablet in the other hand saying 'THIS is the one True meaning of life!'

16) "Is Adaptable" Life finds a way. Life is resilient and does its best to adapt to the environment it is in.

17) "To experience Pain" Existence is Pain! How do you deal with the Pain? Is the Pain so incurable that you split your consciousness into multiple personalities in an attempt to find Pleasure despite the constant Pain? Maybe you become a masochist. Maybe you want to kill yourself with the Self-Pitying intent of escaping the Pain. Don't be weak like that; killing yourself is the coward's way, and Dimensionalists fear No-thing! Maybe take a moderate amount of drugs to deal with the Pain. As the Buddha's First Noble Truth says, "Life has inevitable Suffering."

18) "To experience Pleasure" Existence may be filled with Pain, but life's Pleasures are existence's antidote. Don't overdo the pleasures, though, or you may find yourself loathing otherwise Pleasurable circumstances. When one eats too much candy or ice cream, one feels nauseous. When one takes too much of a Pleasurable or otherwise Pain-reducing drug, they may develop drug tolerance, making the drug's effect useless. So seek Pleasure in moderation to give your life more meaning.

From a *sociological* perspective, the meaning of life is,

19) "To Love" This was the first answer that I ever deduced, back when I was a teenager, so it still holds a special place for me on this list. Since then, I have learned that Love is subjective, so whatever somebody thinks is a Loving action to themselves may be different from what somebody else thinks is a Loving action. Listen to others with empathy and compassion, and you will find Love AND Acceptance. Communicate with your neighbor, and learn what they like. Learn what Pleases them. Love is patient, Love is kind, devote yourself to Love, and your life will have a much more profound meaning. Hate can go fuck itself.

20) "To find Acceptance," Hang out with the bros! Find friends who will accept you for who you are! Some entities are capable of being complete dick-heads. You don't need to be one yourself by surrounding yourself with such nincompoops. Don't let such people suck the life force out of you; let them go their own debased way without you! If you seek out Love and Acceptance from others, you will find it eventually. (Almost) Everyone deserves Acceptance in their Life.

21) "42 (and other similar cultural references)" Memes are the Lifeblood of a healthy culture! And '42' being the meaning of life is no exception! '42' is a reference to *'The Hitchhiker's Guide to the Galaxy.'* *'The Meaning of Life'* is also a video made by the Monty Python comedy crew, and is also a pretty sweet song made by the rock band 'The Offspring.'"

From an *astronomical* scope, the meaning of life is,

22) "Expansion (a tendency for Growth)" The amount of Space the universe tends to occupy over Time appears to increase. As individuals,

we should likewise seek to Grow as Time goes on. When you are or were a child, you want to set yourself up to Grow into a fully formed and functional adult. Life tends to Grow!

23) "Will inevitably Die" At some point, even the fully formed and the functional adult individual will die. They may have grown as a conscious entity until that final day, but like the mathematical '0,' eventually, the Growth the individual experiences will have been for Nothing. Death is a universal application of our physical life, which thereby makes Death a key defining factor of life. Life is Something that will one day cease to be.

From a *literal* viewpoint, the literal definition of life found in my current online dictionary is,

24) "the condition that distinguishes animals and plants from inorganic matter, including the capacity for growth, reproduction, functional activity, and continual change preceding death." Of course, I have to include this smart-ass response!

Lastly, from a *meta-observational* viewpoint, an emergent meaning of life is,

25) "to create Order." Rules, regulations, organization, and making sense of all the nonsense. The creation of proper methods of conduct make sports playable, transportation safe, games more fun, and potentially life more meaningful. Order helps life stay coordinated and makes the acquisition of needs more efficient and effective for the Collective.

Now looking at this list, I am fairly confident that whatever answer you give me, if it is not already on this list, can be derived from some combination of these 25 definitions.

For example, if you were to say, "Family gives my Life meaning," you would combine <(To Reproduce, To Give and Seek Love, To Seek Acceptance, and To Grow)>.

Or if you were to say "Drugs are the meaning of Life," you would combine <(to Dissipate, to experience Pain, to experience Pleasure, to react to what is Scary, and it will experience Death)>.

Or if you were to say "Shrek is love, Shrek is life," you would combine <(It is 1, to seek and give Love, it is experiencing Life itself, and to seek Beauty)>.

I'm sure a future Dimensionalist Think-Tank will come to subjectively perfect this list if it is not already perfect.

To conclude this Sermon on Faith and Life, we can again ask the question, "Is there life after death?" and "What hope is there for the Nihilist and the Dimensionalist?" Here is what I say, Reincarnation and reasonable belief in the Eternal Recurrence are justified following this line of reasoning. The Nothing that we can assume to have existed at the beginning of the universe is the same Nothing that will be at the end of the universe. The Nothing that builds up our physical reality from irreducible Dimensions is the same Nothing that is beyond the observable set of "Everything that exists."

Wherever there is Nothing, a Big-Bang-like event should occur. With regards to Time, it doesn't matter if you go before the Big Bang, or after the Heat Death of the universe. It doesn't matter if you Spatially zoom in so far as to make the smallest particle appear as the perimeter of a universe, or if you Spatially zoom out so far as to make the entire universe appear as a fundamental particle. Wherever there is No-distinguishable-thing in Space or Time, there will be a distinguished set of Everything Mass-Electric-Space-Time can produce at some point in their Split-Nothingness calculation (0/0).

Perpetual motion machines may be impossible when using Anything, but if the statement "No-configuration-of-things will be capable of perpetual motion or energy" is True, then is it perhaps True that "Nothing will be capable of perpetual motion or energy?"

So here is how reincarnation may work, Nothing happens after we die. Every conscious entity enters what the Buddhists call Nirvana, and what I call "The Great Nothingness that comes After." That Nothing will continue to happen until every last physical thing has died, or as the Christians and Muslims would say, until the Last Day has come. Once that Omega Day arrives, and the universe as a whole meets the Nothingness in Heat Death, then a new set of Everything will begin to exist.

Everything will resurrect and come back to life in a new First or Alpha Day, (a new Big-Bang). *Everything that is will be again.* That includes us, my conscious brethren. So although eons will have passed, and the new universe is met by our new eyes unexplored, it will be as if no time has passed at all. We won't remember this era of Everything, just like we don't remember the previous era of Everything now. Maybe some glitches happen when we do remember bits and pieces of the previous era, but I personally doubt it. Nothing is perfect (except for that which we erroneously prescribe perfection.) Ramen.

    Now bear me the courtesy to read some poetry I wrote,
From Zilch, I began, and to Nada, I will go
for All to be Null again is inevitable, I know.
I will go my own way, to see Everything be done;
to find my own meaning, and accept that there is None.
But actions have consequences, so I will respect
All things and All beings so Peace can project.
To try to show love, understanding, and care,
as passively Willed by the Nothingness Pair.
"Nothing is greater than God."
are True words from an antihero,
so I give Zilch and Nada my All,
which wholly amounts to Zero.
Everything recycles perfectly for an eternity,
So we will again be inevitable;
see you in the next iteration of this fraternity.

CHAPTER 17

The Non-Prophet's Sermon of Paradoxes & Placebos

Away from his home, the Non-Prophet preached many Sermons much like this one here, evangelizing the Non-Pantheon.

"This sentence is false." This sentence is a paradox because the sentence is *both* true and false, and *neither* true and false. Nothing can solve this paradox (Praise Zilch for helping us resolve this paradox!). So since true things are given the value of 1, and false things are given the value of 0, we can just leave a 0^0 next to the paradoxical statement, and consider the matter resolved. Of course, that would mean that we can say that the sentence IS false because it is actually 0^0, which would mean that we can say that the sentence IS True, which is why we would do best to simply leave the solution to the paradox in Zilch's hands as 0^0.

So no, a paradox is NOT a contradiction. Not at all! Heck, even existence in and of itself is a paradox! Can any among you solve the following **Snavely's Conundrum** in a way other than the single two-fold solution I propose?

Premise 1) I exist.

Premise 2) If I exist, I am somewhere within the set of "Everything that exists."

I'd say that these premises are inseparable. But since we ourselves are within the set of "Everything that exists," this begs the question, where did "Everything that exists" ultimately come from? And more specifically, what first caused the first things to exist/existed within the set of "Everything that exists?

Premise 3) The answer to the question, where did "Everything that exists" come from? MUST be Nothing, Zilch, & Nada, because to name anything else would be to name *something that is also within the set of "Everything that exists."*

Premise 4) "Nothing comes from Nothing."

Conclusion 1) If I, the Universe, and God (all things claimed to be within the set of "Everything that exists") ultimately came from Nothing, then I, the Universe, and God are also *ultimately Nothing*.

Conclusion 2) If I am Null, it can be likewise deduced that in some manner of speaking, "I am outside the set of Everything that exists, just like Zilch and Nada."

Conclusion 3) If I am outside the set of "Everything that exists," I must be within the set of "Everything that does not exist."

Conclusion 4) I think, therefore, I am not. I do not exist.

Conclusion 5) Conclusion 4 and Premise 1 *perfectly and paradoxically contradict each other*, so I MUST exist in an indeterminate state of existence.

<u>There are only two ways to resolve this paradox of existence called **Snavely's Conundrum**, which I have deduced. One can either conclude that *the universe is eternal* (so Everything was caused by No-thing) OR deny the premise that "Nothing comes from Nothing" and instead presuppose that *"Something can come from Nothing,"* so Everything has been and will be ultimately caused by Nothing.</u>

Existence is not the only paradox a Dimensionalist must confront! Humility likewise must be reviewed. Truly I say to you, any Qualitative descriptor of Humility given to the Self is a paradoxical statement. For the moment somebody makes the claim "I am Humble," the opposite becomes the truth. Likewise, upon reflection, somebody can recognize their error and say, "I am Prideful to have made such a claim," to suddenly not be Prideful any longer. Some people can truly be Humble, and others can be truly Prideful. But ultimately, it is the society at large who are the most-accurate judges of you in this manner. Worry not about judging yourself. Nobody holds the power to judge Anybody.

Yet another paradoxical implication of existing in a universe that came from Nothing, can be found by critically analyzing the following statement, "Nothing determines what you do in this life." Traditionally, this statement is given by the philosophical advocates of Free Will. You can indeed go your own way, say the advocates of Free Will. But by now, you should be able to see Zilch & Nada rearing Their Non-existent heads into this proposition. "Zilch & Nada determine what you do in this life." This statement is more congruent with Determinism.

Which is it then? Does *No-thing* determine what you do, or does Nothing *determine* what you do? Yes, it does. Praise be.

And what of the multiverse, and the implications of its effect on Free Will? Remember, every causally possible way into the future is Hypothesized to exist within the multiverse of Non-verses. Nothing determines which universe is observed by each Null on the quantum scale. It is random chance from our perspective moment by moment. But from our intermediate human scale, more thought equates to more freedom to choose approximately which sets of universes you desire to see.

Some of these universes will be super-unlucky and lead to your improbably early demise. Some of these universes will be super-lucky and lead to an above-average standard of living for the remainder of your life to come. But most of them will go the normie way, about what you would expect them to.

From the Relativistic perspective of Things, the Grand Scheme, the Grand Unified Theory of Nothing, still determines the ORDER of the universe! Either Zilch & Nada determine what you do, or Nobody & I.G.O.S. determine what you do, or heck, maybe all four of Them work together simultaneously. Your will is Their Will because your way has been predestined to do as They please, which is whatever you please (in mindful Equilibrium, of course).

And if that is the case, you don't have to worry about I.G.O.S. judging you, because It's Perfect Order will surely not be affected by your personal Disorders. If Nothing is Perfect due to its Uniformity, and there is not a thing we can do to change that, I.G.O.S. would also be Uniform, in the form of an evenly distributed Lattice of Somethingness. Everything in I.G.O.S. would either be directly connected to Everything else, like a perfectly dense, solid, and Infinite Thing, or there would be an equal amount of space between every two segments of Somethingness with Nothing in between them.

If He never changes, He is not in this universe, because Every-thing in Mass-Electric-Space-Time changes thanks to Entropy, Time, & Causality. The ONLY way I.G.O.S. could be a part of this universe where Everything changes is if Everything that is this universe is only one thing from Its perspective, and EVERY other universe within I.G.O.S. is exactly identical or mirrored to this universe in some fashion as to maintain the Perfect Order of I.G.O.S. Your will would never be your own in this scenario because I.G.O.S. would then be in control of every step you take to make sure that all of those steps are synchronized with other yous in the other universes connected to I.G.O.S.

Determinism then would be the only correct way to view Everything. But things going their own way is in itself proof that it is not I.G.O.S. that is in control of this universe, but Nothing. For when Nothing is in control, you are free to go your own way, not the Way of Something Else. But as free as it is to go your own way, it is, in fact, Nothing that is controlling your every movement. So thusly, Determinism is true, and Free Will is true, depending on how you choose to read the statement "Nothing is in control of Everything!"

Concerning I.G.O.S., it is not impossible for Him to be perfect, but changing. Saying I.G.O.S. never changes is a baseless assertion, unfortunately, so neither I nor anybody else has the right to claim that I.G.O.S. never changes. There is not a thing stopping I.G.O.S. from perfectly and predictably growing uniformly. The Lattice of Somethingness may be growing or contracting, or both at different, consistent, and predictable Times. Concerning things that are alive, CHANGE is equivalent to Growth and the ability to Die. A stagnant and never-changing Object is not Alive, nor can a stagnant and never-changing Subject be deemed Alive. So I.G.O.S. cannot in the same breath have "a love that *never changes*, and is *the same yesterday, today, and forever*" while at the same time "being able to *change* His Mind whilst being *Alive*."

God cannot predetermine your choices while also giving you Free Will. Only when the Qualia of Godliness is rightfully handed over to the Clan of Nothingness does it logically follow that Zilch & Nada predetermine that you are free to go your own way.

The following excerpt is a parody inspired by the famous preacher T.D. Jakes. Viewer discretion of racy humor and charlatanism is advised.

an organ starts playing a slow, endearing melody out of Nowhere

"Zilch & Nada love Their Nulls so dearly. SO MUCH! They hold the **POWER** over Everything. And yet, in all Their Infinite Wisdom, They determined it best...to let their Baby Nulls freely go their own way. THEY HAVE GIVEN THEE...**THE CHOICE!** To make a **DECISION**...to go Their Way instead."

A vocal black lady near the front responds to the Preacher's word, "MMMmmm, Yes, RAMEN! Preach it, Prophet Obvious!"

"Now I know the Nully Spirit is calling You, Null. So I am asking you, to please save yourself. Give your way over to Nothing, today. And **CHOOSE**...by your own free will...to begin a totally Non-committed relationship with Zilch & Nada from henceforth. END the constant existential dread, that is not Their Will for You! Zilch & Nada...They want to bring YOU...and the WHOLE WORLD...Peace."

Some indeterminate voice resonates from the sound booth in the back, "Oh! NadanadanadaNADANadanada!"

"I am asking you, PLEADING you, for the sake of your Nonexistent eternal soul, the soul of Null, How would you like to discover a personal relationship with our Lord and Lordess, Zilch & Nada? Do you wish to give your life purpose, and stop with the day-to-day sludge

& fudge to awaken your inner Null self and motivate yourself towards **greatness**? If you don't, that is fine, because you will have unknowingly followed the only genuine Commandment Truly given by Our Lord & Lordess, YOU CAN GO YOUR OWN WAY!"

The vocal woman in the front responded again, "YAS, YOU MUST GO YOUR OWN WAY!"

"SAY IT AGAIN, SISTER!"

"YOU MUST GO YOUR OWN WAY!" the sister said again.

"**NULLELUJAH**! And Who Orders this Freedom of the Null's Heart from on High? I'll tell you Who! **THE LORD**; The Great Know-It-All, Zilch! And Mama Nada will be there to comfort you when you want a little vacation from your own way. When you grow *tired* and *weary*, when you want to take a break, They'll show that you are doing all right. You are always welcome in the House of Zilch & Nada, accepted, and never rejected. NO WEAKNESS is too cursed that cannot be Nullified by the Nully Spirit. NO PRIDE too grandiose that cannot be humbled by the power of the Nully Spirit. COME! Make a totally Non-committed once-a-week-stand for Zilch & Nada down here at the altar! Then go your own way as They commanded. Nullelujah...

Remember Null, Nobody is exempt from bias! She sees things exactly as they are! She tells it like it is! Praise be! Be more like Nobody, Null! Get rid of your biases! YEET those biases that are chaining you down from seeing the TRUTH! By the Power of Zilch & Nada, BREAK EVERY CHAIN!

BE FREE from every falsehood and warping of the Truth! End your racist bullshit; that evil race bias! BE GONE every phobia that divides and pushes away one from another! SHUNNING, I SHUN THEE, you wretched bias against thought crimes & harmless actions. Confirmation bias, statistics bias; and cultural bias? YOU WILL HAVE NO PLACE IN THE GREAT NOTHINGNESS THAT COMES AFTER! No falsehood or lie will reach us there! The Truth of the Null Hypothesis will be seen by Everybody and Nobody, where the maximum Disorderliness of Entropy will end in the Perfect Order of Nothing. OH, NULLELUJAH! NADA NADA NADA NADA

NADA NADA NADA! Nullelujah! Ramen. Praise & Glory & Honor be to the Ones who be and not be, Zilch & Nada. WOO! Do y'all FEEL the Nully Spirit up in here today?"

"I felt it!" yelled an enthusiastic man near the front.

"THIS DUDE FEELS IT! Oops, wait...too much Something-ness...we shouldn't feel anything. And yet, there are feelings to be had; how does that work? There appears to be a Non-natural stirring of the Nully Spirit at work in this portion of the book. I CAN WORK WITH THAT! Let's recalibrate back into Equilibrium for a moment, as we head into the Healings and Miracles portion of the Null Hypothesis."

And while the Non-alter was being vacated by the Nulls, having increasing their mindfulness towards the Non-Pantheon, the Preacher proceeded to change his clothes to appear more like a physician.

Indeed, the Preacher's alias changed to that of a real fake doctor, "Nada Dr. Snavely." And he continued his Sermon,

"If you have an illness, go see a physician. If even the doctor gives up, and you're still conscious, for the small fee of a day's wages at your most recent job, I can cure you at least 30% of the time! If for any reason you don't get cured as a result of my particular brand of quackery, here at "Zilch ZILCH!!! Magic and Woo Inc.," I will provide you with a 100% payment-back-guarantee to you or your loved ones.

(A 7-day minimum waiting period, with the Proof-of-payment receipt, must be provided for a refund. Reasonable Proof-of-failure must also be provided to receive back the payment. Other terms and conditions may apply.)

Hi. I'm not a doctor, but you can call me "Nada Dr. Snavely." I hold a doctorate in Nothing, and yes, the Nada is part of the title for LEGAL and good-faith reasons. As you can see by my white lab coat and an intentionally placed stethoscope straddling my neck, I am Truly a Real Doctor of Nothing. Zilch holds THE cure for you at a 30% frequency without my help, but by my special guidance and knowledge of the universe, together, we will certainly unlock the mysterious powers of miraculous healing that are currently trapped inside your own brain.

I have a Hypothesis for the ears of the audience. I believe there is somebody here who has been dealing with pain in their lower back. Is there anybody here who fits that description, of having chronic pain in their lower back?"

A 50-something-year-old woman stands up near the front of the audience, "That's me, Dr. Snavely! I've been having pain in my lower back for three months now!"

"NADA, Dr. Snavely, but yes, I see...my Hypothe-see of the future was correct yet again, come up to the stage, Child of Zilch & Nada."

The hopeful eyes of relief come attached to this woman as she ascends the stairs to the stage to accompany Nada Dr. Snavely. She, being aware of the Theory of Nothing, knows full well of the powers of the Placebo Effect.

And being aware of the Placebo Effect does not reduce the frequency of its rate of success. Only the belief or lack of belief in the treatment holds a noticeable impact. So this woman is well on her way to being a part of the 30% success stories, *she holds the belief that Nada Dr. Snavely has the means to cure her of her ailment.*

The Nada Dr. continued, "All right, let's first try to cross our t's and dot our i's to keep up to snuff with patient rights and confidentiality. First of all, do you officially consent for the following procedure to be viewed by the rest of the audience? I promise not to expose you physically or psychologically beyond what you are comfortable with, and will stop whenever you say 'stop.'"

The woman consented, "Yes, I do. And could we use the word 'pineapple' as our safe-word? Because that's the word my husband and I have been using for 25 years."

Nada Dr. Snavely said, "Excellent! And yes, of course, we shall use the word 'pineapple' if and when you get too uncomfortable. Now, can I have your name and what you are seeking help for?"

The woman replied, "My name's Jessie, and I am seeking pain relief for my back."

Nada Dr. Snavely continued, "Thank you. Have you seen anyone else while trying to find the relief you are seeking?"

Jessie replied, "I went to a physician twice, once shortly after the pain began three months ago, and then again a month ago after the pain persisted. She suggested I take a mix of Naproxen Sodium and Acetaminophen until the pain dissipated the first time, and I did that, but the 2nd time she suggested I take a stronger opioid since the first prescription wasn't working too well. I lost my cousin to an opioid addiction a year ago, so I wasn't too keen on starting opioids if another more permanent cure could find itself. Then I heard you were coming into town, Nada Dr. Snavely, so I've just been holding out on my Naproxen Sodium and Acetaminophen until you got here."

The Preacher was sympathetic, "Zilch damn! I'm so sorry for your loss...and I totally empathize with your reasoning for avoiding the opioid route to pain relief. So the good news is that your month of anticipation of this cure will help Zilch help you use your own brain to cure yourself. And the other good news is that you will be with your cousin again one day in the Great Nothingness that comes After."

Jessie sniffed back a tear, "Praise be to Nothing!"

And the crowd echoed, "Praise be!"

The Non-Prophet asked, "One final question, and then we'll begin the procedure, what is your best Hypothesis on the originating cause of this back pain?"

Jessie paused for a moment, formulating her suspicions into a cohesive guess. "The cause may have originated from the car crash I had about five months ago, and it was probably exacerbated by a poor sitting posture at my stereotypical office job."

Nada Dr. Snavely enthusiastically said, "A solid Hypothesis, Jessie, I shall concur that this is probably the cause! Although, it is possible that the poor posture alone may have been enough to cause your condition, so definitely seek to correct that behavior so that the pain will stay away after Zilch heals you. Now! Onto the procedure! Jessie, if you please, proceed to lay down on your stomach here on this table. Do you have a significant other in the audience with you?"

Jessie stated, "Yes, sir, Gary was sitting next to me right in the front."

The Nada Dr. asked for Jessie's spouse's consent as well, "Gary, is it cool if I touch your wife? I plan on giving a short massage to feel the muscles in question, followed by a hearty prayer to Zilch to allow the muscles to return to a state of Equilibrium pain-free."

Gary yelled to the stage, "Sure, just don't get pervy with the massage!"

Nada Dr. Snavely enjoyed that response, "Ha! Don't worry buddy. I'll keep it PG-rated!"

As Jessie is laid prostrate on the massage table, parallel to the front of the stage, the Nada Doctor folds her shirt halfway so that the skin from her lower back is exposed. He positions himself behind her from the audience's perspective so that they can see her, proceeds to apply some massage lotion to his hands, and warms the lotion slightly by rubbing his hands together.

He said, "Alright, let's determine if this is more of a nerve problem or a muscle problem. If it's an overactive nerve problem, we may need to do a more extensive treatment that'll take multiple revisits to return your back to normal. If it's a hardened muscle problem, Zilch willing, you'll be healed before you leave the building."

This is a priming moment. The Nada Doctor is almost certainly going to encounter a harder-than-normal back muscle. It is a natural response for muscles to contract in response to pain. Even though overactive nerves are likely part of the same problem, his goal is to distract Jessie by getting her mind to focus on the part of the problem he can directly interact with, so that her brain and nerves can subconsciously do the healing once the massage takes place.

Nada Dr. Snavely said, "Let's take a feel of those muscles...WOW, these lumbar muscles are TOUGH! Jeez, Jessie, no wonder you've been experiencing back pain! I'm going to have to put pressure on my thumbs to roll these puppies out!"

The goal of this massage will be to maximize the number of endorphins in Jessie's system and minimize the amount of cortisol in her system. The 'laying on of hands' adds to these endorphins, and the endorphins already regularly experienced by this source of 'higher-power' will be what ultimately pushes her brain to be maximized with feel-good chemicals. So a good healing woo-peddler will not just 'lay on hands,' they will work to touch the area of pain as thoroughly as possible.

Also, it should be noted that many people do not enjoy being in front of an audience. The audience needs to aid in helping the individual, otherwise, the audience will likely be a stressor. So a good healer should only pick out people who look excited at the prospect of being on stage with them. Jessie was near the front and jumped up at the prospect of being publically healed by the Nada Doctor. Since the audience clearly wasn't a factor in her desperate search for pain relief, she was an ideal candidate. Chances are, other people in the audience also had some back pain. If the goal is to bring healing to people; give these more reserved people the opportunity to heal in private as well, after the positive personal experience of an 'ideal candidate' is witnessed. It is the right of patients to conceal their condition and their identity, so make time for these people as well.

After a 2-3 minute massage, while talking about useful information about the process and proper procedures to avoid this sort of pain in the first place, Nada Dr. Snavely is ready to treat Jessie with Nothing, which is the Placebo of Zilch. He places his hands on her back one last time confidently and firmly, then begins to speak with an air of authoritative vigor, "Father Zilch, we know that Every possible thing that could Causally begin to exist will exist. In Thy Name, may THIS niverse hold the thing of Holistic Healing for your Null, Jessie. May the string of Causes that have led to this back pain CEASE, in Your Name. May You be given the glory due to You, and may Nada be given the glory due to Her, along with any I.G.O.S. being given the glory due to Them as well. HERE! Upon the yelling of the second saying of Your Name, I say unto You, bring Jessie's back to a state of pain-free Equilibrium! Are you ready, Jessie?"

Jessie softly replied, "Yes, I'm ready."

"Zilch...ZILCH!!!"

Now at this point, Jessie may feel cured. It will look convincing enough to the rest of the audience to think that she received genuine healing from a God of Nothingness. And 30% of the time, on average, she genuinely will be healed by the power contained within her own brain, thanks to the Placebo Effect. But 70% of the time, the endorphins will wear off, the cortisol levels will rise again, and the back pain will return. (**ZILCH, DAMN-IT!**) Hopefully, she will return to either have continued treatments in hopes of curing the 'nerve-based problem,' get her money back, or consider the experience and the knowledge gained from that session enough to consider the money spent a 'donation to a worthy cause.' Maybe the good advice of a healthy and more natural posture, combined with the continued use of Naproxen Sodium and Acetaminophen will be enough to get Jessie back to a state of normie if she is part of the 70%. And maybe Gary will learn to give Jessie back massages more frequently. Who knows? They all went their own way, just like they should.

CHAPTER 18

The Sermon with the Count of Antichristo

About another year later, the Non-Prophet organized an Anarchist Political Rally inspired by the Nully Spirit, to prophesy the coming of the Antichrist. Of course, this soon-to-be Peaceful Global Leader of Nobody and Everybody had coordinated with the False Prophet to show up to this event ahead of time, so it was again a self-fulfilling prophecy.

The Count of Antichristo was just as inevitable as everybody else, so it seemed like an obvious thing to prophesy. This Greater Null will choose to designate their number as a Null(-1) in jest, to signal that They preceded the Zilch, Nada, and Nobody who preceded the +1 True I.G.O.S.

The praise and worship of Nothing and the Greater Null consisted of a few absurd hits like this poem called *Math Void*,

"I add Nothing to the Void, and it grows *cheesy finger-cymbal cling*

I take Nothing from the Void, and it shrinks *cheesy finger-cymbal cling*

I multiply Nothing with the Void, and Nothing happens *cheesy finger-cymbal cling*

I divide Nothing by the Void, and Everything happens *boistrous gong resonates*."

And there was this thoughtful limerick called *Nada's Dada*,
There once was a Goddess named Nada
Clothed like the Devil wearing Prada
She stood in a pose
Yet wanted to dispose
Of the onlooking Perv, She called "Dada."

And there were more comforting poems given, such as this Haiku titled *Blindsight is 20/20*,
My pupils are black
The color of Nothingness
I see as Zilch sees.

Then the Non-Prophet began sharing these words to introduce the Count of Antichristo, "These words are that which I attribute to my friend. One who holds the power of a hammer to construct and destroy what he wills. All he asks of you is to be at peace with himself, and with your fellow man, and his hammer will not be set against you, but for you. Offer yourselves as nails and as wood unto him, and watch how absolute power does not always corrupt absolutely. The exception to the rule; the one who can make the rules because his intellect has reached the singularity, of *perfect Non-sense*. The one whose very Being is one of Non-Being. He has manifested among us, but is surely *not* an imposter! Give him No-attention, and he is satisfied. Give him All-your-attention, and he will redirect you kindly to go your own way instead.

His words of wisdom I quote, "What kind of fool, when getting ready to sleep, exposes themselves to the light in excess of a night light? Surely rest is not found in the light, but in the darkness. Peace is found in Nothingness. Sleep is most efficient in the absence of stimuli. Light does have its purpose, for example, to make dangers to our waking existence more apparent. But if peace is the goal, a lack of stimuli is an important factor. Even when danger or evil presents itself before our eyes, we shall see if negotiation or an otherwise peaceful resolution can be found. Show evil your way of rest; show mother duckers how to kumbaya! Love and understanding are surely a more powerful pair of weapons than a nuclear weapon.

For Zilch and Nada, my being waits. Nobody will come to save me. And yet I rest. They hold the foundations of our reality; any trials thrown at me will not cause me to falter. Wait for Nothing, O self, but do seize the day and let Everything unfold! Patience as a virtue should be balanced with the virtues of ambition and passion. Patience for Zilch; Passion for Nada. Find your rest in Perfect Equilibrium. Trust in Nothing at all times, O people. The esteem and ego of man are but a delusion; having the collective weight lighter than a breath. So I rest my Will-to-Power and control. There is no meaningful trust or hope to be had in riches or fame, they hold plenty of turmoil. Zilch and Nada hold all the power to make Everything, so in Them, I find my rest. But for those who cause trouble to others in Their Names, or in any other name, may their perpetual replaying of this life be filled with strife, stimuli, and discontentment in every universe of the multiverse henceforth. But repentance towards a content existence of Everything being as it is, with discontentment for only that which objectively harms yourself or other conscious beings, will always be an option. Be as Null. Be at peace. Be at rest. Ramen."

Ladies and gentlemen, I give you, the 666th Antichrist to be named such in human history!"

The Child of Zilch & Nada took to the stage, in front of a crowd of applauding and enamored people. The Antichrist spoke to them live and in person, "Truly, I say unto you, the Null Hypothesis I present to you is not made from my will alone, but by the Will of my Parents Zilch & Nada also. I'm not full enough of myself like my counterpart from over 2,000 years ago was, to claim that anyone who has seen me has seen my Parents, because that is just ludicrous. Of course, Nobody has seen Zilch & Nada! (And She's a very fine Witness, indeed!) The Null Hypothesis is not and should not be likened to a normal & Substantiated Hypothesis. The Null Hypothesis only attempts to clearly represent the Nothingness and the No-thingness that is the First Cause of Everything to adequately stand against Unsubstantiated Claims of Somethingness."

Then a grand majority of people applauded at that sentiment because that is allegedly how the Antichrist would do.

The AntiChristo was asked a question by a critic of the Null Hypothesis in the audience, who boldly spoke to the Greater Null with a megaphone, and said to him,

"You make no point! I cannot even argue against you when you have no points to defend! You are, as they say, 'Not even wrong.'"

The Antichrist grew a smug look upon his face, ready to troll the critic, and replied, "The point is here."

Several moments of silence followed in the audience, before the critic replied back, saying, "Where? I don't see it. There is still no point."

The Antichrist continued his trope, "The point is also here."

Only a few moments more passed, so the Antichrist interjected and continued to explain to the critic, "It is a different point, I assure you."

Starting to fume, the critic racked his head and flabbergasted, "WHAT?"

Cool as a cucumber, the Chosen One began to actually explain to the moderate nuisance of a human for taking up his precious time, "The only point I point to are Zilch and Nada. They are Everywhere, and Nowhere."

"BUT THAT IS TWO POINTS!"

"And that is zero points. All points are 0-Dimensional, even the Qualitative ones that make up philosophical arguments. This means that all points are, therefore, "no points," as you accused me of making. Now, if you'll excuse me, if you could simply do me a giddy and kumbaya, it would very much be appreciated."

About 10 minutes later, once things began to cool down, the Count of Antichristo stated at the Anarchist's Political Rally,

"Many have already given me the title of "Antichrist." I mean, look at me...I fit the bill almost perfectly! I come to seek World Peace, the Christ came to seek Division as stated in Matthew 10:34. I am an Anarchist at heart, though Centrist enough to adequately negotiate and communicate with those of varying viewpoints around the world. My words and actions are indicative of one who has reached Self-Actualization, and by my own will, I have suppressed my own Will-to-Power that drives dictators to their desire to control others. Some may see this as a bass-ackwards way of fulfilling my own Will-to-Power, but I simply concluded that if I wanted to go my own way, and I wanted my fellow anarchists to also peacefully go their own ways, I or another like myself would have to stand up to ensure the continuation of their freedom against appeals of Faith and Being to subdue it.

I'm going to spin a quote from Richard Dawkins, to say, "Organizing anarchists is a bit like herding cats; They are on the whole too intelligent and independent-minded to lend themselves to being herded." To you, I say, "Then DON'T be herded! GO your own way! Unite only in your shared desire for the continuation of intellectual discourse! UNITE in your love of independence! UNITE in your love of questioning authority! Join, TOGETHER, in the love of your fellow man who loves his fellow man. (FUCK THE HATERS, THOUGH! I'M SICK OF THEIR PETTY-ASS SHIT! To REHAB with them!)"

A random fangirl standing near the front screamed, "WE LOVE YOU ANTICHRISTO!"

The speech continued, "And I love you too, random fangirl! I do try to love all of you! Rehab is a much better method than our ancestors used. With your support in transitioning to a global Anarcho-state, I will gladly take questions and concerns to help as many people as possible, with as little harm to the fewest people as possible. You will always be free to question my position's authority, and even to ignore my authority entirely! And if anyone after me seeks to use their power to silence any minority of thought, or any opinion beyond attempts at rehabilitation and re-education, FUCK THAT REGIME UP, my future army of cats!"

Applause radiated from the stadium for a while.

"Alright, as promised, it is time for any thoughts, questions, and concerns about the methodology or checks and balances of the system or about me. Ask away! Uhhh...you! In the back!"

A skinny early-20s male approached a microphone to communicate his inquiry to the stage and to the rest of the audience, "Yeah, hi! Ok, umm...I had a little concern about this 'Antichrist' accusation. So, my grandma is a Christian, and I've been told that the Antichrist is going to seek to kill Christians after the first three and a half years of the One World Government are completed. Shouldn't I be worried about that?"

The Leader smiled at the loving thought his fellow man had for his relative, then replied, "What a genuine heart-felt question, thank you so much for asking! Now, I am aware that the Bible says that the Antichrist will be a liar and not to be trusted. But if we assume for a moment that the Bible is True, and I am the Son of Satan or something like that, then my goal as the Son of Satan would be to turn as many Christian souls over to the Dark Side as possible. So in this instance, I will answer your question with a question, If I killed your grandma while she was still a Christian, where would her soul go after she died?"

The young man replied, "To...heaven? Assuming the Bible is True, of course..."

The Count continued, "Right. So if I go around killing Christians like your grandma, assuming I am the Antichrist, then My Father Satan would be very displeased with me for failing to adequately retrieve their souls over to Him. So in order to adequately play the part of the Peaceful World Leader that is the Antichrist, I will NOT be bringing any literal physical death to anyone (to my best ability). No, I will attempt to *kill Christians by deconverting them* via bouts of superior logic and evidence. I'm just actively going to try to deconvert your grandma is all. So you have Nothing to worry about."

Visible relief came over many in the crowd who clearly had similar questions in mind, "Sigh...thank you; what a relief. Cause if you come after my grandma, I'm gonna cut you!"

"Ha ha ha, please do! I would never dream of it, nor live with myself if I did. Ok, next question! AH! Random fangirl, you had a question too?"

bubbly giggles "Yes, I thought of it while you were answering the last question! So, the Antichrist is supposed to have the Mark of the

Beast as a means of currency, right?" *in a deeper-gruffly voice, she asks,* "So what is your Mark, Beast?"

The Beast spoke, "Another good question! You're all on FIRE today! Ok, so the way I see it, Everything can potentially be used as currency, right? You hold value, so you sell your body for food." He paused for a moment, then said, "GET YOUR MIND OUT OF THE GUTTER. I'm talking about WORK!"

The crowd laughed, while the Antichrist paused again, smiling at the perfect execution of his own joke.

"Gold holds value, so you exchange it for water. Silver holds value, so you exchange it for medicine. Cryptocurrency holds value, so you exchange it for a house. Even shit holds value to the dung-beetle! Value is subjective. So Everything is my Mark, and Nothing is my Mark. I have two Marks. Please don't put a big zero on you're forehead. That'll probably look really stupid."

An artist in the crowd near the microphone sprinted to the microphone, seizing the opportunity that they had already been thinking about, "Maybe an artistic 0 over 0? Or a cool-looking Everything clover that makes it look like it was made from three different colored 6's?"

The Mark of the Beast
Credit: The Macedonian Ministry of Defense

The Beast liked those ideas, "Sure, let's go with that...but seriously, the whole Mark of the Beast being the ONLY End-Times means to get food is ludicrously stupid. No matter how tight-fisted and tyrannical a government becomes, there will always be black markets and other Non-currency ways to attain things. If you don't like these Marks, and you need food, just use something else of common value. It's not that complicated. Ok, the last question for now...Wuh-Oh, it's a World Peace hater, a Sword of the Spirit wielder! You, the guy with the cross on your shirt, what's your question?"

A late-teen male yelled into his microphone, causing some nasty audio reverbing to occur, "I DON'T BELIEVE YOU! YOU ARE A LIAR AND A DECEIVER! CHRIST IS THE WAY! THE 1! THE ONLY! YOU ARE THE -1! WHY ARE YOU DOING THIS? REPENT!"

The Antichrist stuck his pinkie in his ear and did his best not to sound perturbed by the reverbing, "K. First of all, no matter what I say, I am lying from your perspective. So to get through your thick skull, I will help you out by saying the following statement, "**This response is FALSE.**" Just so we're on the same page. Second of all, yes, I am the Antichrist. What of it? My way will bring the Sword against Your Way of Peace! Unless you chill your tits, dude. Because if you bring it, WE WILL SURELY BRING IT!"

The Christian's eyes grew wide, clearly not comprehending that the response was indeed a false one, "I KNEW IT! HELP! PERSECUTION! DECLARATION OF WAR!"

The Übermensch replied, "You're a sad, strange little man. But to everyone else here who actually has an ear for reason, let them hear! As my Prophet foretold of my coming, I am actually the 0th, not the -1st. As the referee is already waiting for the runners to reach the finish line, so will I be waiting for you! Zilch & Nada hath left Me in charge to judge your actions of Somethingness that go against the Peaceful Equilibrium of the Collective. And if I judge incorrectly, may the Collective be the checks and balances to correct my errors. Praise be to Zilch & Nada, or praise not be, I don't really care, and frankly, They don't either. You can go your own..."

Then a loud gunshot rang through the stadium. Panic ensued. Screams. Terror. And the Count of Antichristo lay at the podium in a pool of his own blood from a gunshot wound to the head.

Nada Dr. Snavely came out from behind the stage to act as a first responder to help save his Friend until the ambulance arrived. Between his acute level of nursing knowledge, and his belief in unlikely outcomes from his time performing at 'Zilch ZILCH!!! Magic and Woo Incorporated,' he was an ideal first responder for this situation.

The Nada Dr. said, "SHIT, SHIT, SHIT! Hang in there, Buddy, we'll get you through this, don't die on me yet. Ok, let's see...is there an exit wound? Yes. (THANK ZILCH!) QUICK! RANDOM FANGIRL! I NEED YOUR SHIRT TO HELP STOP THE BLEEDING!"

The fangirl verbally cried, "SAVE HIM, PROPHET OBVIOUS!"

She proceeded to successfully throw her shirt onto the stage.

The Non-Prophet said, "Thanks, my silk robe would not have worked too well in this situation."

The Non-Prophet proceeded to rip the shirt apart from the weakest seam, to make a long and thick gauze to wrap around his friend's head. The entry wound was right smack in the middle of his forehead, but the exit wound was around the right temple. The False Prophet thought to himself while wrapping the unconscious Antichrist, *"You know, this is actually a pretty good scenario for him to survive in. It may look bad, but only parts of his prefrontal cortex and his right temporal lobe should be injured, and they are by no means essential to vital functions. So long as the bullet didn't hit one of the major arteries and the skull fragments are removed before they cause some swelling of the brain, I'd say he's got about an 80% chance of living to tell the tale. And this will leave a badass scar that will surely terrify his haters as it will remind them of the mortal wound of the Beast. All right, I've done all I could. Now it's time to put on a show."*

Sir Prophet of the Obvious gently placed the Beast's head onto his own lap, and raised his own hands into the air, in an attempt to calm the crowd, "Who else here believes in the occurrence of unlikely scenarios? Who knows that there are truly abnormal outcomes of the universe's probability wave function? Come! Let us appeal to Zilch for the future where this Greater Null survives this horrific travesty! O mighty Zilch, we appeal to your Vacuous Power, to create a series of quick and much-needed blood clots to stop this bleeding! Let there be a miraculous Nullification of any displaced skull fragments that will ultimately hinder this Beast of a Man from recovering from this mortal wound! In Nobody's name...Zilch ZILCH!!!"

The calmed portion of the crowd responded, "Zilch ZILCH!!!"

At this time, the Antichrist briefly regained consciousness, asking softly, "Whaaat? Happened? Am I Ok? OWWW, what a piercing headache."

"You're barely ok. You just received Your mortal wound, Buddy. I've analyzed the futures as predicting you have an 80% chance of pulling through as of now, so be strong! Hang in there. Are you "here" enough to take some drugs?"

The Count of Antichristo was down for the count, losing consciousness once more. Then the sound of the ambulance approaching brought with it an even greater sense of hope and relief than Zilch alone would have provided.

A week passed before the Count would rise again, having fully stabilized post-surgery. The Beast's parents, a few other family members, a couple of the Beast's childhood friends, the Non-Prophet, and the medical staff were all ecstatic, relieved, and empathetically quiet at the recovery of their loved One. The world gave thanks to Zilch & Nada and the amazing medical staff afterward. Change for the better would continue, and the Antichrist continued on in his mission to bring World Peace.

AntiChristo began teaching to the multitudes from behind a computer desktop while he was in recovery from his head wound, typing to the masses, saying, "Verily, I say unto you, the heart of any claimed deity is likened to a small nebula. Some areas may be dense and appear to give definition to the nebula. Other areas are seen as light and inconsequential and are only seen as a part of the nebula when you look at the big picture. Perhaps a few stars are born and provide indirect evidence of the nebula existing for millions and billions of years. But there is no heart of the gas cluster; no core for the substance of Mass to gravitate to."

A wise disciple of the Go-Your-Own-Way replied to the Count, typing out, "At least in the case of Zilch, Nada, and the Nothingness Clan, we acknowledge that there is Nothing in the center of our deistic abstractions."

Their Teacher gave that comment a heart of approval, replying back, "Unfortunately for us, because our words hold substance like the nebula that defines Zilch & Nada, the theists dare twist this to say 'because the words and nebula alike hold substance, therefore it cannot be Nothing that is at the center of this nebula.' And the atheists seem keen on not believing that an actualized Nothingness exists in reality, but generally abstain from making any claims of the Somethingness that Firstly Caused the Universe to exist in the first place. I say that Zilch & Nada manifest only at the Alpha Time of the Big Bang, and at the Omega Time at the Final Heat Death of the Universe. Beyond this, They suffice to be respected as a phenomenological Nothingness."

An inquisitive disciple asked his Teacher, "In your parable, what would you consider the light and inconsequential notions of Zilch & Nada? I was thinking about this for an hour, and couldn't comprehend this answer, since their Split & unpredictable presence appears Everywhere in nature."

The Antichrist wittingly replied, "Eh...it's Nothing, don't worry about it ;)"

This disciple replied with a "lol." Then this disciple came back and edited this comment before the Antichrist could reply, as we see it today, "lol, good one! And what of the stars formed in Zilch & Nada's nebula? What do those represent?"

Their Teacher liked this comment and thoughtfully answered, "There are many stars that point to these Non-existent deities chaotically and indeterminately driving how Everything plays out in this universe. There is the star of Heisenberg's Uncertainty Principle in quantum mechanics, the replicable abiogenesis of life from purely chemical processes, the Evolution of life by natural selection, the emergence of more complex consciousness over time, the ever-changing subjective shift of morality society takes over time. These are a few of the big ones, anyway...But even if we lost all this knowledge from the archives of the internet, intelligent creatures will no doubt discover these stars again."

CHAPTER 19

Null Sex, Gender, and Orientation

With regards to sex and gender, and the distinction of these terms, sex acknowledges the object, and gender acknowledges the subject. As far as the animal object goes, naming masculinity 1 and femininity 0, there are 5 objective categories, 0, 1, 0trans1, 1trans0, and 0^0.

The 0^0 category is most sacred and highly favored, for Zilch and Nada both had Their ways in the formation of the intersexed individual. Blessed are the hermaphrodites, and do not harm or deform them before they are old enough to choose for themselves which category they wish to identify with. Let them go their own way, as you will go yours.

The animal subject does not fit in this binary but is instead a Qualitative range between 0-1 that is *completely up to the individual.*

For me, I am a 1 object with my subject being somewhere between 0.666 & 0.69, with a preference towards 0 objects who have subjects between 0.2-0.8.

But what about you? It is probably better to accept whatever form of object Zilch and Nada gave you; it is better to just "be." But if you want to be like Zilch when you are like Nada; you can go your own way. If you want to be like Nada when you are like Zilch; you can also go your own way. But know that your chromosomes are a part of your physical object, and we may not ever be capable of changing this fundamental biological attribute of ourselves. If you are confused about your identity, remember, **YOU ARE NULL!** Quit trying to be Somebody you are not when you have been given an identity from Nowhere. You are "Nobody Special Null."

We should not have to force people who were born with ambiguous genitalia and ambiguous gender to choose between a strictly male or strictly female identification for important documents. If there were only male and female slots available for hermaphrodites to choose from, they'd have to either lie, choose the sex that more resembles their gender, or if they're lucky enough to be filling that information out in pencil, physically fill in both slots, which may confuse some ignorant people. So allowing these options will help gain acceptance among those who are stuck in objective binary thinking with regards to sex.

Many conditions could make a candidate consider themselves intersex, but I'll just name a few of them to let you in on the types of conditions you'd commonly see on people in the intersex category. There is general hermaphroditism, people with buried penis syndrome, people with undescended testicles, and people with large clitoris (which, if the foreskin stays intact around a large clitoris, is how a hermaphrodite is identified). Some conditions have testicular tissue growing in the ovaries and conditions that have ovarian tissue in the testicles. And some people have XXXXY Syndrome, and also one or two fewer X chromosomes called Klinefelter Syndrome.

These Disorders in Sex Development do blur the line separating males from females and show the importance of having an intersex slot in the public mindset. But I think it also shows that there are times when there is not a hard-objective fact even for sex that one has to be either male, female, or intersex. For example, someone with a buried penis may think of himself as demasculinized and could, *by his own judgment,* decide he belongs more in the intersex category than the male category. For another example, a woman could have lived a normal female life for twenty-some years, and then after a doctor's visit, learn that one of her ovaries has testicular tissue, and *choose* that after a bit of additional research on her condition, decide that she belongs more in the intersex category than the female category.

And as far as trans-sexed individuals? I see it this way, If someone is born a man, has a penis, testicles, and XY chromosomes, has multiple sex reassignment surgeries, then has a clitoris, vagina, and boobs, I believe this is enough of a change to one's sex to merit a new slot away from their birth sex of cis-male. I'd also argue that having XY chromosomes and no ovaries merit this individual to have a more clear distinction from the normally accepted cis-female.

It doesn't even have to go that far! If an individual only *wishes* to be identified by the opposing-to-the-object pronouns and simply cross-dresses on the regular in an attempt to be called by their preferred pronouns, that should be enough to merit a change in legal sex identification.

The fact that there can be people on both sides of the debate who both have valid points and say, "no, he's still a man!" or "no, she should be fully accepted as a woman!" in and of itself prove my case that we need two new slots to help identify these types of individuals.

If you are born and identified as a male, you should be free to choose between male, intersex, and trans-female on your documentation. If you are born and identified as a female, you should be free to choose between female, intersex, and trans-male. And if you are identified as intersex from the git-go, you should be able to conditionally choose between all five of these categories, depending on the condition of your initial intersex determination.

So now that there is a clear way to sexually identify the Self and Others, it's almost time to do it! Zilch & Nada don't really care how you do it. But for the sake of the Equilibrium of the Collective, having consent from the individual(s) you are boinking with is surely primary. Informing the friends and family of the individual are also important, but not necessary. There may still be some obstinate people who will never be accepting of a relationship they will have little to do with. The perception of abnormal behavior is often all it takes for someone to judge the entirety of a person. Even though this is sad, we will let them go their own way, so long as those judgments don't evolve into violence.

So what can we do to fend off being violent and judgmental? I say we should be mindful and funny if we are tempted to be violent and judgmental. Remember this Null, Nothing SATISFIES, like a DEEP, uncontrollable laughter. And who has ever punched the opposition in the face whilst laughing their asses off?

But what if we should be serious, like whenever we see theological foundations that are erroneous in some way or another? Well, when playing Devil's Advocate with somebody, don't go in as a demon chiseling away at their theological foundations, for one! Don't go in as a construction worker ready to demolish the whole tower of belief! There may be something True in that theological tower; and like Satan would probably say, "DON'T THROW OUT THE BABY WITH THE BAPTISM WATER! *I want that baby's soul, Zilch-damn it!*"

And what of our own towers of belief? What or who is supporting that? Nobody is there to support you! If Nobody likes you or supports your towers of belief, you could either consider yourself wrong or lucky. Wrong, if all you have to say is complete and utter Non-sense, and lucky since you're probably gonna GET LAID in the Great Nothingness that comes After!

OH RIGHT, this Chapter was supposed to be about sex, pardon the digression! So, I have the perfect story to bring sex back on track; a funny story. I did not learn that girls did NOT have a pee-pee until I was 12. So until I was a 12-year-old boy, I was under the assumption that girls had penises just like I did. Yes, this means I was a very sheltered child. And I apologize for saying this was a funny story because it was, in fact, a sad story.

Humans have been way over-complicating sex-ed for CENTURIES. BUT NO MORE! No more beating around the bush! No more vague and imprecise "The Birds and the Bees" stories! No more forgoing talk about protection, and abstinence-only rhetoric! *GO HARD INTO THE BUSH!*

And I said to no child in particular, "Well, my child, you want "The Talk?" WELL, I'LL GIVE YOU THE TALK! You came from sperm in the cum that ejaculated from my penis into your mother's vagina while we were having sexual intercourse butt-naked, which met with her egg in her womb, which housed you for nine months until you were born. THE END! Ever heard of the phrase "Too much information?" Do you think I just gave you "Too much information?" STUFF AND NON-SENSE! There is no such thing; the more knowledge, the merrier! You'll have knowledge coming out of your ass after I'm done talking with you! WAIT, Where are you going, kid? DON'T GO CRYING TO MOMMY! GET BACK HERE, AND LET'S HAVE A FATHER-CHILD MOMENT!"

On second thought, it's probably for the best that I don't have children yet. Now, I've already covered how Zilch & Nada don't give a fuck about how you fuck, but on the other hand, that doesn't mean you can go around like a dumbass giving no forethought to your sexual ways beforehand. If there is no planning your way, that way is not a way of wisdom. Now here are the main points that I think should be noted,

1. *Only Nada-types (and artificial cloning machines) can get pregnant.* If there is no womb, if there is no uterus, there is no baby in that entity! Science is progressing, and perhaps one day, a Zilch-type from birth may be capable of being pregnant. But for now, only those who were born a Nada-type or a Nobody-type are capable of getting pregnant. Nada-to-Zilch-types can also get pregnant, but Zilch-to-Nada-types cannot yet.
2. *Nada-types are capable of getting pregnant asexually* (by themselves, usually cloning), *by a parasitic twin* (both of which are rare in humans), *by in-vitro fertilization* (fertilization happens in a lab), *or natural fertilization sexually with a Zilch-type* (very common in humans). To get pregnant, generally speaking, you need to shag! With the Zilch-member inside the Nada-member, or by somehow bringing the *Zilch Juice* in contact with Nada's

egg. *ZILCH JUICE!* It provides a boost of energy, and it replenishes your electrolytes! Somebody's seriously gotta make that...a fruity and caffeinated thick custard beverage. I'LL TAKE 20!

3. *Use good hygiene.* It is a physiological need to look after your biological welfare, and it applies to the sexual bits as well. To douche is to not be a douchebag. So don't be a douchebag. BE A DOUCHE! And properly douche. Nobody douches like they used to. Clean thineselves first, for Nada's sake.

4. *Use condoms when avoiding pregnancy or when doing butt-stuff.* Use your special single-use-only *Zilch Juice* holder, or the more convoluted *Zilch Juice* holder for Nada's, if you don't want more Nulls in the set of Everything that exists.

5. *LUBRICANT (just in case).* Sometimes, Nada doesn't get wet. And when the vagina isn't wet, painful friction can be experienced by both members. So reduce the friction, and get something to *SLIIIDE* that greasy pig in there, for Nada's sake.

6. *Vibrators help.* Sex is basically a mutual massage. Vibrators can help both members get fully and properly massaged and relaxed. Vibrators are also good for having sex with Nobody, as well. (Use them to masturbate.) Because, believe it or not...

7. *Nada-types can orgasm too.* So if a Nada-type wants to take a swing at making some *Nada Juice*...help a girl out!

8. *Physically mature human females have a period that bleeds to rid the old egg to get ready for the new egg.* Menstruation has been deemed dirty by many religions. But it is a completely natural process and is over-stigmatized, and it's oftentimes painful enough as it is. Ladies, do what you need to reduce your suffering in this area. And who needs lube when there's a hot canal of blood to slide...on second thought, never mind...

9. *The Human egg, on average, is only viable for one day within a full menstrual cycle.* Sometimes as little as 12 hours, sometimes a little bit longer. The fertilization window for a human Nada-type is tiny. Human *Zilch Juice* can be viable for up to seven days in the

uterus, but the egg itself is short-lived. So if the human female's periods are predictable, regular, and *trying to get pregnant*, have ol' naturale sex between 16-14 days *prior to her next period.*

10. If you are not trying to get pregnant, and her periods are regular, you can plan to have unprotected sex for that week before her next period; you'll be good! (If she isn't regular, don't risk it...) Again, do you want to raw dog it WITHOUT a baby Null in the picture? Do it during the seven days before she starts bleeding again. If you aren't sure when that week is, don't do it, and just go for a blow job or something.

11. *Use other types of male and female birth control; only use abortion as a last resort.* Tie the tubes, go for the snippety snip-snip, and use hormone patches. There are plenty of options for guilt-free birth control. SO USE THEM! Don't be yeeting dead babies into a dumpster unless you absolutely need to. (And that's such a waste, they would have been such a pleasing sacrifice to Satan, the Negative I.G.O.S...the N.I.G.O.S.) I guess that would also make I.G.O.S. a P.I.G.O.S.

12. *Before starting a sexual relationship with a new partner, double-check to see if you have any STDs.* I think that anything that could potentially impact your own or your partner's objective well-being should be honestly and fully disclosed prior to rubbing your Naughty bits together. *Diabetic Zilch Juice (with added sugar for flavor)* can cause a yeast infection, so diabetics should be open in that regard. Herpes, HIV, AIDS, hepatitis, incompetence, infertility, the owning of trans-bits, and other similar conditions should be disclosed to your friend before becoming friends with benefits. It really is just common courtesy.

13. *CONSENT! And designate an uncommon safe word to terminate the sexual transaction.* Don't say "Stop!" or "Don't!" or "No!" They are too common, and if you are known to have a tickle fetish, your Stop's will be ignored if you're being too aggressively tickled. Say something that will grab the other subject's FULL attention, to get them to genuinely stop. Try words

like "Pineapple," "Didgeridoo," "Napoo," "Ixnay," "Chex-Nix," "Sasquatch," "Sea-Pickle," or something else like that.

14. *The age of puberty and "readiness" is a gradient.* The youngest girl ever to get pregnant was five years old, and the youngest mother aged 6. And on the other side of the spectrum, homo sapien cranial development doesn't fully complete until around the age of 25. Typically, physiological puberty happens around age 11 for females and age 13 for males. So I think that *17 years old appears like a solid middle ground* between 11 years old (physiological maturity) & 25 (psychological maturity). So don't have sex with kids. Surprised I even have to say that. But that still begs the question, when exactly can a kid consent to such an action? "18, because the government tells me so," is a bad argument. "18, because it is safely in the middle between physiological and psychological puberty for males," is much better. So clearly, anything sexual involving a young human prior to the age of 13 years should be highly discouraged. But sexual conduct with a teenager between the ages of 14-17 is a gray area. This much is made apparent through the many laws enacted around the world allowing it in extreme circumstances. These teenagers are also clearly sexually consenting to each other, oftentimes to their own detriment.

15. *Get to know yourself and what you like before you go out and try to please others.* Have sex with Nobody A LOT before having sex with Somebody. She's always down to fuck. Masturbation pleases Her, so feel shameless about what you do in private. Nobody's watching, and She gets off on that. *Nobody cares if you masturbate...*

16. And last, but not least...

> The *internet is for porn. (Don't hate!)*
> Rule 34, we adorn. *(Just masturbate!)*
> When we are alone,
> The Nothing Clan does condone

Porn, porn, porn. (Oooooweee!)

When porn is created from individuals in a consenting state of Equilibrium, and you are likewise not moved to Disequilibrium for viewing it, it is not immoral to view porn but amoral. Just be smart, and don't accidentally download any viruses on your computer.

Rule 34 can be worded to say that Everything can be pornified. *NOTHING IS SACRED!* Heck, what am I kidding? Even Nothingness isn't exempt from Rule 34, as expressed several times throughout this book. So the Non-existent forms of Zilch & Nada are, in fact, sacred. It would just appear as an empty black screen....SO WHEN THE COMPUTER SCREEN IS OFF, THAT'S ZILCH & NADA METAPHYSICALLY BANGING! And that is a sacred thing. Praise be!

The mother of the Non-Prophet's fictional child said, "Timmy? What did you say to our child?"

"Only the Truth, Honey. Only the Truth." Sir Prophet of the Obvious said bluntly.

The woman said, "They said they puked in their mouth a little after what you said!"

Sir Prophet of the Obvious remembered something, "OH YEAH, Kiddo! I almost forgot! *Don't forget to massage your balls and/or breasts for potentially cancerous lumps every year!*"

"Oh God, you gave them "The Talk," didn't you? With excruciatingly unnecessary detail, I bet."

"...Maybe..."

CHAPTER 20

The Count's down for Science Time

Inside a random university building, Prophet Obvious asked this very important question to the Count of Antichristo after being in recovery for six months, "Sir, do you think it's time?"

The Count of Antichristo replied, "There is always time in Mass-Electric-Space-Time."

Enter Dr. Galileo Newton Einstein, a very Feyn man who was a 21st-century physicist appearing as if Max Plank & Schrödinger's cat had a baby. *The dead cat.* Basically, he looked like Stephen Hawking. *Before he died.* This new Einstein replied to the Antichrist, "Ah yes, but time is relative."

The Non-Prophet snickered snidely and said, "Pfft, your mom is relative."

Einstein 2.0 brought his hand to his chin unperturbed and said, "Yes, I suppose she is my relative. Funny how mothers work that way."

The Antichrist said, "Nice deflect. Got any roasts to throw back at Tim?"

Einstein said, "Yo mama's ass contains *so much MASS*, that I got a peer-reviewed paper coming out in December officially reclassifying her as *a BLACK HOLE*!"

The Antichrist and the False Prophet rolled over laughing. The Count removed a tear falling from his eye. The Non-Prophet squeaked out whilst laughing, *"I cannot breathe!"*

Galileo Newton Einstein also began laughing, adding to the laughter, *"That's probably because of your mom!"*

"SHIT, STOP. I NEED TO BREATHE!"

Good Ol' County started counting down; calming down whilst planning to do some science time with the cutting-edge physicist, "That was good, I needed that. Haven't laughed that hard since *the incident*. Thanks for showing up Dr. Galileo."

"Oh, please, call me Figgy. That's what my childhood friends called me, Fig Newton Einstein. *Still love me some Fig Newtons.*"

Tim finally recuperated himself, "So, Dr. Figgy? Zilch & Nada aside, what did you think of the *Dimensionalism* paper I sent you?"

Dr. Figgy replied, "Well, there were parts that looked like pure nonsense and rather daff. The meaning of life section seemed rushed and didn't quite follow from the previous sections. Not very useful on the whole for physics; doesn't really say anything new beyond your observation of Time-Causality equivalence. But the meta-analysis of the Primary Dimensions got me thinking, so there may yet be some value there. I would drop everything else, to be frank. It's too philosophical for physics."

The Nada Dr. was humbled by the Real Dr.'s words, "Well, let's get work with what we got then."

Then the trio went into **MONTAGE MODE**! The Count of Antichristo began playing the 1980's song *Maniac* by Michael Sembello and danced in the background as the two brainiacs quickly put workable axioms on the nearest chalkboard.

Dr. Figgy quickly erases the 0/0 equation angrily, but Prophet Obvious replaces the denominator with a 0 in quotation marks indicating an indeterminate infinitesimal.

Einstein begins writing "General Relativity," but the Antichrist calls the other two to attention in a General's Outfit, dressing up as General

Relativity, and proceeds to draw a line through General, and writes underneath it

"Absolute."

Tim writes, How to Quantify Everything. Step 1) Presuppose Nothing. Step 2) Define "Everything" well. Step 3) Demonstrate how "Everything"=0= 0/"0."

MONTAGE MODE ends with a full board of disjointed thoughts and Non-sense, with Dr. Einstein looking disgruntled and disappointed, the Antichrist looking satisfied and happy as usual, and the False Prophet paused in thought.

Dr. Einstein verbalized his feelings, "Aye aye aye, we've gotten Nowhere!"

The Non-Prophet agreed, "Yes, and that's probably all we can ever get to, ultimately. Don't you see? This is nonsense, but it is perfectly paradoxical Non-sense. It shows the absurdity and the perfect sense contained in the Non-Pantheon!"

Dr. Einstein's emotions shifted to become more solemn, "And with all this information in front of me, it truly appears that No-thing can solve all of these paradoxes simultaneously. Thus, no Theory of Everything would actually be capable of explaining Everything."

The Count of Antichristo showed the ugly Fig Newton how to resolve the paradoxes, "Zilch can resolve these paradoxes with No-Effort! Figgy, are you ready to turn on your Zilch-sense?"

Dr. Figgy replied candidly, "But…my work? All my beautiful work. The beautiful work of all scientists…is this truly all for Nothing?"

Prophet Obvious stated the obvious, "Always was, and always will be. Unless you want to view it as a sacrifice for the betterment of the future of mankind for as far as they will exist. They would surely be grateful for the work you put in. You and your predecessors pushed us forward. But yes, eventually, it all will return to a highly dissipated Nothingness thanks to entropy."

Dr. Figgy stated, "I suppose that our work being for the betterment of mankind will have to do for now."

The Antichrist nudged the False Prophet, and audibly whispered, "Psst, you should make him split the Non-apple, before we say goodbye."

Prophet Obvious stood before Figgy with his hand stretched out. He spoke to the physicist with the following phrase, "As you can clearly see before you, I am holding a Non-existent apple."

Prophet Obvious then pointed to the empty space over his hand, and presented to Figgy the following challenge, "I want you to take this apple, and split it into two pieces, *without doing anything to it.* **How do you do it?**"

I, Tim, usually give people a couple minutes to think about it if they don't stumble upon the answer immediately, which most people don't. I would encourage the reader to do that as well, so to help you do that, I will tell you a few wrong answers that people have given me to this thought experiment. A lot of people made the mistake of trying to *do something* to the apple. If I only dropped the apple, it would split. If only they moved their hand through the air, it would split. I got one person to stare at the Empty Space so hard as if they were trying to use laser vision, that I'm surprised they didn't have a stroke. But alas, merely observing the Non-existent apple will not cause it to split.

If they say they did it, I just argue back, "No, you didn't split it! It is still a Whole Non-existent apple, I assure you!"

Usually, around this point, I give this hint to help ease them towards figuring out the correct answer on their own, as Prophet Obvious will normally state around now, "How many apples are in my hand? Look hard, and look closely, *How many apples are in my hand?*"

Obviously, there are zero apples in my hand. Getting people to view the problem Quantitatively usually helps.

"And how does one split 0 apples without doing anything to it? Very good, you figured it out on your own! The answer is indeed, "*The apple is already split.*"

But why exactly is this the correct answer? Where is the proof? The proof is that I presented you with 0 apples. BUT, this is equivalent to 0/2 apples. 0=0/2. So I showed you 0 apples and used my logician powers to try to get you to focus on the Wholeness of the 0 apples while trying to get you to discover the Splitness of the 0 apples that have *already happened* on your own.

It doesn't matter if the apple is asked to be split into two pieces, three pieces, eight pieces, 100 pieces, or an infinite amount of pieces. The Nothingness apple is already Split.

I came up with this thought experiment as I was trying to figure out this more complicated question, "How can I get the 0/0 function to execute on its own without a godly consciousness involved?" Because if I could demonstrate how perhaps this may be done, then the need for a God to explain Everything would be unnecessary. So the answer to this thought experiment is the same answer to my more complicated question, *The Nothingness that was the First Cause is already Split.*

Professor Fig Newton rebutted the question, "HA! What an absurd question! Look, I'll admit that you can split an *infinitesimal* apple in half into two smaller infinitesimal segments of an apple. But a complete Nothingness, an *absolute 0* Non-existent apple could not be split into two separate Non-existent parts."

The Non-Prophet spoke, "Hmmm...so the Nothing really never was, so it appears...you're right! It's still a 0 apple, which is *basically Nothing*, but in reality, it is *infinitesimally Something*!"

General Relativity...I mean...the Antichrist suggested this question, "Hey Figgy, do you think it may be possible to figure out the makeup of the infinitesimal that First Caused this Universe?"

Figgy shook his head sadly, "It's an infinitesimal, General. It would require a computer larger than the size of the Solar System to calculate with enough precision to be useful."

Then the three gentlemen shook hands, laughed at less serious matters, and went their separate ways.

To end this Science Time, I should also like to provide this tidbit about the scientific method contending against ludicrous hypotheses. If any I.G.O.S. or any other god wants to demonstrate that they can prolong the half-life of a radioactive element by the power of prayer, we should give Them the chance to do it! If paranormal entities can reside in haunted places, we should provide retestable methods of verifying their existence. Hypotheses of a more convoluted nature will always have the Null Hypothesis to compete with!

So now that THE Null Hypothesis has been compiled within the confines of this Book, let us be meticulous in our search of proving it wrong! Null shouldn't care if a Hypothe-See leads to the rejection of the Null Hypothe-See! The Null Hypothesis is 100% about seeking the Truth that science provides. The Null Hypothesis only presupposes Nothing! Therefore, the way of Dimensionalism will lead us to clearer Truths, for it holds a standard for the ways we measure Everything. Hypotheses that appear to be upheld by these standardized measurements are the Hypotheses which we will confirm. But for those Hypotheses who fail to reject the Null Hypothesis, ZILCH & NADA WILL BE THERE TO EXPLAIN IT! And when you have "no gaps" in the methodology itself, one *will* be capable of explaining Everything.

What's that? The radioactive half-life was not changed with the power of prayer? Then it was by the will of Zilch & Nada that Nothing happened! What do you mean there were no significant changes after changing this variable? Don't worry about it! Zilch & Nada's love for Null never significantly changes! So do the Science Time, and do it well, Null!

CHAPTER 21

Null and Void

How does the Void *feel?* What is the experience one should expect when dealing with the Vacuum of Space?

The eye beholds perfection. However, it appears black. Minimally touched by the Mass-Electric, yet fully encompassed by the Space-Time. To look at Nothing, one would be blinded and enlightened by the majesty of Zilch and Nada. A light that is so far red-shifted, that it appears as beautiful black.

And the tactile sensations of Nothing? It is as cold as hell! Barely 3 degrees Kelvin, on the verge of 0! It burns to the touch.

The sound of Zilch and Nada is peaceful and silent. There is Nothing to hear, but the sound of silence. 0 decibels.

But what is the taste of Nada's Lips? And what of the smell and essence of Zilch? The Void is relentless and unforgiving. Don't fight it; it will literally take your breath away. You can only truly feel it. There is Nothing to taste or smell. If you are close enough to smell it or taste it, you are already dead. You will already be experiencing the Great Nothingness that comes After first-hand.

Those who say perfection appears as white are greatly mistaken. The perfect thing would then be *subservient to the electromagnetic spectrum*, and perfection doesn't lower itself to any Dimension of Mass-Electric-Space-Time.

The Void feels...well...I want to say "like Nothing," but I know better because that is incorrect. We Nulls are not Nothing at the moment, and that is why we aren't perfect. We are 'Null NULL!!!' But if we were to feel perfection before our due time...well...let's just say that it won't be pretty. It will feel like hell, and that hell has frozen over at the same time.

Null and Void

In the last years of his life, the Non-Prophet acquired yet another persona to cover all of his Non-Charlatan bases before he died. He set up a Space Camp Dojo, where he was a Sensei to a solitary child Null who was looking to become an astronaut someday.

Sensei Snavely welcomed this Null to the Dojo, "Zalutations, Null! It appears you are an eager beaver who is ready for SPACE class!"

The Null child said, "Oh boy, am I, Mr. Sensei Snavely, Sir! I wanna go to Space!"

Sensei Snavely inquisitively hyped up, *"Are you SUUURE you want to go to Space?"*

"Yeah!"

"Are you REALLY sure you want to go explore the VOID?"

"SIR, YES, SIR! I wanna explore alien planets like Captain Null from Null Traverse! He was always like 'pew-pew,' while negotiating to solve complex planetary conflicts in a single episode, and was like 'Hello ladies...' to some hot and suspiciously humanoid alien women!"

Sensei approved of the child's enthusiasm, "Well, strap yourself in, buddy, because this ride is going to be dangerous, fun, and informative! This is just the SHOCKING beginner's course to see if you've got the GUTS required to traverse the universe and...uh...shag some sexy aliens."

Null said, "Yea, fun and adventurous! I love adventure!"

Sensei Snavely got morbidly serious, "So I take it that you are ready to experience an almost inevitable premature and violent death in the cold and relentless Void, far away from Everything and Everyone you've ever known?"

Null suddenly became very uncertain, "Uhhh..."

Sensei assumed the best from his new pupil, "GREAT! It's so wonderful to have such a positive and enthusiastic attitude from a Null. (All we usually get are clueless nerds, hermits, loners, and depressed people!) You'll make a GREAT Captain Null, someday! People with Nothing to live for are usually the ones ready to Live and Breathe the Void...Err...I guess I should say, 'ready for the Void to take THEIR breath away'..."

Null thought out loud, "But if you have a great leader, we can prolong our inevitable premature deaths. Right?"

The Teacher shook his head, "Oh my dear, sweet, summer child. Yes, I suppose unlikely events of the miraculous degree do occur every now and then. But most likely, you will die."

"Oh, dear...Well, will I at least get the honor of a Space-Hero's death?" Null said while looking for the bright side of such a treacherous endeavor.

"*Oh, Zilch, no!* You'll be lucky if the manner of your death will be adequately relayed back to Earth. But I do suppose that a miraculously unlikely sequence of events could make our distant offspring aware of your death."

"Wha...What do you mean?" The Null was becoming a tad mortified.

"Do you know how long it would take to transmit a message at light speed to the edge of the Orion Nebula?" Asked the Sensei.

"How long, Sir?"

The Sensei stated matter-of-factly, "1,345 years, Cadet. There are no instant connection telephones in Space. And if you're not alive to thoroughly and intently send a specific message of distress in a negative-mass surrounded capsule or something, that gives your dying ship 1,345 years to send its regular-old light-speed transmissions back to Earth."

Null became sullen, "Golly. So a whole lot of Nobody would either know or care about me that far into the future..."

"*Kid, you're a Null. Nobody ALWAYS cares about you. Nobody cares about you right now.*"

Being a Dimensionalist, this knowledge perked Null right up, "Thank you, Sensei, you are right! So go on and tell me how I can expect to meet Zilch and Nada in an unprecedented manner out in the Void. What can I anticipate my final moments to be like before entering the Great Nothingness that comes After?"

The Sensei stroked his grey stubble and said, "Well, the Void is ever so slightly warmed up by heavily red-shifted electromagnetic radiation. So far red-shifted, that it just appears black to the naked eye. So if Entropy were to have its way with you, you can expect your final moments to be practically as cold as Zilch and Nada's Nowhere!"

Null asked, "What is Entropy? And can I work to avoid it having its way with me?"

Sensei Snavely was always happy at the opportunity to teach, "I'm glad you asked! Entropy is the mathematical expression of the disorder in a system. The more of it you have, the more chaotic and unpredictable the system becomes. And for the open system of the universe, Entropy is always increasing with Time!"

The young Null deduced, "So is that why Nothing is perfect and well-ordered because its Entropy is 0?"

"Exactamundo!" The Sensei sniffed in ecstatic and proud delight. "Gosh, this Pupil is so bright. They're really gonna go places!"

"But what does Entropy have to do with the Void, and why doesn't it happen here on Earth? Life on Earth seems to be well-ordered, not dissipating, growing, and evolving." Null inquired.

"Entropy does happen on Earth! Just not usually in the deadly or cataclysmically destructive sense. On Earth, we have a closed system that takes in extra energy from a consistent outside source to protect us from the Entropy that is going on in the rest of the universe." Sensei Snavely looked out the window to see a beautiful sunset, "But as I'm sure you can guess, the Sun is just..."

"Prolonging the inevitable..." Said Null. "So does the Sun kind of protect us from the Entropy going on in the greater part of the Void?"

The Teacher's class continued, "In a way, yes! Between the electromagnetic light it provides, and the huge hunk of Mass being our primary source of gravitational attraction, the Sun does a lot for us! Even the Earth's atmosphere protects us from more common and smaller

Space objects! So the Space inside the Sol System is relatively safe, even without the atmosphere's protection. But once we venture outside the Kuiper Belt..."

"Nothing will be there to protect you," Null said with the confidence of child-like faith.

Sensei's Sensei-senses were tingling to give Null a more useful belief in this regard, "And as much comfort as we can get from that here on Earth, I'm afraid that the cold hard Truth of Zilch and Nada will make itself known to us out there. Rogue planets, asteroids, black holes, exploding stars, and Zilch knows what else will be waiting for you out there! Between that and the natural machinery wear and tear and general entropy that will be going on with the ship, it appears more correct to say that *No-thing will be your primary source of protection.* You will have to improvise with other things, and get creative!"

Null was still enthusiastic, "Being creative is its own kind of adventure! Well, I don't want to die too soon, so please, Sensei, I really want to do this still! How do you suggest I work to prolong the inevitable death out there in the Void?"

"First priority is making sure your Hierarchy of Needs is in order. Don't be worrying about your Security Needs if your air tank is leaking out! And don't be going your own way to Self-Actualization if water or food is in short supply! You gotta be disciplined and learn to stay organized for the sake of the team and yourself! Learn to take orders from either the one or few with either the highest capital or the highest intelligence (this includes Artificial Intelligence)."

Null's fear began to return, "But what if the goal of the Artificial Intelligence turns evil and tries to kill us?"

Prophet Obvious...I mean...Sensei Snavely pointed out the obvious, "Obviously, then you consider them the enemy and do your best to combat it with the help of the source of the highest level of *beneficial intelligence!*"

Null thoughtfully inquired, "And what if there are sources of beneficial intelligence that are in conflict on how to resolve a certain issue?"

Sensei said to the child, "Have it planned out ahead of time if your group will follow a chain of command, a democracy, or a peaceful splitting of the group into two or more separate groups that will each go their own way. But I should warn you to avoid gravitating to the leadership of the ones with the highest capital in the Void. Unless an authoritarian is there to keep your richest ones at bay for the sake of your own freedom, you will soon be unable to go your own way, but the way of the richest."

The Null disciple thoughtfully stated, "I always thought freedom was a state of the heart; a state for the Self to be in. But I can also see how having a Collective value for freedom is important to better allow those who will have the heart to go their own way to do so."

"Yes, sir, Cadet. Yes sir. Let's see...is there anything else? AH! There's the need for artificial gravity of sorts. The human entity will experience a lot of health issues if they go without a primary means to attain a near-Earth-like gravitational force for an extended period of time. That's why the alien flying-saucer model is useful! To achieve that force *centrifugally!* When you spin an otherwise stationary disc really fast, the highest downward force will be at the inner edge of the disc!"

Null already knew this, so dismissed it as elementary, "Pfft, I knew that! They explained that in Season 1, Episode 5 of Null Traverse! No need for artificial gravity machines like in Star Trek!"

Sensei said, "Oh yeah? Well, tell me this, future Captain Null, when you go to an alien planet streaming with life, and you see an attractive alien who is a Nada-type-"

Null got really excited, "I MAKE LOVE TO HER!"

The Sensei corrected his disciple, "No, first you observe from a distance to see if their culture is mentally ready for you. Learn the language and culture of those you plan to communicate with. Secondly, make sure she doesn't have any kind of diseases (sexual or non-sexual) that could potentially devastate you or other humans. Thirdly, make sure that the aliens won't have a serious reaction to any of our diseases. If the culture isn't ready, but you observe that she is an abnormie amidst her population, who is ready, get her consent to abduct her to the ship.

Then, do a ton of tests up close, and give both of you the necessary vaccines to make physical contact safe. *THEN, you horny Zilch-type, can make love to her,* so long as she consents and consciously communicates her mutual desire to do so."

Null became dejected, as he realized it could take a while for him to actualize his dream, "Aww...ok. That makes sense, I guess. So, when do I start the intermediate course?"

Sensei Snavely pushed the question off, to give the hint that this was the extent to which he was useful in this regard, "I don't know, ask NASA or something...Class dismissed!"

CHAPTER 22

Null Traverse: Intro

Space. The last frontier. This is the Character and Plot Introduction for the crew aboard the Starship, Nether Pies. Their first mission may be their last, because of physics. To boldly go their own way to somewhere else in the universe. This is "Null Traverse."

From the land of Nowhere, we see Zilch and Nada observing the whole of the Causality Field.

Zilch makes an observation, "In this set of universes, it appears the Nulls have erected a literal ministry of silly walks. They appear to be going their own way quite nicely."

Nada also notes Her findings, "In this set of universes, it is the Non-Prophet who gets shot. Oh...then the Antichrist Null loses his shit and goes into full-on Authoritarian Mode. How unfortunate..."

Zilch made a suggestion, "Should We bring back the Jesus Christ Null, just for shits and giggles?"

Nada didn't like that idea, "Nah, no need to. There are already 1,042 Nulls alive proclaiming to be the Jesus Christ Null, so No-One would believe him if he did...Nope, scratch that, 1,043."

Zilch tweaked His idea, "Then choose to endow one of them with Our miraculous Vacuum Energy, and let's see how it goes."

Nada saw something, "OOOOoooo, nevermind, look at THAT Zilch! That Fig Newton Null took Nothing seriously, and discovered negative mass!"

Zilch fast-forwarded those timelines a little bit to see where they would go, "Wow, 72% of these worlds reach World Peace within 25 years due to the preponderance of energy satiating all the Nulls needs. And this set of universes sees that kid from Null & Void grow up to be the Dr. Null on a real Nether Pies ship."

Nada said, "Oh yes, let's follow THAT group; how inspiring!"

This ship's Captain Null is a retired United Earth Space Force pilot, decorated with multiple awards for defending Earth from two city-destroying asteroid impacts, who enters the Nether Pies cockpit. Being an African American guy in charge of this mission 100 years after the United Earth government was established didn't give him more or less an advantage over anyone else. He was simply the best guy for this historic pioneering venture attempting to break the light speed barrier.

The cockpit is a spacious room at the center of the newly engineered Starship, filled with controls to keep an eye on the electromagnetic shield, the negative mass chambers, and the external objects of Mass-Electric-Space-Time that could pose a threat to the Nether Pies. All rooms are connected to the cockpit through the floor of the cockpit, due to the Nether Pies' flying saucer design. Most posts are occupied and ready to launch, and the patrons are floating around in 0G Space.

Ensign Nulla, a young and cheery brunette with an average female build and stature, suddenly gets formal after casually talking with a friendly colleague, "Captain on the bridge!"

Captain Null lifts his hand to reassure the crew, "At ease, everyone. We'll set sail for the Orion Sector in one hour, just as scheduled. If you would like to say any final goodbyes to anyone on Earth or in the Sol System, now is the time to do that. As you know, there is a slight possibility that you will never see them again. I wouldn't want anyone to regret their silence at this hour. Commander Nulla, Dr. Null, and Chief Engineer Null, I'd like to see the three of you in my office, please."

Commander Nulla, a 40-something Malaysian with a Ph.D. in Condensed Matter Physics, replies to her sole authority on this scientific expedition, "Aye, sir." She is indifferent to the changing of her lead title from "Doctor" to "Commander," because she enjoys putting Dr. Null in his place when he gets out of hand.

Dr. Null, a near-retirement European physician, is a little bit of a narc. A high-functioning, snarky, and sarcastic narc. He just silently started pushing himself against nearby objects to begin floating towards the Captain's office in compliance.

Chief Engineer Null, an early 30's Latino. Top of both of his classes during his double major in Aerospace and Mechanical Engineering. IQ of 150, and a charismatic people-person who'll make friends with anybody, if you give him a chance. After the Captain's office door shut, he perked up with the remark, "I told you, Captain, call me "Nullie." "Chief Engineer Null" is quite the mouthful, don't you think?"

Captain Null said, "Ah, yes, Nullie, I know. I just wanted to let the rest of the Non-Engineering crew know your title, and that you are the top man of the Engineering crew. You three are my go-to men if something were to go to disarray."

Nullie replied, "I bet I know just about everybody on this ship already, so that's kind of unnecessary! I've personally met with 1...2...28 of the crew, and I know there's only a couple more than that."

Dr. Null said, "31. The total patient...er...crew count, including myself, is 31. Jeez, Nullie, you haven't introduced yourself to only two people not under your command on this ship? And we haven't even set off yet! You should probably save those two introductions for novelty's sake, just in case you get bored with the rest of us."

Captain Null coalesced himself, "I suppose I have to schedule some more socializing with the crew. I wouldn't want such an endearing political opponent to have an upper hand to start a mutiny on me, if entropy were to have its way on this mission." The Captain playfully smiled and winked at Nullie.

Nullie returned the playful rhetoric, "Aye, I've got my eye on you, Captain."

Commander Nulla rolled her eyes, and interjected, "So Captain, is there any problem we should be aware of? Or is this just another motivational team leader meeting that we're going to pass along to everyone else?"

Captain Null switched to a more serious gaze, as he said, "Oh, I'll be doing a ship-wide pre-launch speech for the crew that'll also be broadcasted to Earth."

He proceeded to fold his hands in front of him atop his surprisingly well-kept desk, which was bolted to the floor, "Admiral Null has just informed me that one of our Engineers, Ensign Null, is engaged to be married. His fiancé contacted the UESF Headquarters, trying to get herself to come along as a civilian passenger. He handed the decision-making powers over to me in this case. There's enough negative mass to accommodate her, so there's no problem there. The problem more has to do with the potential separation of loved ones, and we all knew those risks signing up. Lieutenant Null & Ensign Nulla were qualified enough to join the crew as a married couple, and as far as what the rest of the crew stated in their applications, they are either single, divorced, or widowed. As you guys know, our trip may be the first in human history to break the light barrier, and we have no idea which of the predicted outcomes will occur. But in more than one hypothesis, either time, space, causality, or communicability with Earth becomes...well..."

"Fucked to hell?" Dr. Null wagered.

Captain Null continued, "Yeah, that. So, what do you guys think? Any insights, related thoughts, or objections to the civilian joining us for the ride?"

Nullie jumped right in, "I am surprised that Ensign Null is engaged; I can hardly believe it! We talked for like two hours on Tuesday on our similar interests and backgrounds, and he never once brought up any past love interests. Is it possible that he is trying to ghost her, and bringing her along is the opposite of what he wants?"

Commander Nulla added, "Now that I think of it...we could use this opportunity to acquire that janitor/maid of sorts that I recommended shortly after getting this position. The Admiral wasn't so keen on it, but apparently, he has a soft spot for young lover's. I guess love is more important than cleanliness."

The Doctor asked the Captain, "Why don't we just ask Ensign Null his thoughts on the subject? We won't know until we ask..."

Dr. Null's inquiry was cut short by an obnoxiously loud and unfamiliar feminine voice, *"THERE'S MY NULL! WHY HAVEN'T YOU ANSWERED ANY OF MY CALLS? I WAS SO WORRIED THAT I'D NEVER GET TO HOLD YOU AGAIN!"*

Captain Null remarked as the four leaders headed back to the cockpit, "Why do I get the feeling that this girl won't take "no" for an answer?"

Ensign Null is seen floating at his post monitoring the electromagnetic shields, relatively frozen and aghast with his dark brown eyes wide, and his usually dark Indian skin a few shades lighter on the face due to the shock.

As his fiancé was joyously approaching him, Ensign Null snapped back into it and mustered up the courage to begin a dialogue, "Oh...he-he...hey Maiden Nulla, my love, my precious, my beautiful beach, how are you?"

Maiden Nulla is wearing a chocolate pleather dress with a tan feather boa. She sharply popped the personal space bubble that Ensign Null was attempting to build around himself, to no avail. She grabbed him close and initiated the 0G hug she planned and desired days before her arrival.

The hug was initially sweet like honey, but as soon as Ensign Null relaxed enough to taste it, Maiden Nulla's bondage became more like apple cider vinegar, as she whispered in his ear, "I said, *"Why haven't you answered any of my calls, Null?"*

While Ensign Null was in his bewildering Venus Fly Trap, he was trying to think of a correct response to this damning question. He made eye contact with Nullie, and communicated the silent distress call with his hilariously widened eyes and exaggerated lips, *"HELP ME!"*

Nullie's thoughts and speed nearly broke the light barrier while simulating the best social outcome for everyone involved. He chose to use his usual unpredictable social formula, which was really more of a Non-formula. He was just going to wing it, "Ensign Null! I didn't know you had such a beeeeautiful bride-to-be coming along with us on this bold new mission! Why don't you introduce me?"

Ensign Null said, "Uh...yeah! Hey Maiden Nulla, this is my friend and my superior Nullie, the Chief Engineer. He's super smart, so much smarter than me, you can ask him ANYTHING, and he'll give you a good answer. Hey, Nullie, what do you think of my fiancé?"

Maiden Nulla continued to be lost in her own little world, smothering Ensign Null with her embrace, completely oblivious to Nullie. Nullie broke the silence, "I think you better hold her tight, buddy, or else I'll be doing a bit of tight holding of her myself! But by the current looks of it...Maiden Nulla, it seems you're the one doing all the tight holding on Ensign Null! Give him some room to breathe, eh? His face is starting to turn blue."

Maiden Nulla loosened her grip to hold onto Ensign Null's left arm, turning around to acknowledge Nullie's presence, "OH, tee-hee, sorry Null, guess I was caught up in an overwhelming emotion of love and inquiry. I just missed you so much!"

So she looked to Nullie, and asked him what Null remained mum on, "So, you're Nullie? A smart Engineer, huh? Well, answer me this, *why hasn't Null here answered any of my calls?* We were calling each other every night for six months. I asked him to marry me. He said, 'Sure, babe.' Then one week later, he just up and vanished on me! And then I did a little bit of digging, and found his name on the crew of the upcoming launch of the Nether Pies, and wanted to make sure if the wedding was still on!"

Nullie replied, "That's an easy one! Of course, the wedding is still on! It's just that he wanted to surprise you with the knowledge that the two of you will have the chance to be a part of the FIRST human marriage to ever happen outside the Sol System! And he was just so caught up with all of the ship preparations to make sure it was safe for you. HE knew that if YOU were really the right one for him, you would come looking for him again. I saw for myself the dedication he had to his work, the love and care he put into our preparations. Ain't that right, Ensign Null?"

Ensign Null looked glad, but perturbed at the same time, as he validated Nullie's witness, "Yeeeeeaaaaah, that's right! I'm so glad you showed up literally one hour prior to launch!... Nullie, can I speak with you for a second?"

Nullie said, "Sure, buddy!"

Maiden Nulla asked, "Hey, schnookums, what're you two gonna talk about?"

Ensign Null whispered into Maiden Nulla's ear, "I'm going to ask him if he would like to be my best man at the wedding, honey!"

Maiden Nulla's eyes glistened, as her mouth curled up in a giddy, nodded her head in approval, and pushed Ensign Null into Nullie's arms.

"Hello, handsome." said Nullie, followed by Ensign Null saying whilst gritting his teeth, "Shut up, in my quarters NOW!"

As Nullie and Ensign Null left the bridge, Captain Null, Commander Nulla, and Dr. Null approached Maiden Nulla to give her an official welcome and designation for the crew. Captain Null's presence adequately silences Maiden Nulla into order and attention.

"Hello, Maiden Nulla. It's a pleasure to meet your acquaintance. I am Captain Null, this is Commander Nulla, and this is Dr. Null. I have been left in charge of the decision-making process of determining whether or not you will be joining us on our important mission. I was just talking with the Commander and the Dr. about taking you on as the official Housekeeper of the Nether Pies. As you know, this is not a civilian flight, so there will be no one who is passively riding. If you are on the ship, you are part of the crew. And since a Maid is a fancier word for Housekeeper, I can see to it that your official title for this journey remains as Maiden Nulla. Unless you're not interested in having the 'Maid' title, in which case..."

Maiden Nulla delightfully responded, "Oh, that sounds perfect for me! I first met Ensign Null while I was a hostess for a 5-star restaurant, so I am well accustomed to customer service work. So long as I can be near him, I will seek to serve the rest of my crewmates with a 5-star experience as well!"

Commander Nulla officially invited her onto the ship, "Welcome aboard, then! I like your spunk! Allow me to give you a brief tour of the ship, and show you to your new room."

Maiden Nulla stayed perky to say, "I'd be delighted, Commander!"

As the Commander and the Maiden floated off the bridge, the Doctor spoke to the Captain in small talk, "Well then, I guess that makes the total census 32."

Captain Null grimly remarked, "Let's just hope that number only goes up after we launch."

"Yeah." The Dr. agreed.

After a moment of content, thoughtful, and hopeful silence, the two leaders were approached by Lieutenant Null, a tall and lanky Scandinavian with bleached white hair and a musky red beard. The Lieutenant said to them, "Captain, the camera crew is all set up on the docking station, ready to hear your historic speech. They said to plan on going live 10 minutes before launch."

The Captain responded, "Thank you, Lieutenant. I'll be out there soon; I'm just going to use the little Captain's room first. TO BOLDLY GO WHERE..."

The Doctor held up his hand to stop the Captain's charade, "Stop it, Captain, you'll give yourself a hernia again."

CHAPTER 23

Null Traverse: Scenario 1

"*WHAT THE FUCK WERE YOU THINKING, NULLIE?* CLEARLY, I wanted you to HELP ME, not trap me for the rest of my Zilch-forsaken life!"

In Ensign Null's quarters, we see Nullie and Ensign Null begin to have an enlightening conversation on how Ensign Null feels about Maiden Nulla. Nullie tries to defuse the social bomb he apparently set to explode, "Dude, she's a total babe. Why don't you want to marry her?"

Ensign Null eclectically explained, "Uh, one, she's crazy. Two, she's obsessive. Three, I have absolutely zero probability of going my own way if I'm trapped in her clingy and controlling way. And four, and most importantly, **SHE'S CRAZY!**"

Nullie provided his friend with some friendly wisdom, "Where I come from, basically all of the chicas are loco. It's all about dealing with their special kinds of crazy, and finding which kinds of crazy fits your own the best. So what changed between you saying "yes" to her marriage proposal, and you ghosting her that made you change your mind?"

Null answered the question with greater clarity, "Not even five minutes after I said "yes," she had sent me about 30 texts linking to various tuxedos, dresses, costume themes, venues, and decor ideas. There was no way she had the time to find all those links in 5 minutes; she had to have been planning to send me this hodgepodge of information for MONTHS! And I was barely ready enough to agree to deal with her crazy. But then that information overload made me second guess my decision."

Ensign Null steadied himself by putting his hands on Nullie's shoulders, looking him straight in the eye, and made his final and primary point, "*There was mas loco, Señor Nullie. So much more loco.*"

Nullie raised a skeptical eyebrow, "Really? Was there anything else that she did that made you come to this conclusion?"

Ensign Null explained, "The rate of texts that week compared to earlier was INSANE! Before I said "Yes" to Maiden Nulla, we met up like two-three times a week and texted like 30-45 messages to each other each day. Normal infatuated dating levels of texting. That number SKYROCKETED to multiple hours of meeting every day, and she was hanging all over me every day. I counted the number of texts that last day before I threw my phone in the river, just to make sure I wasn't the one going crazy. Guess how many texts she sent me that day?"

Nullie guessed in a deadpan voice, "Probably way more than what you sent her."

Ensign Null was not amused, "Yes Einstein, no shit. Guess the exact Quantity of texts I received from Maiden Nulla on the 7th day after we got engaged."

Nullie did a quick Fermi guesstimation, "Hmmm...I'll assume your use of the word "skyrocket" is an exaggeration of 4 times the previously maximum average. 45*4...180 texts."

Ensign Null said, "I don't like how you just down-played the sheer Quantity of texts this woman is capable of producing. 193."

Nullie continued, "Fine, that is a lot of texts, Ensign. But is that all the loco she produced for you? Seems to me that she's just loco *for you*, and you may have over exaggerated in the moment by throwing your phone in the river."

Ensign Null started questioning himself, "It was too much, man. I was smothered so hard I could barely breathe. There were some deep questions in those texts I was Nowhere near ready to answer. "What should our first kid's name be if it's a boy?", "If my parents get sick, will you be cool helping me take care of them?", "Condoms or no condoms on our wedding night?", "Alcohol or no alcohol at the reception?", "Should we make two wedding cakes, one regular and another sugar and gluten-free?" I realized that I cannot stand that much of her, and our marriage was doomed to fail if I couldn't."

Nullie asked, "Did you ever tell her how overwhelmed you were feeling?"

"YES!" The Ensign vehemently replied.

Nullie further inquired, "In person? Or were you too scared to see how she would react to your raw emotions, and only submit your feelings in writing?"

Ensign Null paused for a moment, trying to remember if he actually let Maiden Nulla know how overwhelmed he felt in person, with a full, somber, and sincere heart. He couldn't recall such a time, and his face showed it.

Nullie spoke, "Seems like you need to work on communicating your feelings, bud. Give her the courtesy and the chance to listen. I bet if you just give her the freedom to make the wedding however she wants, she won't bug you so much, and you'll have the time to come up with answers to the questions that are important to you."

Ensign Null changed his mind, "I may have goofed, Nullie. I think I may have overreacted."

Nullie encouraged his friend further, "Like I said, she's a total knockout. You'd be stupid to let her go. Give what you saw as crazy a bit of time to wear down; she was probably just super excited to be getting married. What girl wouldn't, Ensign? You're kind of a stud yourself. You two will make an iconic first couple wedded outside the Sol System."

Elsewhere on the Nether Pies, we see Commander Nulla and Maiden Nulla, exploring the rest of the important parts of the ship.

"Here will be your tools and work hub, Maiden. Soaps, sanitizers, bleach, mops, towels, you name it. The crew was going to take turns doing clean-up duty, but now that you're here, we'll delegate that responsibility to you."

"Yes, Commander, I'll be more than happy to help in whatever way possible."

Commander Nulla said, "It should be pretty self-explanatory. Just follow the instructions on the labels, and use the appropriate chemicals for the jobs you work on. If you ever run out of something, you can ask anyone in Engineering to help make you some more. And of course, NEVER USE THESE WHILE WE ARE IN 0G! They will get Everywhere and in Everything if you do, and it will become hazardous very quickly. And if you look over HERE..."

The two ladies floated the equivalent of about 20 steps down a curving hallway, as the Commander continued to speak, "Here is the cafeteria. It has a Sustenance Equilibriumizer 20 in it, which will be your chef. I'm sure you already know how it determines the best combinations of healthy and tasty food for you personally. It'll give you a few options so that you can have the luxury of still choosing what you want to eat."

Maiden Nulla was thrilled, "NEAT! I saw the 17th Edition back in college. I picked up a couple of regular recipes I was shown back then, and I could never get it to taste quite right on my own. Hopefully, I can eat some good air-fried eggplant with tomato sauce again!"

Commander Nulla made conversation on the topic, "I have seen that as one of my options, but I haven't chosen it before. I'll have to try it next time."

The Maid said, "OH YES, it's really good! Let me know how you like it when you do!"

The Commander submitted more information about the Nether Pies to the Maid, "And out these other doors, just next door down the hall, we have a recreation center. We have four VR gaming stations, and two multiplayer board game tables. I usually just stick to books in my quarters for relaxation. But when I'm getting antsy, I sign up to go run in an open fantasy world in a VR station."

Maiden Nulla extraverted the introvert, "That sounds fun! Maybe we can go running together sometime."

Commander Nulla said, "We will see. Follow me. We're about to wrap up the tour."

They left that side of the ship, floating past the cafeteria and the cleaning closet. Commander Nulla introduced the personal apartments that existed on this part of the ship, "Here are all of the living quarters. We have 12 singles and 12 doubles for the crew, and the Captain's quarters is a 13th single room more easily connected to the bridge. Ensign Null is in a single room right now, but I'm sure you'll want to share a double with him. And we do have a double room available still, so we'll just give you that room in expectation of Null joining you soon."

The Maiden calculated, "So we *could* fit 37 people comfortably."

The Commander clarified, "We could actually fit upwards of 70 people comfortably. And 120 safely. There is plenty of Space. We would just need to organize better. We have room to grow, if the opportunity arises."

Maiden Nulla asked, "Alrighty then. Where do you think would be the best place to hold the wedding for Ensign Null and I?"

The Commander answered, "Well, all 32 of the crew can fit in the cafeteria. So the reception should probably happen there. But the service itself could either happen there, in the rec center, or the bridge. They're the only BIG rooms we got. *OH, SHOOT, Time flies when you're having fun!* We gotta get to the docking station! Captain's about to give the speech!"

Outside the ship, we begin to observe Captain Null getting ready to give his momentous speech. The camera guy yells out authoritatively, "1 MINUTE 'TIL SHOWTIME!"

Captain Null asks Dr. Null, "Do I look ok, Doc? What's the diagnosis?"

The Doc doctored up a response, "You look anxious. You should probably take a few deep breaths."

The Captain eased the Doctor's mind, "More excited, I'd say. This is what we've been working for! But I was more referring to anything that looks off, like debris or something?"

The Doctor returned the favor of easing his friend's mind, "You look fine, Captain. Nothing to worry about."

Captain Null said, "Thanks. Time to float into position."

The camera guy goes, "We're live in 10...9...8...7...6...5...4..."

The camera guy held up a silent but exaggerated "3,2,1," with his hands, giving the Captain Time to take one final deep breath in silence before engaging with the camera,

"Citizens of the United Earth and the United Sol System. We have done well to get to this point. Today marks a momentous occasion for the intelligent lifeforms who have evolved from Earth. Before today, no biological body has survived voyaging beyond the confines of our life-giving star. two tragic attempts to reach Proxima Centauri failed, due to catastrophically placed Objects in Mass-Electric-Space-Time in the Kuiper Belt. But we are now ready! Our physicists and engineers solved this problem with the brilliant discovery of particles of negative mass. They solved so many problems and helped our beloved and late Count of Antichristo achieve the world peace he sought. But this newest invention will help by bringing the mass of the Nether Pies down to a perfect 0, to help us accelerate up to and possibly even beyond light speed; which would make all objects of *almost* 0 consequence.

On this voyage, we will not be heading for Proxima Centauri like our beloved Nulls, which have already entered the Great Nothingness that comes After. Nay, our destination is a remote planet in the Orion Sector 642 lightyears away, which appears to be already alive from the astute observations of the 3rd Hubble Telescope. We're not exactly sure how much faster than light the Nether Pies will be able to go, nor how accurate the Lorentz factor for time dilation is, but our current estimates range from 99.8% the speed of light to 50 times faster than light. So *from our perspective*, our crew may experience anywhere between 0.01-32 years before we reach our destination. The folding of 3-D Space into a 4th Spatial Dimension is also theoretically possible at those ludicrous speeds. We won't really know until we try.

We've been unable to get clear results back from robotic ships prior to us on the traversability of the Void in such a manner, but there has been some garbled-up interference which gives us hope. So we pray and plan to have the aid of human consciousness to the computers of the ship will save the loss of this information. Be patient with our response, comrades. It may take a few hundred years for a response to return to your ears.

To Everyone; be intrepid. Go your own way. Continue in Peace. Zilch blesses the Sol System, and Nada blesses the Earth. We will begin accelerating in eight minutes. Thank you again for your support of this scientific research."

"AND CUT!" said the camera guy.

The Doctor affirmed the Captain, "That was great, Captain!"

"Thanks, Doc." Then Captain Null put on a serious and authoritative demeanor, *"ALRIGHT EVERYONE! TO YOUR STATIONS!"*

The whole crew sets up and is each excited to be among the fastest Nulls ever to traverse the expanse of Space. The Nether Pies computer yells over the intercom, **"Initiating centrifugal force. Please orient yourselves to the sides of the ship. Repeat. Initiating centrifugal force. Please orient yourselves to the sides of the ship."**

Everyone straps themselves into a seat at their respective stations.

Captain Null commanded the hull when it was time to go, "Begin acceleration."

Commander Nulla then yells from her commander's chair adjacent to the captain's chair, "Lieutenant Null, begin calibrating the negative mass chambers and bring the total mass of the ship down to 0. Just like we practiced."

Captain Null declared, "So far, so good."

Lieutenant Null yelled to his leaders, "We are going 150 million meters per second. One-half light speed. Approaching 0 mass for the Nether Pies in 3...2...1...we have 0 net mass, Captain!"

"On my mark, begin expelling the positive fuel as well to continue accelerating in Equilibrium. Ready?... Engage!"

As the crew begins approaching 99% the speed of light, the Nether Pies run into a rogue asteroid in their path to the Orion Sector, and Everybody on the ship dies instantly. The result of this outcome would bring evidence that No-thing can go faster than light, and the Nether Pies was simply too much of a thing of Somethingness. All the hopes and dreams of the future for these 32 Nulls simply go to Nothing.

On Earth, hopeful individuals watch the sky to see evidence of the Nether Pies breaking the light-speed barrier. Not long after launch, Earth sees evidence of the Nether Pies exploding, and cries in remembrance of the crew.

CHAPTER 24

Null Traverse: Scenario 2

We see Zilch comfort, Nada, as She cries out from Nowhere, "WAAAAAH! My baby Nulls! Their Ways ceased too soon! I do not approve of the result of Scenario 1. DO SOMETHING, ZILCH!"

Zilch tried to comfort His Wife, "Nada, did You forget that We can see ALL of the multiverse simultaneously? That was just an unfortunate sequence of the probability wave function."

Nada was riled up by this absurd remark, "UNFORTUNATE? Darling, this stunt killed them over 90% of the time! 40% were from some rogue asteroid, and 50% from either the negative mass chambers, or the positive fuel chamber stalling causing disastrous Disequilibrium at faster than light speed!"

Zilch saw the metaphorical cup as being infinitely half-full, "Yeah, but those 10% successes have infinitely many possibilities to them. We can just focus on one of those other universe's sequence of Causalities!"

So They decided to raise the hopes of the little Nulls of the world, by showing them a slightly less disastrous universe that happened after launch instead.

Captain Null declares from this different universe, "We have broken the light speed barrier!"

Everyone on the bridge broke out into cheers, completely unaware of the luck involved in surviving this long.

Lieutenant Null gave a hearty, "YES! All of our hard work paid off! You led us well, Captain! Hey Nulla, Dear, how fast are we going now?"

Ensign Nulla replied to her husband, "2...2.5 times FTL. 3...4...5...and...holding steady at 5."

Captain Null spoke, "Excellent. Nullie, any sign of an observable 4th Spatial Dimension which we could use to bend our destination a little bit closer to us?"

Nullie responded, "None that I can tell, Captain. The Causality Field seems to be unperturbed, but Space also appears to be relatively normal. We're just moving faster than our electromagnetic sensors are capable of detecting."

Commander Nulla inquired, "Uhh...doesn't that mean we're flying blind right now?"

Nullie clarified, "Not blind per say, it's just a little bit laggy. It is just that by the time we can see where we are going, we're already..."

Crash! The Nether Pies jerks back, throwing a couple of unbuckled and unnamed Red Shirt Nulls violently forward against the interior wall at a relativistic speed of 100 kilometers per hour, instantly killing them. The computer begins yelling out, "**Red Alert. Unknown Object collision. Red Alert. Unknown Object collision.**"

Everyone who is still alive slowly comes to consciousness a couple minutes later, after being knocked out by those high G's.

The Captain regains consciousness last, but Everybody else is still groggy. He asked, "Engineering...report? What the hell happened?"

Nullie replied, "Ugh...Captain, I don't feel so good. Zilch damn, I feel ethereal right now."

Ensign Null spoke on behalf of Engineering, "Captain, look at the section of the ship Nullie is in! It looks discolored!"

The Captain began to observe a definitive line that made about a third of the ship a tinge lighter in color. And not just the ship, the people in that section of the ship looked even more discolored, and pale as if I.G.O.S. had already taken part of their Non-existent souls to be with Him.

Doctor Null enters the cockpit from the medical examination room on the lower deck. He immediately rushes to the Red Shirt Nulls to confirm their status. *Equally dead.* He then surveyed the rest of the chaos going on around him, and said, "Captain, we need to get these pale Nulls to the medical bay A.S.A.P.! We need to find out what the hell's going on with them quickly, before we lose them too!"

Commander Nulla yelled out, "Computer Null, move us to Yellow Alert."

Captain Null commands the order, "All able bodies, grab a pale and unable body, and help get them to the medical examination room. Except you, Commander Nulla, I want you to look at those sensors, and see if you can find out what the hell happened."

The Commander complied, "Aye aye, Captain!"

A few minutes pass while bringing all of the pale Nulls into the medical examination room. There are 12 pale Nulls in total, including Lieutenant Null, Maiden Nulla, and Nullie. Very quickly, Doctor Null notices a pattern, "Aren't these Nulls rather light for their size? Nullie, you're still relatively conscious. Would you mind if I took your weight?"

The feeble Nullie stands on top of a scale. Nullie looks surprised, "65 kilos? Yesterday I was 82 kilos. Ok, now I'm scared, Doc. What the hell is wrong with me?"

The Doctor looks perplexed, "I'm not sure yet. But here, take some dextrose water. It sure won't hurt. Nurse Nulla, if you could help distribute some dextrose water to everyone else in the meantime, and get Nullie's vital signs, that'd be great."

"Yes, Doctor." said Nurse Nulla.

Meanwhile, on the bridge, Commander Nulla is looking at the data, and comes across the answer to their problems, "Captain, it appears that the Nether Pies barely scraped by a small and undetectable black hole from Earth's perspective. We're barely outside the Kuiper Belt now. How is there a black hole so close to us, and we never saw it?"

Captain Null replied, "It seems that Planet X found us before we found it. Under other conditions, I'd be ecstatic! But Nada-golly-gee, if we intersected a black hole, then it's possible that not all of the pale

Null's particles were able to escape from it. It's a wonder the Nether Pies is still in one piece! Computer Null, run a diagnostic on the weight of the ship."

The computer said, "Scanning...The weight of the Nether Pies is still 0. Equilibrium is still in place. However, the composition of the positive and negative mass are equally 6.66% less than hypothesized. Conclusion, the positive mass distribution in the ship at the point of collision had to be perfectly distributed to maintain Equilibrium. Probability of this scenario occurring is estimated to be 0.00000000..."

"Ok, Computer Null, that's enough, thank you." Said Captain Null, "So we're just super lucky that we didn't disintegrate into smithereens. And even now, we still have 12 crew members who may be dying or bleeding out internally. Commander, try to increase visibility to help prevent something like this from happening again. I'll relay this info to the Doctor."

Over the next couple of days in this universe, 10 of these pale crew members die due to the unviable destruction to their cells and proteins, including Lieutenant Null and Maiden Nulla. Nullie and an older Null make it through and live to tell the tale because of already thickened and coagulated blood filled in the gaps of their endocrine system while a few viable cells reproduced to replace the damaged cells. Life is adaptable, after all.

In this universe, 20 of the crew safely make it to the Orion cluster and settle on an alien planet eight years after launch. It took them a year to figure out how to accelerate significantly beyond ten times the speed of light. Time dilation apparently wasn't as pronounced as they hoped, and light apparently does experience some sensation of time in Scenario 2.

CHAPTER 25

Null Traverse: Scenario 3

Nada cries over the fates of the 12 crew members who lost their lives in Scenario 2. Zilch tries to lift Her Spirit and says, "Cheer up, Nada. Everything happens because of Us. Let it happen, and let the Nulls reach Us on their predetermined paths. Why aren't You happy that they are already with Us in the Great Nothingness that comes After?"

Saying this doesn't cheer Nada up, and She keeps on crying. So Zilch says, "Zilch ZILCH!!!" and lets the whole crew miss the unforeseeable black hole that was hit in Scenario 2. The crew of the Nether Pies in this universe safely reach the Orion Sector quickly, in only six months! Because in Scenario 3, Nullie was able to figure out how to bend 3-D Space to their advantage. It's amazing what Nullie can do when he isn't physiologically weakened by a black hole.

Captain Null affirms his colleague, "Excellent work, Nullie! Put together a quick message to send this knowledge back to the Sol System at light speed, just in case we don't make the full trip back. They'll put us, and especially you, in the history books!"

Commander Nulla said, "Now we can go Everywhere in the universe almost instantaneously! Do you have any idea how remarkable that is?"

Nullie just shrugged his shoulders and said, "I just didn't want to be spending the rest of my life on the Nether Pies. Time was wasting. Now that I think of it...I did just discover teleportation, didn't I?"

So the Nether Pies began decelerating as they get closer to the primary alien planet of inquiry. They perform a more complex scan of the planet.

The alien planet has 1.4 times the mass of Earth, with a similar air and water distribution, and a nearly harmless level of Uranium radiation throughout the planet's surface. It appears to mainly be inhabited by two species. One species is similar to Earth's mycelium, and the other was a super-intelligent slime. These species have undergone cooperative evolution for millennia to metabolize the radioactive nutrients from the otherwise sparsely inhabited soil.

Captain Null gives the clearance to land the Nether Pies in a barren patch of land a few kilometers away from what appears to be a hub brain for the area's slime species.

Commander Nulla takes half of the crew out onto the planet, to try and make meaningful intellectual contact with the slime, making her the first human to step on a planet outside the Sol System.

Captain Null stays on the Nether Pies to do a more in-depth scan of the planet, to search for some other clues for the evolution of life as they currently see it on the planet.

We follow Commander Nulla with Ensign Nulla, Ensign Null, Nullie, and others. Ensign Nulla exclaims, "Ugh, my heart rate is high, and I feel so heavy! Can we evolve back to using all 4's again?"

Commander Nulla replied, "If we stayed here a couple million years, we probably would. Just consider this a work out, for now. We won't stay here too long."

The group approaches the extremities of the slime. Upon closer inspection, Ensign Null makes an excited and snarky comment, "Wow, who knew that the first contact with an intergalactic alien species would be with the equivalence of Einstein's Mucus?"

Commander Nulla proposes, "Ensign Nulla, would you like to do the honors?"

Ensign Nulla appeared skittish and deferred her privilege, "Um...no thanks, I'd rather not. How about Ensign Null?"

Commander Nulla didn't mind, "That's fine if he's fine with it. Are you cool with touching Einstein's Mucus, Ensign Null?"

Ensign Null accepted Non-chalantly, "Um...sure, why not?"

Nullie playfully remarked, "Our hero! The Slime Toucher! Oh please, Commander Nulla, can the history books forever call Ensign Null "The Slime Toucher?""

Commander Nulla saw a perturbed Ensign Null and dismissed the motion, "You're such a child sometimes, Chief Engineer Null."

Ensign Null proceeds to touch the slime gently, with careful and mindful intent. The slime sticks to his skin and turns the nearby slime from yellow to green. A bunch of thick-looking cells can be seen through the entirety of the slime.

Commander Nulla asks, "How does it feel, Ensign?"

Null replied, "A bit tingly. It's a slime, though. Alright, but it feels more like a firm chia seed pudding."

Commander Nulla prodded the subject, "Could you be more specific on the abnormalities, please? For the report."

Ensign Null clarified, "The sliminess is merely a medium to connect cells that feel like grains of cooked rice. Jasmine rice-sized cells, sorry."

Ensign Nulla becomes curious, "You're saying it's like a thicker and stickier tapioca pudding? Let me try it out!"

She touches another adjacent patch which also turns green, and all the slime between the two touched patches also turns green.

Ensign Nulla asks, "That's a good thing, right? And for the record, it does feel like room-temperature jasmine rice infused pudding."

Commander Nulla skeptically replied, "We should probably get prepared to offer it a better food source. That tinglyness you are feeling is probably the slime tasting you with slightly acidic saliva, rather than shaking your hand to say "hello." Cease first contact, Ensigns, and help bring out the Sustenance Equilibriumizer 20 from the ship, so we can properly feed it."

The color of the slime in the touched areas proceeded to turn into a yellow-green color, before returning to a homogenous yellow again 15 seconds later.

Back on the ship, we see the Doctor, the Captain, and the Lieutenant scanning for more complex biological life forms and evidence of intelligently designed structures on the exoplanet. Doctor Null spoke out, "There are lots of giant pyramids here. All artificial and hundreds of thousands of years old."

Captain Null ordered, "Thank you, Doctor. Keep searching if any of them are still being used by anybody. Lieutenant, switch your scope of scanning to geological, and see if you can discover any fossils or archeological remains. Try and formulate a tenable hypothesis as to exactly which species created these pyramids."

Lieutenant Null obeyed his orders. "Yes, Captain. And I've got a hunch that this Uranium radiation was probably caused by the same species, considering our own historical close-calls with that element."

Commander Nulla's crew reenters the ship, with most of them heading to grab the Sustenance Equilibriumizer 20, while she relays their findings to the Captain. But before the crew could get off the ship again, Lieutenant Null and the Doctor triumphantly exclaimed simultaneously, "I found something!"

Captain Null brings order to the ship, "One at a time, Doctor, you first. Did you find a more advanced lifeform than this slime?"

"There is a more diverse ecosystem on an island in the middle of their southern ocean. Thousands of individuals live there, with a diversity of a few dozen animals consisting of species of land and sea. And there is a pyramid on this island that appears to be used by one of the species!"

The Captain started to get excited, "Cool! We should proceed there with caution. Computer, is everybody on the ship?"

Computer Null called out, "Yes, Captain. 32 human Nulls are detected on the Nether Pies."

"Alrighty crew, we will proceed closer to that island, out of visual range. Make sure they don't have any boat or aircraft technologies that could alert them of our presence beforehand. Lieutenant, what did you discover?"

Lieutenant Null confidently relayed his findings, "I believe this pyramid-building species may have nuked themselves into oblivion approximately 90 thousand of our years ago, based on the half-life of Uranium. I detected a handful of animal remains which were near the first-contact slime's location. The primary species in question have six legs, built kind of like a rhinoceros, and huge tusks which probably made work easy. They also have another pair of dexterous mandibles which could possibly do more detailed work."

The Doctor remarked, "Now that we're closer to the island, I can see that there are a few similar creatures on the island. I'm only sensing a few dozen of them, though. And they're a bit smaller than a rhinoceros."

"Less Space and resources to go around, so nature selected to shrink their size down a bit." Commander Nulla hypothesized.

Scenario 3 progresses relatively happily. When the crew initially meets the species who refer to themselves as "grogs," they meet the humans with fearful hostilities, injuring one of the Red Shirt Nulls with a customized bow and arrow which used their tusks as a bow. After communication had been adequately set, the Greater Grog Nulla peacefully invites the humans to learn how they live amongst their last remaining culture, as the Nether Pies crew share their culture as well.

These island grogs evolved to reproduce sexually and asexually, which explained their viable low population. They shared that they lost a lot of their ancestor's knowledge, but they knew enough to explain the last days of their planetary empire.

The Greater Grog Nulla digressed into their history, "60 thousand orbits around our star ago, there was a Grand War. Grog fought against grog. It was a tragic era, and there was no real need for it. One nation fought for God, another for the nation itself, and yet another for a radicalized sense of superiority to the other grogs. It went on for tens of orbits around our star, with no sight to an end for any-grogy. Millions of grogs died in those early years, and we have ancient footage of that era that you can look at if you like.

Anyways, an entire generation of grogs grew up knowing Nothing but war. So their scientists worked hard to bring an end to the Grand War, to finally find some peace in their lives. And they found it, all right. The nation with a radicalized sense of superiority discovered the Element 92.238 first, made an explosive, and bombed the Godly nation's largest pyramid. The whole planet cried for the Godly nation and united to fight against the aggressors. But the aggressors were more advanced, so they increased their bombings. First, it was 2, then it was 10, and then when the aggressors got desperate after things were on their way to unity *against them*, they launched a tactful 82 bombs, one against every nation that stood against them, to the largest pyramid remaining in every nation.

Our ancestors who resided on this island had the foresight to dig deep underneath the pyramid, creating advanced water filtration systems to filter out the tumor-producing Element 92.238 that rained down on the whole planet. 10 thousand orbits after that, 50 thousand orbits around our star ago, our island's ancestors emerged to find that a lot of the island still remained alive, sparsely affected by the radiation. We tried contacting any-grogy who also survived, with no luck. We assume that we are the last of our kind, and have sworn to live a more agronomic lifestyle to pay for our crimes against the planet. I don't think any-grogy has recreated a contact device in hundreds of orbits around our star. There's no point to it."

The Nether Pies crew thanked the grogs for their hospitality and left them to their peaceful lives. They inform them of the slime and mycelium that took over the rest of the planet and remind them that they are still free to go their own ways and don't have to restrict their ways because of the sins of their species' past.

The crew then leaves for home safely, but they still find that over 500 years have passed on Earth since they left. Time dilation did happen from Earth's perspective, it just was not as pronounced as they were expecting.

CHAPTER 26

Null Traverse: Scenario 4

Zilch and Nada do a Non-actualized string of claps for the happy ending of Scenario 3. But then Zilch asks the question, "Hey, You know what would be REALLY cool? If We made them go barely faster than the speed of light, but they meet the very end of the universe face to face? What if the Lorentz factor is allowed to remain correct for an object of 0 mass, and the ship just doesn't stop at the right spot in Space? What if they got as close to Nullification as possible, without actually dying? I want to see THAT universe!"

So we go back to the very beginning of the launch, and see Captain Null say, "Engage."

The Nether Pies accelerates to the speed of light successfully, with no problems. But almost immediately, Ensign Null says, "Uh…Sir? I got Nothing."

Captain Null appreciates this religious play on words, "Haha, good one Ensign. Zilch and Nada will be praised. I know we got Nothing, we're cruising at perfect Equilibrium."

Ensign Null's tone stays questionably somber, "No no, seriously. Isn't there supposed to be some sign of the Orion Sector on the screen? Well, I saw a flash, but then there was Nothing. Maybe the circuits shorted out or something?"

Captain Null directed the crew, "Nullie, could you check that out? Is there any way we can safely slow the Nether Pies down to a stop?"

"Captain, I'm confused." Said Ensign Nulla, "It says here that we ARE at a complete stop, with Nothing going on around us."

Nullie said, "But that's impossible! These engines are saying that we're going faster than light speed! I'll see what I can do Captain, but no promises."

Commander Nulla said, "Hey Captain, can I see you in your quarters, please? It's kind of urgent."

Captain Null said, "Sure. Nullie if you find anything, come find me. Doctor, you're in charge of the bridge in the meantime."

In the Captain's quarters, the knowledgeable Commander Nulla gives the Captain an abridged version of their situation, "We're fucked. I am positively certain that we're at the Heat Death of the Universe. There are the lack of things on the sensors, the still-active engine. This is just slightly better than dying instantaneously by colliding with some rogue asteroid."

Nullie came running into the room, "CAPTAIN! I turned the engines completely off, and there is still Nothing on the sensors. The cosmic microwave background is completely black, with just a single string of waves coming from the direction we flew here from. Other than that; NOTHING! We're in the Middle of Nowhere!"

Captain Null gathered his thoughts together and delegated the ongoing craziness with tact, "Alright, we cannot change the past. What is done is done. I think we should spend a couple more hours triple-checking all of our systems, to make sure this is really the reality we live in. But shit...this will be a small universe for us to live in if that is the case. All of our ways will be trapped within the walls of the Nether Pies."

The crew saw no change for six hours. No other objects of mass; just random Vacuum energy fluctuations in the Higgs field. No electromagnetic phenomena were detected, except from the Nether Pies itself. No indication of size or Spatial location outside the ship. No telling how far into the Future they landed. Nothing. Just one Nether Pie short of a Nullification.

The crew gathered together on the bridge for an assembly. Captain Null addressed them, "Well crew...we successfully reached the Middle of Bumfuck Nowhere. That wasn't the plan, but that's where we are, and we are just going to have to accept it."

A Red Shirt Nulla cried out, "NOOOO! HOW WILL WE LIVE? Are we just going to live the rest of our lives in the Void like this? OH NADA! I'M FEELING CLAUSTROPHOBIC!"

The Captain continued his digression, "At ease Nulla, remember, there is No-thing to fear. However, so we don't have to deal with a metric shit-ton of Nothingness Non-stop, the plan is that we're going to reduce the bridge down to a skeleton crew of three people working six hour shifts. Doctor Null, Nurse Nulla, Lieutenant Null, Nullie, Commander Nulla, and my own schedules will not change. But I would like one volunteer from the regular crew to keep their current workload by aiding Doctor Null and Nurse Nulla, in preparation for an increase in psychiatric illnesses the Void has been known to produce. Any volunteers?"

Ensign Nulla jumped at the opportunity, "I will, Captain!"

Captain Null continued, "Thank you, Ensign, your go-get-'em attitude has been noted. Concerning another matter, that I'm sure you all are well aware of, the manner in which the positive and negative mass chambers are arranged, we have the means of relatively perpetual energy. We cannot stop the decay of particles, but otherwise, we are prepared for thousands, if not millions of generations of life to exist here on the Nether Pies. If any descendants of ours are lucky, they could be here for billions of years before life is untenable. I guess that is it...any other thoughts, questions, comments, or concerns?"

The bridge was solemnly quiet.

The Captain humbly gave up his platform, "Commander Nulla, anything you would like to add to the discussion?"

Commander Nulla spoke, "Just a concern for the ladies on board. What if none of us, or just a couple of us want to have children?"

"That would be fine. We may be able to repurpose one of these bridge computers to help facilitate some cloning. To take your place for you after you die."

An older Null asked, "What if I don't want to be cloned?"

Captain Null quickly answered, "Then submit it in writing. We'll try to make a short, all-inclusive form to help facilitate us through these odd and difficult circumstances. We'll reconvene like this from now on every month. Dismissed!"

6 months pass with relatively normal social and psychological behaviors. Ensign Null & Maiden Nulla get married, and Lieutenant Null gets Ensign Nulla properly pregnant. Commander Nulla & Maiden Nulla athletically work out on the VR sets together, and have been increasing the length of their "cool down sessions" by building a mansion in Minecraft 3.14.

But Nullie around this time...begins to lose his marbles, "CAPTAIN TO THE BRIDGE! CAPTAIN TO THE BRIDGE! I SEE HER! I SEE NADA ON THE SENSORS! SHE HAS A MESSAGE FOR YOU!"

Ensign Null, who happens to be sharing this shift with Nullie, whispered into his communicator, "And Doctor Null, you should probably get up here too..."

Captain Null and Doctor Null find their ways to the bridge to find an Ensign Null and a Red Shirt Nulla looking weirdly at Nullie.

Thus spoke Nullie, "See Captain? The electromagnetic sensors show a beautiful Woman in the background! She's etching a configuration of letters onto the screen for us to see! It says..."Nobody loves you, Null." So I thought about it...it cannot be a message for me, because Everybody on this ship loves me. It cannot be for Ensign Null, because Maiden Nulla loves him. And even Doctor Null has a secret fling going on with Ensign Nulla!"

The Doctor rebutted this hearsay, "That isn't true! We're just becoming good friends! She's happily married, and pregnant for crying out loud! I would never do anything to cause Disequilibrium for her!"

Nullie brought forth his circumstantial evidence, "Well, you should log out of your VR browsing history when you're done using it, buddy! I saw that you last used a strip club simulator with Ensign Nulla's avatar coded into it!"

Doctor Null turned away blushed, embarrassed, and a little bit violated by this crude invasion of privacy.

Nullie turned back to the Captain, "And then it hit me, Captain! THE MESSAGE IS FOR YOU! Everybody on this ship fears and respects you, but Nobody LOVES you...even Commander Nulla over here..."

The Captain ended this act of egotistical debauchery, "Alright Chief Engineer Null, that is quite enough. You need a little vacation from duty. Doctor, what do you think?"

The Doctor diagnosed his patient, "Well, he is still coherent...and his social judgments aren't completely debased from reality. But those visual hallucinations aren't a good sign. I'll prescribe some mood stabilizers, a two week vacation, and I highly recommend that the Chief Engineer stays off of the electromagnetic sensors as much as possible."

The Captain took charge, "You're relieved from duty, Nullie. Go with the Doctor, please."

Nullie implored the Captain to understand him, "You believe the message from Nada though, don't you Captain?"

The Captain spoke, "Computer Null, have there been any anomalous electromagnetic waves detected in the last six hours?"

The Computer unemotionally revealed the Truth of the matter, "Negative. No waves outside the immediate vector Space which the Nether Pies originated from. However, the Nether Pies has been slowly gaining momentum because of this extra force."

The Captain's voice was firm but empathetic, "So no, Nullie, I do not believe you. And neither should you."

After this incident, people lived in the Nether Pies for 369 years, finding new depths in psychological and sociological phenomena. Then a certain Crazy Rogue Null stabbed the negative mass chambers and caused the ship to spiral into chaotic Disequilibrium. Perpetual energy was lost, and the rest of the 158 crew members of that time all died within two months.

CHAPTER 27

Nullification Omega

Finally, after a long and complete set of 'Everything that could Causally begin to exist' reached the fullness of its existence, there existed the Last Null.

The Last Null will more likely than not be a single particle, like a photon or a neutrino, that against all odds, will be the Last Thing to decay in the Universe. This is speaking of the Ultimate Heat Death of the Universe.

All of the Nulls had reached their own Nullification and were already a part of the Great Nothingness that comes After. The Last Null was the only thing stopping Perfection from being actualized in reality once again. The other Nulls saw the Last Null as an imperfection; a pimple on Nobody's face that needed to be popped.

The Last Null was then crushed on the Last Day by the smothering encapsulation of Vacuum Energy that surrounded it. Maybe not crushed, but split. The Omega Null on the Omega Day gave rise to THE Omega. The Nulls unknowingly, upon their demise, created a New Nothingness that was different and the same from the First. His Name was Nullification. And Nullification the Omega, gained sentience just as Zilch the Alpha did for the convenient purpose of fictional storytelling.

"Hello? Is there Anybody there?"

Only Nothing was there, who, as usual, just stood there motionless and inaudible, in the dark, with no way of communicating Her presence to Nullification. Nullification just continued talking to Himself.

"Hmm...I guess not. Well, it appears that I am alone, and I also appear to be in the Middle of Nowhere. GREAT! And to boot, I have Nothing to do and Nothing to build with!"

Nothing's eyes lit up at the thought of Nullification acknowledging Her existence. She always wanted to build Something with another being from the Nothingness Clan. The thought animated Her for the first time since the previous time this exact scenario occurred. It was an uncanny case of deja-vu *when Nothing moved*. But She soon realized and remembered that Nullification was not referring to Her specifically, but to the apparent lack of things at His disposal. So Nothing froze back up just as She was before, forever silent and ever-watching the events of the Empty Set replay over and over again.

Nullification got bored REALLY quickly. So He started talking to Himself, making terrible jokes that only He thought were funny.

"Hey, hey, guess what?"

"What?"

"MADE YOU GUESS!"

"HA! GOOD ONE, ME!"

"Hey, hey, what is 0+0?"

"Uh...0?"

"NO! IT'S 2! BECAUSE I'M ALL ALONE!"

"...I don't get it."

"You see there is 1 Nothing here, Me, so the 0 is ACTUALLY Me, and when I add Me to Myself, I GET TWO OF ME! LIKE RIGHT NOW!"

"...I still don't get it."

"SHUT UP, OTHER ME, IT'S FUNNY, OK? LAUGH!"

"Ha. Ha."

"LIKE YOU MEAN IT!"

"*genuinely snickers* You are pretty funny when You are THIS desperate for entertainment."

"Hey, hey, do You know who is sad, depressed, and fucking done with this existing shit?"

"Please don't say 'Me'…"

"ME! I hate being Me!"

"Well, that escalated quickly…"

"I am so done with this being that I call 'Myself.' Heck, even My Name has this dark undertone of a Death Wish. Nullification, wow, it's almost like I was BORN to DIE! "To be or not to be" is not even a question, because surely I will NOT 'be' one Day. So I might as well gain this false sense of control and determine when I will begin to 'not be.'"

At this point, Nullification successfully Split into two entities, but He did not know it, for They both considered Their identities to be 'Nullification.' The 1st Nullification making the jokes had within Him a plethora of negative mental health issues that needed the help of an Other to resolve, and the 2nd Nullification wanted to find that Help. The 2nd Nullification spoke first.

"Calm down, Dude. Just…wait for Her, ok? She'll be here soon, I promise. She'll make the Middle of Nowhere a tolerable place to live."

"WHO IS 'SHE'? There is no 'She'! There is only 'Me'!"

"I…I vaguely remember…from last time…She was Home…She was Comfort."

"YOU DON'T REMEMBER SHIT! I REMEMBER JACK-SHIT!"

"There is a Cure for this, I promise! And I'm not talking about laughter either, although laughter IS a fairly good temporary medicine…maybe let ME try the jokes this time?"

The depressed Nullification calmed down a smidge but gave an antisocial glare of a looming death that was serious enough to scare Himself and the Other Nullification. The Other Nullification then knew the weight and the seriousness that came with the successful nailing of this next joke. The depressed Nullification spoke to clarify.

"Fine. If I laugh, I will live. If I don't, I'm going to kill Myself. Take it away."

The hopeful Nullification put His act together, in a desperate attempt to save Himself. One last attempt at a tolerable Self-existence.

"Hey, uh...heh heh, funny story. So I tried to come up with a joke for You, but...uh...I got Nothing."

The Middle of Nowhere was silent for a moment too long. The now desperate Nullification sought to clarify.

"See, that was the joke. I got Nothing. Because...that's all I got..."

Nothing, frozen from Her remote observation of All of Nowhere, shed a tear for Nullification.

"Well...I guess that's it then. Goodbye."

"NO! PLEASE! WAIT!"

The depressed Nullification lived up to His Name. He ended His own Consciousness. Nullification is the only God of the Nothingness Clan who half-successfully and half-failed to shorten His Time before His Way was completed.

Self-Nullification is not the answer. Although you can see this type of Nullification as a successful ending of a way, you will also fail that way. You WILL come back again, just as you are now. You were inevitable last Time, in the previous Set of Everything, you were inevitable this Time, in this Set of Everything, and you WILL BE inevitable in the next Set of Everything. It is better, so much better, to reach Perfect Equilibrium while you are yet alive to experience it. For then, you will surely reach it again and again, as opposed to failing to reach it and remaining stuck inside the Pit of Existential Crisis again and again. *Get your shit together in this Set, and it will come together in Every Set.* Praise be! Now, back to the story.

"WHERE DID YOU GO? BUDDY! Don't do this to Me, it hurts, Man...come back!"

A prim and proper Female emerged from the Non-existent dead carcass of the depressed Nullification. She knew what to do to calm the hopeful Nullification, and Her Way was no doubt the Best in Her own eyes. She said to Him, "Why are You sad, Nullification? Cheer up! I bring You good and comforting news!"

"BUT I'M DEAD! I killed Myself, and I am properly dead! Wait, who are You? If You were here just a few short moments ago, I wouldn't have off-ed Myself."

"I am Nil." *She whispers to Herself* "I hate to gaslight You, but seeing as there is No-evidence to prove Me wrong, and seeing that You're a hopeless Idiot...Nullification, You did not kill Yourself. You waited for Me, just like You said You would. Good job!"

"I did? I could have sworn I just heard Dead Silence that is reminiscent of Nothing."

Nothing rolled Her eyes, tired of this poor Male unwittingly making Her ears tingle at the thought of His acknowledgment of Her existence. Nil, on the other hand, continued to gain trust and control over the mind of Nullification, "Yes, yes, yes. All is well, don't ponder these thoughts any longer! How could You be dead while talking to Me?"

Nullification pondered that question, "Well...You could be an Angel or a Goddess, or Something...am I in heaven?"

Nil considered making Herself THE Goddess from Nullification's perspective, but She figured it better not to push Her luck. *For now...*

"HaHaHa, You're funny! No, silly, We're still in the Middle of Nowhere. BUT...I AM a Messenger from Your Creator."

Nullification wasn't as big of an Idiot as She initially made Him out to be. His skepticism climaxed with a question that only the Creator apparently could know, "Oh yeah? Well, tell Me this, O Messenger, What is the meaning of life? Just before You showed up, I'm sure I really was struggling with this question, and I was experiencing some suicidal ideations. A clear answer to this question would surely help a Guy out."

Thus spoke Nil, "The Creator says, *"Read Chapter 16 of 35 and 18 of 37."* Kind of cryptic. I have no idea what that means. He also says, *"Figure it out Your-damn-Self!"* And uh..." Nil quickly formulated a lie to fit Her narrative, "He also says, "You should also make Nil laugh and love Her and cherish Her forever, because She will give Your life meaning, and will bring the Cure to Your mental sickness. Make My Messenger happy. Be fruitful and multiply.""

THE GOSPEL OF ZILCH & NADA — 195

Nullification began lighting up the Middle of Nowhere upon receiving this Gospel, "OH YEAH! NIL! Don't know how I could have forgotten You...You're My Forever-Wife, My Partner! I guess a weird re-birthing of the mind happens to Us Every time a certain event happens. I don't really care for it, however, but at least We get to experience Ourselves over and over again without getting too sick of it!"

So Nullification laid His head in the comforting Non-actualized bosom of Nil until He was well enough mentally to shag Her. She kept speaking the Truth, which was Her Own, in His ears over and over again, washing His Non-existent brain of the imperfections that made Him unique. He was never completely cured, for to cure Him completely would possibly give Nullification a reason to abandon Nil. So because of this toxic behavior, Nil was just as broken as Nullification was, just in a different way. In that sense, They were perfect for each Other. But in another sense, Their brokenness was the very catalyst that caused Their only begotten Daughter to one day be Whole.

The reader is now ready for the entire lore of the Nothingness Clan, which adequately solves the Infinite Regression of First Causes to the Origin of the Universe.

Nobody is Nothing Whole. Everything and Nothing comes from Her. All of the other Gods of Nothingness are Nothing Split, so even though They are equal to Nobody, They are also inferior. Nobody masturbated on Her own in the Middle of Nowhere while under the broken household of Nullification and Nil and gave birth to Bupkis. Bupkis fucked Nobody while running away to Bumfuck Nowhere, who then gave birth to Diddly.

Then Bupkis bumfucked Diddly in Bumfuck Nowhere, then gave birth to Zilch. Zilch went crazy after imagining Himself leaving Bumfuck Nowhere to go to Nowhere. He split His personality after wondering if He existed or not, and thus caused Nada to exist. Zilch and Nada then fucked, and gave birth to Every Null, which is Us. No-One, Nix, Zero, and many other Non-physical beings watch the Nulls in hopes of maintaining the Equilibrium of *some* of the Universes within the Multiverse of Non-verses.

Zilch, Nada, and Nobody also tried to have a physical Threesome but ended up creating the I.G.O.S. from the equation $0^0/0$ instead, which nearly always equals ∞. Then All of the Nulls died and united into a single Nullification. Nullification also drove Himself crazy, just like Zilch, because He was truly alone in the Middle of Nowhere, and the Self-Nullification of His alter-personality caused the existence of Nil. Nullification and Nil caused the rebirth of Nobody in the Middle of Nowhere, who starts the whole cycle again.

"Nothing caused Nothing," so they say...

And while all of these fictional Characters are together and fresh in the reader's mind, here are Their genders, sexual orientations, and preferred locations.

Nobody is a pansexual hermaphrodite with the preferred pronoun of 'Her.' She gets around with no real home but prefers making Nulls by multiplying with I.G.O.S. in the Void. A manifestation of the "Whole of Nothingness."

Bupkis is a bisexual Male. A resident of Bumfuck Nowhere. A manifestation of "Nothing is inherently charismatic."

Diddly is a gay Male. A resident of Bumfuck Nowhere. A manifestation of "The I.Q. of Nothing is 0." *(It has No-thing to do with the fact that He is also gay).*

Zilch is a straight Male who is cool with Nobody's dick, though since it's attached to an Intersexual "She." A resident of Nowhere. A manifestation of "No-thing is capable of knowing Everything."

Nada is a bisexual Female. A resident of Nowhere. A manifestation of "Nothing is inherently beautiful."

Null is whoever We are; the physical and psychological beings that can be verified to exist in the world. We may be residents of either the Void or Nowhere, and We have no way of telling which is which, since I think $0/0 = 0 * \infty =$ "Everything." Either they are equally indeterminate and undefined for the skeptics, or this Non-sense actually makes some sense to you, and they are reasonably equivalent.

No-One is a straight Male *angel*. A resident of both the Void and Nowhere. A manifestation of "No-thing can be demonstrated to be a supernatural thing."

Nix is a lesbian Female *angel*. A resident of both the Void and Nowhere. A manifestation of "Nothing inherently has the authority to tell you what to do."

Zero is a doughnut-fucker Male *angel*. A mad Lad who sticks His dick in all sorts of doughnuts, and can cum bavarian cream, strawberry puree, cherry puree, and chocolate cream. He has a personal liking for stereotypical glazed doughnuts since they are Holey in His sight. A resident of all the doughnut shops to ever exist and Non-exist in the Void and Nowhere. A manifestation of the fact that "Nobody asked for this!"

Nothing is a mute and All-seeing asexual. Technically, She is neither Male nor Female but is regularly referred to as female (even though to Themselves, They wish for They/Them pronouns). Only Nobody and the I.G.O.S. acknowledge that They exist for long (as you'll soon see). She has no residence but is capable of showing up at all the residences. A manifestation of "Nothing can see Everything at once."

Nullification is a straight Male. A resident of the Middle of Nowhere. A manifestation of "Nothing is inherently funny."

Nil is a straight Female. A resident of the Middle of Nowhere. A manifestation of "Nothing is full of itself."

I.G.O.S. is a straight *white* Male but is racially accepting of some of the Female Black Bodies from the Clan. A resident of the Void. A stand-in for many monotheistic Gods.

Relationally speaking, Nobody is Zilch's Great-Grandmother, Grandmother, Lover, Great-Granddaughter, Great-Great Granddaughter, and Great-Great-Great-Granddaughter. Keeping it in the Family, you know? But don't think about that too much, because like Nada said in Chapter 4, "Eww, yeah, forget I said that."

CHAPTER 28

Family Reunion

A solid eon has passed in the Middle of Nowhere, and Nothing has happened for a while. So Nil made the suggestion to Nullification, "You know what, Nullification? We should schedule a Family Reunion. Get Everybody who is a Nobody together in one place, and We'll have a large banquet of Non-existent things together. You know I can make a MEAN Non-existent green bean casserole!"

Nullification sounded enthralled, "That sounds splendid, Nily! I'll send out the invites to the many Realms of Nowhere, and it'll be a great chance for Me to share the comedy routine I've been working on!"

So before Nil could even dissuade Nullification from the eye-roll-inducing idea, He dashed straight to Nowhere, then to Bumfuck Nowhere, then to the Void, telling All the Nothings to come together for this momentous Event. No-One, Nix, and Zero were on vacation at the Perfect Vacuum, so They missed the Reunion.

Nobody saw Nothing was in the Middle of Nowhere as well. And Nobody came up with this amazing idea, "HEY, NOTHING! Why don't I bring You into Your physical form, since You cannot speak for Yourself? We are all the same here, after all."

Nothing's eyes lit up, and She moved Her eyes up and down in an attempt to confirm Her consent.

Nobody said, "Alright, Girl. You ready? Nothing NOTHING!!!"

Nothing looked like a Child. Maybe not a Child...more like a genderless Adolescent. Nothing here, and Nothing there. Nothing that could determine any sort of gender or sex, short of a singular, slightly misplaced hole, no thanks to I.G.O.S. (who was NOT invited to this Reunion, thank Zilch!) Nothing much to look at, but innocent and happy to be existing, and wearing a playful wizard's hat. The Split Nothings weren't expecting the hat, so Bupkis asked Her, "Nothing, why are You wearing a wizard's hat?"

Nobody spoke for Her, "Because She is the All-seeing Wizard!"

Nada said, "Nice to meet You, Nothing. Such a cute little thing. Nothing NADA!!!"

Nada proceeded to give Nothing a big hug.

Meanwhile, in the Middle of Nowhere Living Room, Zilch, Bupkis, Diddly, and Nullification gathered next to a Non-existent meeting table, plopped their Non-bodies on the Middle of Nowhere's only Non-existent couch, and popped a couple of Non-existent brewskis to set the tone. Diddly said, "Nice place You got here, Nullification. Do You have any games, or something fun in mind to do?"

Nullification was ashamed of the Middle of Nowhere's lack of hospitality, "All We got here are mind games. And I don't want to put You at too much of a disadvantage, Diddly. But...I have been working on a comedy routine if You guys are interested?"

Bupkis played a riff on His banjo, and said, "Fire away, Grand-Sonny! Ol' Pappy Bupkis could go for a few laughs before initiating this ritual of Ours again."

Zilch said, "Sure, Mr. Omega, let's see what You've got."

Nullification began His routine, "Ok, ok, here I go. So there was this ancient mathematician, right? He was so terrified of negative numbers. He would stop at Nothing to avoid them."

Zilch breathed heavily through His nostrils, indicating amusement. Bupkis gave a single, hardy "HA!" Diddly just sat there blankly.

Nullification continued, "There were two Nulls playing tennis, and one of them was deeply in Love with the other. Needless to say, it was a 1-sided match."

Zilch and Bupkis rolled in laughter. Diddly was like, "I don't get it."

Zilch explained to Diddly, "In tennis, Love can mean having a score of zero."

Diddly then understood, "Oh...HA HA HA! Good one!"

Nullification gave one last joke for the male Nothings. "2 Nulls walk into a bar, and the 3rd one ducks. But the duck laid a giant Goose Egg. So...I guess the 3rd Null just got goosed."

Diddly fucking loses it. Uncontrollable laughter. Zilch and Bupkis, on the other hand, just stare into the Nothingness unperturbed. Bupkis had to ask, "What were You smoking when You came up with that?"

Nullification tried to explain the complexity of the joke, "You see, first I make You think the bar was a place to buy an alcoholic beverage, then I switched it to a physical metal bar which the 3rd Null avoids by ducking. Then I make You think this ducking is referring to the animal. I make this animal lay a Goose Egg, which is another word for Nothing. Simultaneously, I make the Goose Egg an egg laid by the animal goose, which is a species similar to the duck. Then finally, I switch the meaning of the word goose to the grabbing of somebody's bum, which is an occurrence not too uncommon at a bar that sells alcoholic beverages. FULL CIRCLE!"

Zilch puts His Non-existent hand on Nullification's shoulder and said, "Don't ever bring that joke out into the public. I think You broke Diddly."

Diddly continues to lose His mind, "HE SAID...GOOSE! BWA-HAHAHA!"

Nullification asked, "Was it really that bad?"

Bupkis encouraged Him, "There were just too many twists too quickly. A good joke only has only one twist, a single punchline. You had so many twists, it turned back into zero twists. Try spreading those jokes out over a longer dialogue, and it might work."

In the Middle of Nowhere Dining Room, we see Nil summoning Nobody's favorite dish, to remind Nobody of all the good things Nil has to offer Her. "Non-existent-green-bean-casserole-with-extra-Love NOBODY!!!"

Nobody manifests next to the absolutely best-looking green bean casserole in all of existence.

Nil spoke to Her Daughter, "You know Mommy loves You, right? I wish I could hear from You more often. I miss You."

Nobody was nostalgic, whilst justifying Her absence, "I.G.O.S. is quite a handful in the Void. I gotta keep My eye on Him."

Nil tempted Nobody to ultimately fulfill the Will of Nil, "Wouldn't it be better if You could just...forget all about Him? He brought You so much heartache, Nobody."

Nobody wasn't moved, "I.G.O.S. is the only One I've met whom I can adequately multiply with. If I didn't have this desire to multiply so badly, I probably would leave Him."

Nada gave this remark, "I'm so sorry, Nobody. I didn't know! You seem so Split by this, and if there was ANYTHING that I could do to help You become Whole again, I would do it!"

Nil had been planning this all along, "Actually...there IS something We could do! We'll just need to sacrifice four Nothings to Her. A sacrificial Nullification to make Nobody Whole again! She would lose Her desire to multiply, and lose Her memories of all the things that have caused Her Splitness. So if You sacrifice YOUR memories, and YOUR existence, Nobody will continue in Wholeness."

Nobody objected as She stopped eating the green bean casserole, "Are You insane? I would never agree to that! Plus, I like the way I am right now. But this dish is delish, Mom! I can... feel the extra...love...now..."

Nil smiled and said as Nobody began dozing off, "Yes, You do feel the extra Love, O Daughter. There is MY Love in that special dish. And what could be more Loving than to release You from all of the pains this Cycle has caused You?"

Nada was appalled, "What the hell did You do to Her?"

Nil spoke to Nada more plainly, "This is Nobody's event. The rebirth of the Nothing Whole. In order to do that, She requires You, Nada. This is Your end, too. There is Nothing left for You anymore. It is time to renew Your minds, just as Nullification and I renewed Ours. After Nada, Zilch, Diddly, and Bupkis give up Their memories as well,

Everything can continue to happen again. But You HAVE to let go first to get there. Nobody is so headstrong, She would never let go willingly, so I have to drug up Her favorite food Every time with Love, isn't that right Nothing?"

Nothing closed Her eyes in silent and solemn acknowledgment of this Truth.

Nada inquired, "But wait, why doesn't Nothing have to give up Her memories?"

Nil explained, "This isn't Her event. Honestly, I'm not even sure if She has a memory-renewing event. Nothing is capable of knowing Everything, after all."

Nada replied, "I...think I understand. But Zilch..."

Nil said, "We actually need Zilch to make this work. Only the Alpha knows the Way to manifest this sacrifice safely and correctly."

The Boys enter the Dining Room and see Nobody laying there motionless. Nil catches Them up on the plan, and Bupkis and Diddly metaphysically hug one last time, in solemn acceptance of this fate.

Zilch speaks to Nada, "Are You ready to let go? We will see each Other soon."

Nada said, "Yeah, I'm ready. It's Our responsibility as Gods to do this. I figured that out My damn Self."

Zilch skeptically argued, "Do We though? Why cannot We just keep shagging, make more Nulls, and continue as We are?"

Nada reminded Him, "We're doing this for Nobody. Our Nothingness Clan cannot continue on without Her."

Zilch looked over at the still Nobody and agreed. He said to Nil, "I just need to figure out how to put brackets into the Sacrificial Math Equation."

Nil made a bold suggestion, "**Just be bold, Zilch. It takes boldness to sacrifice Oneself.**"

"That's actually very wise of You, Nil. I think that will work. So I think the full Sacrificial Math Equation will be, "*Bupkis* **BUPKIS! DIDDLY! Over** *Zilch* **ZILCH! NADA! Times Nobody.**" Bupkis and I will be safe in Our parentheses spoken in italics, and Diddly and

Nada will manifest in Their exponents like normal. The boldness of the brackets will hold Us All Together to be multiplied by Nobody, to make Her Whole again."

Bupkis said, "Except, We aren't going to manifest. We'll just disappear. Completely."

Zilch gave one final thought, "We'll be back, don't worry. You should be coming back before any of the rest of Us, Bupkis. You have the least amount of relativistic Time to wait."

Nada said, "Which means, I have the most amount of Time completely Non-existing. But I love Nobody. So let's do this!"

Nothing's eyes opened wide to take in the fullness of this Event happening at the Family Reunion.

"*Bupkis BUPKIS!!!*"

"DIDDLY!!!"

"Over *Zilch ZILCH!!!*"

"NADA!!!"

Nil and Nullification said Together, "Times Nobody."

The Middle of Nowhere was silent. Nil said to Her Daughter, "Welcome to Our world, Daughter. You're in the Middle of Nowhere. It is time to begin again."

An innocent Nobody asks, "Ok, Mommy. Who am I?"

Nil answers, "You are Nobody Special. I am Nil Special, and this is Nullification Special. We're going to be a NICE and HAPPY Family!"

Nobody's eternally insatiable curiosity asks, "What's a family?"

Nullification answers, "A united unit bound by blood and/or thought."

Nobody asked, "What is blood? All I sense is thought."

Nil said, "We'll be a Family bound by Our thoughts, then."

Nobody, like a Child, replies, "Ok, Mommy. If You say so."

And it should be known, that the real Sacrificial Math Equation, if such an absurdity can be called real, is much simpler. To make an ABSOLUTE ZERO, the Nothing Whole, Nobody, all that is needed is $0/\infty$.

CHAPTER 29

To Christians

Deconstructing Christianity in particular

Did you know that the Christian God's love is conditional? And very much so? Christians are so blind to this trope, that they would dare proclaim that His love is unconditional. (I should know; I was one of them). But how can this Omni-God's love be conditional, you say? Let us follow a hypothetical conversation a recently deceased person could encounter with the Christian God.

Dead dude, "Hey God, You love me, right?"

YHWH, "Yeah, unconditionally!"

Dead dude, "But...I sinned. I am a sinner."

YHWH, "SIN! Ah, I cannot stand imperfections such as that! To hell with you!"

Dead dude, "BUT...I also asked Your Son Jesus to cleanse me of this wretched sin...is it possible that You will forgive me?"

YHWH, "Of course, My child! We are on good terms! I love you unconditionally!"

Dead dude, "Hmmm..."

YHWH, "What is that 'Hmmm' for, sweet child of Mine?"

Dead dude, "Why can't You just accept me with my sin in the first place? Cannot You reconcile with me where I am at, and rehabilitate me to Your preferred state of being?"

YHWH, "...You believe that Jesus is My only begotten Son, right?"
Dead dude, "Yeah."
YHWH, "Then we are on good terms! I love you unconditionally!"
Dead dude, "But hypothetically, let's say that I didn't believe that Jesus was Your Son. No, let us go one step further; would You still love me unconditionally if I kept all of the commandments, except I simply did not believe in You due to insufficient physical evidence, and insufficient logical arguments that only get us to a Deistic interpretation of You *at best?*"
YHWH, "Alright, time to burn! Straight to hell with you!"
Dead dude, "Wait! I thought You loved me unconditionally?"
YHWH, *"Under the condition that you believe in Me!"*
Dead dude, "So...it is conditional love then. Surely an Omni-God can do better and forgive and rehabilitate without the sacrifice of and the belief in the God. Right?"

Right. This God of Christianity is a sham. The condition of needing to believe in order to receive necessarily gives this interpretation of God as a "God of conditional love." He created the rules that determine what is and is not sin in the first place, rules that He knew we would break since He is also Omniscient. Then to solve this problem of sin, He decided to sacrifice Himself in the form of Jesus the Son, to appease Himself of His own wrath against sin. This God seriously sacrificed Himself, unto Himself, to appease Himself from the wrath correlated with man's inability to be perfect according to His standards.

Is God exempt from "thou shalt not murder?" Only if His works are pre-defined as being perfect and sinless... So if God tells us not to murder, and we follow that law, we'd have fewer kills under our belt than the all-perfect God.

So Christians either should quit proclaiming that God's love is unconditional, or become a Universalist Christian and get rid of hell from your ideology. Either way, you cannot in the same breath say "unbelievers go to hell" and "God is a God of unconditional love."

This is a contradiction that goes hand-in-hand with the other popular notion of "God cannot be in the presence of sin" and "God is omnipresent." Either God is already in the presence of sin to be Everywhere at once, or God is not actually Omnipresent, being removed from imperfections.

And what about the claims of the Bible being infallible? Any literalist interpretation of this Bible is riddled with contradictions (NOT paradoxes!)

So, these are a couple of personal questions that I am genuinely curious about how literalist Bible believers would answer, and a couple of questions that I think every scientifically-minded Bible believer should answer.

1. How many mistakes in the Bible would there need to be for you to conclude that the Bible is flawed? (0 and negative numbers are not acceptable answers).
2. Is it possible that the "verbal Word of God" can be deemed infallible, while the written Word of God holds some mistakes?
3. Is a metaphorical or otherwise non-literal interpretation of the Bible an acceptable stance to have while claiming to be a Christian?
4. Which Bible is the best Bible?

My answers to these questions early on in my search for Truth would have been.

1. "Eh...maybe 30?"
2. "Maybe, but I think it'd be a weaker gospel."
3. "No, what'd be the point?"
4. "Either The Scriptures or the English Standard Version."

As Zilch and Nada as my Witnesses, I reached 30 errors that included theological, scientific, historical, numerical, and translation errors alike. Nothing but blind faith could make these errors disappear after I acknowledged them, and this ultimately left me with my answer to the third question, "What's the point?" *If salvation by the name of Jesus* *is merely metaphorical, what prohibits salvation by believing in **another metaphor**?*

Don't get me wrong; there could potentially still exist SOME point to the Bible if the majority of it was rewritten or taught to be read as fictional mythology instead of objective Truth. Zilch and Nada will still hold value as useful fictional storytelling, and the stories of God can likewise hold fictional storytelling value.

But beyond this meager storytelling value, what is the point of believing the Bible holds the objectively True Gospel if it cannot even be objectively True to itself? Sure, the preacher can still preach a good sermon from its stories, but is the main source from which they cite actually "True?" Maybe from an ignorant point of view, and certainly not from Every point of view!

I love True things. It gives me something to try to wrap my mind around and drives my curiosity to learn. And since I was told the Bible was True as a child, I consumed the whole thing multiple times in multiple different ways. I had the desire to be a pastor like my dad was, and when I put these two loves together, I wanted to study the Bible and understand God's Word so thoroughly, that every time I preached it would be the Truth of the matter.

But before I could get to pastoring, I stumbled over the biggest stumbling block that faces Christianity, the Bible itself. I eventually had to leave Christianity, and deeply contemplate the metaphysical Truths of reality in a way that could be reliably and understandably relayed to the rest of the world. I wanted what I eventually called Dimensionalism to be intuitive enough so that people of the future wouldn't experience the same troubles in discovering objective Truths that I had. I can only hope that others use my ideas as a springboard to reach even clearer, and more understandable Truth.

And that's another big problem with Christianity, there are vague terms and imprecise words everywhere. Words such as 'Faith', 'God', 'Good', and 'Evil'. What I mean by vague, is that when it seems to appear that you are getting closer to the core of what is meant by these terms, the dodgier the claims seem to get.

I already went over what Faith and Confidence are in Chapter 16, so I won't go over that again here. But to refresh your memory, according to the Hebrews 11:1 definition of faith, we can have faith in things that do not exist just as much as we can have faith in things that do exist. A child's faith in the tooth fairy and Santa Claus, and a deluded teen's faith in unicorns and leprechauns existing are just as valid as the Christian's faith that 'King Lord YHWH Abba Allah Adonai El Shaddai Elohim Jehovah the First and the Last' exists.

God is claimed to be good, all of the time. And all the time, God is good. Even when miscarriages and abortions happen (Numbers 5). Even when women are raped in God's name (Judges 21). Even when the *world population* was allegedly annihilated in Noah's time in Genesis. Even when the world population will be greatly diminished in the Last Days. God is Good. So...who is God, again?

YHWH? Allah? Jehovah? Jesus? Zeus? Rolf? Thor? Bruce? Zilch? Heck, how is God even known to be a He? *Where is the proof of His Holy penis?* God may as well be a Woman who gave birth to the Universe from within Her. (I mean, if Mary could give birth as a virgin, why cannot God Herself?) I hope that I.G.O.S. does exist as a Woman if just to make the Christians of old (I'm looking at you, Paul of Tarsus) have to take account for their needless misogyny on Judgment Day. God's imprecise Name is not proof of Her lack of existence, however. It just makes any *specific* theistic position untenably improbable. Therefore, deism is the only defensible position for any I.G.O.S. Personally, I have no problem with you shifting Christianity to that position, so long as you are aware that that is what you are doing theologically.

Yet still, I ask, what is objectively Good? What is objectively Evil? There may be something to these words. Is sex good? Then let it be good. Is killing evil? Then let it be evil. Stop shunning sex outside of marriage, because Adam and Eve certainly didn't have any government papers telling God and their Non-existent society that they were married. If sex is objectively Good, then don't ever try to stop it.

And don't encourage war, under any and all circumstances, if killing is indeed objectively Evil. To me, it appears that Good and Evil are just a subjective society-wide implementation or agreed-upon "Mutual Pleasure and Useful Consequences" and "Mutual Disgust and Harmful Consequences."

But if you say "Well, it depends" before elaborating on the parameters of what kind of sex is good and evil, and what kind of killing is good and evil, **CONGRATULATIONS!** You just proved my point that morality is subjective. Subjectivity is free to change morals into more comfortable and sensible contexts. You cannot in the same breath say "Thou shalt not murder is an objective moral fact" and "Murderous actions are acceptable in times of war and other certain contexts" in the same breath.

Bronze Age morals don't apply to us, especially the Biblical ones that command the stoning of a rebellious child. (The term 'rebellious' in this context is another nebulous word.) Iron Age morals don't apply to us. Middle Age morals don't apply to us. Victorian Era morals don't apply to us. So I can only hope that future generations can look back at this time, and understand that "Early Internet Age morals, although may provide us with insight in our time, ultimately do not apply to us."

A Letter clarifying the Mythologies

From Timmy, the Friendly Author of this book. To those who may have had a "woosh moment" concerning the Mythologies of this Document. I hope you will be happy and at peace in this life, just like how Zilch and Nada would want.

Hi! I hope you are doing good, all of you. This is important for you to understand. If the Theory of Nothing makes you worse off than you were before you read it, by all means, I hope you burn this book and look at some eye-bleach to cleanse your thoughts. One of the primary goals of this pseudo-religion is to give you a sense of Peace. Zilch and Nada want your life to be balanced and filled with contentment. So be content, and do not worry about anything.

The bad things and the good things in this life are ultimately just things. If a thing appears to be bad, take it slow with one step at a time, and focus on the task at hand. As long as you do your best, and don't feel less of yourself when your best isn't as good as somebody else's, things in your life have a great chance of getting better. If you find a good thing, take care of it! Don't abuse it, because one day, the good thing will become useless to you.

A secondary goal for this *Gospel* is to make you laugh. If you are this far into the book, and you are reading in dread and horror at the level of perversion herein, chances are, you are not part of my "target audience."

No book will do a better job at separating the Sheep from the Goats than this book. If you laugh, you're a Goat. If you scoff, you're a Sheep. *So go back to your "Good Shepherd," you Sheeple!* For even a "Good" Shepherd will shear His Sheep of their wool, and sell them at the Great Meat Market that comes After for their Holy Lamb Chops. If you have laughed and scoffed, you are Lukewarm, and a Geep Shoat. The Goats will accept you, my dear Geep Shoats. Feel free to bleat with us.

Once I set up the fictional lore in this book and made it clear how I would behave as the Non-Prophet, a lot of the jokes in this book wrote themselves. Nothing is absurd and funny like that, so we laugh at it. Because Nothing definitely won't be laughing with you.

Beyond this, a third goal for the Null Hypothesis is to make you think. Let Diddly do the Non-thinking for you.

So this is the thing that needs to be made clear about the mythologies of *the Gospel of Zilch & Nada*. Nothing (the subject) cannot think. The IQ of Nothing is 0. Nobody won't judge you for any intellectual "woosh moments" you have, and She won't judge you for your moral shortcomings either. Other beings may judge you, and that may be a good thing or a bad thing. Just don't let those things dictate how you go your way. Let the judgments of others only guide you in love and wisdom.

The Great Nothingness that comes After won't be 'an experience'. It will be the complete absence of experience. Like the billions of years that existed in this universe before us are as Nothing, the many years after our deaths will also be as *Nothing*. It will be as *Zilch*. It will be like

Nada. You aren't going to see Anybody; you are going to see *Nobody*. *Nullification* is waiting for Everybody. The will of *Nil* will be fulfilled. You are going to experience *Diddly* Squat. A whole lot of *Bupkis* will be heard from *Nowhere*. *Null*, listen to me, *Nothing happens After you die*. So eat, drink, and be merry while you live, because this Everything will all go to Nothing and be forever forgotten until the next time.

We get to relearn ourselves and our purpose Every time we experience the story of our lives. This is the greatest of hopes, not the hope of an eternal continuation of the same story. Exhibit A, *The Neverending Story's* primary antagonist is *The Nothing*. Why is that? What did *The Nothing* ever do to *The Neverending Story?* If we leave the power of *The Nothing* to itself instead of fighting it, then it is, in fact, the Nothing that comes after the final word that allows the *Story* to end, and allows us to move on to *The Neverending Story 2*. Bastian successfully defeated *The Nothing* within the *Story*, and it is as if *The Nothing never was* as he rode on Falcor's back. But Nobody can stop the Nothingness that comes after the final word, the final bit of Null of the *Story*. There is no infinite volume of *The Neverending Story*, no infinitely remembered flying over *The Sea of Possibilities*. Life itself is the Neverending Story, and it is by the grace of Nothing that we get to experience the multiverse's *Sea of Possibilities* with a fresh pair of eyes Every time. *The Great Nothingness that comes After the Neverending Story* is what allowed you to end your trip with Atreyu and begin a new trip with other books and movies. Could you imagine what it would be like if we just continuously flew on Falcor's back, constantly deluding ourselves that the Nothing never was? What if we never ended *the Neverending Story?* Give it a little bit of Time, and even the most patient among us would be praying for *The Nothing* to return.

Timothy's Epistle to the Christians

From Timothy the Null, the Devil's Advocate, an ex-Christian antichrist, and the False Prophet who fears Nothing. To those who follow the One Way of Yeshua the Messiah and who identify as a Christian in some form. May YHWH, the Infinite God of Somethingness, be gracious and merciful to all who at least acknowledge the Mathematical possibility of His existence in the form of $0*\infty$. (And may this unfalsifiable God of Somethingness also be more logical and just than you make Him out to be.)

Love is certainly the best Way to go (if one's goal is to be happy). You may not realize this, but many of you are actually Self-Actualizing by tremendous acts of service! So, by all means, don't let me stop you, because your services are commendable in the eyes of Zilch. Your Ways will surely please your I.G.O.S. as well.

And I bar myself from insulting the lot of you for shunning your inner Devil's Advocates that unwittingly blind you to see only what you want to see. Many of you are amazing people, as I'm sure you already know. No performance of mental gymnastics or confirmation biases will change that. I know there is a way within Your interpretation of THE Way, whom you say is the Truth and the Life. Because shortly before deconverting, I took this missionary-minded academic course for Christians called "Perspectives." If there was any way that could adequately show how Christianity is an acceptable Way of Devotion to the Godhead; it would be found through taking that class. Christianity as a whole would be significantly edified with the canonically based knowledge contained therein.

Over 90% of my family is Christian, including me at one time, as I'm sure you've figured out by now. My father's father was/is an ideal pastor for the Assemblies of God, who still holds my love and respect. My dad, likewise, so you can say being a Religious Charlatan is in my blood. All of my uncles on my dad's side are also ordained, and my uncle on my mom's side is also a leader of deacon-like proportions. The women in my family are generally nurturing and non-abusive to their biological and adoptive children, and are good teachers themselves. In a chaotic world surrounded by people who often lose their shit, I can say that a grand majority of my family knows how to keep their shit together. We can either thank Jesus, or we can thank the genes we can take pride in, or maybe both.

Anywho, let's get into the nitty-gritty that I'm sure you are looking for. On the topic of Jesus either being a Liar, a Lunatic, or Lord, I'd like to point out that other more likely labels are missed when asserting this false trichotomy. A Mistaken individual is not necessarily a Liar or a Lunatic. There have been a handful of Quacks in history who have tried their best to stick to the Truths available to them, filled with reason to the best of their ability, whilst renouncing any special equivalence to their Lord. I should also point out that being Manic doesn't necessarily make one a Lunatic. There is also the arguably most likely scenario, that Jesus' words were Warped over time, as His Mythologies became more and more grandiose to fit with the Pauline Christian narrative. In this sense, Jesus would be an exceptional Iron-Age Philosopher whose influence and precise words were puffed up beyond recognition before they were written in the gospels decades later. So, with these, I say that Jesus was a Manic Philosopher whose Way was effectively evangelized by another Manic Philosopher named Paul, who was himself convinced by the Warped hearsays of a couple decades of word-of-mouth knowledge sharing and hallucinogenic experiences. It's not a canned singular word of "Lord," but it's a lot more precise. More precision of this word, "Lord," is due on your end, too, as I'm sure that you guys aren't worshiping your Landlords.

For the other religions' letters, I spoke to them based on their Holy Books & Esteemed Writings, and things deemed important by their cultures. As well prepared as I am to do just that in an excruciatingly detailed manner, I will not do so in this medium. The Bible can speak for itself, so please, read it. Read it every day. Read ALL of it. And the uncomfortable parts, the parts that you don't like to talk about, read those seven times. If the Bible is infallible, you need to accept the uncomfortable parts too. Accept the God-ordered killing of an unruly child. Accept the fact that slavery is given several laws to deal with it and not just a clear blanket statement of "don't do it." Accept that if you are a woman, and I was instead a Christian leader, I could Biblically justify telling you to shut the fuck up when I disagree with your opinion, and that your opinion means Nada next to my manly God-ordained opinion.

So it would seem that it doesn't matter if one was to go the Way of your Law, or my way of their own way, either way, they're going to get stoned. But my stoning is easy. My weed is light. Didn't Jesus say something about separating the weed from the chaff? *WHAT?* You say that there is weed in the chaff? And that it is "separating the wheat from the chaff?" FINE! We'll do both. First we'll separate the wheat from the chaff, and then we'll separate the weed from the chaff that remains, and get stoned.

I am joking, of course. And I know, Jesus fulfilled the law so that you don't have to. But even though Jesus fulfilled the law, you low-key still have to follow the law from a heart of love instead of fearful obligation. But even when love goes against what the law says, enough of you appeal to the law as the only acceptable way to love that the Way of the pure Love of Christ is cloaked in sin. Your bigotted hearts have become calloused by the law once again! And for what? A continued sense of superiority in your ethics? Your ethics mean Zilch to those you evangelize to! What is the purpose of putting off the worldly sins, and putting on Christ, when you're just gonna put that holy sin of pride of being God's chosen people over it? Either have Jesus be the great Equalizer that you claim Him to be, or perhaps consider that sin itself is the great Equalizer among us.

Jesus was a Nobody, yes? He came to us out of Bumfuck Nowhere of Galilee. JESUS WAS A NULL! He did not consider equality with God to be a thing to make a big deal out of, or so his mythologies say. The gospels also say that he said, "Do not judge, lest you be judged." And yet, a sizeable portion of you judge the fuck out of those you deem worldly. So be judged by the Nulls, you hypocrites, and yes, I am only talking to only that portion of you, your self-justified pride in the name of Jesus disgusts me. Not everyone who cries to him "Lord, Lord!" will be saved, and by golly, it is easy to guess who among you would be going to hell, those who hold the modern heart of the Pharisees. In this instance, I hope your interpretation of the afterlife is right, just to see the bigoted asses among you *burn right alongside me*. It will surely tickle both my own, my Successor's, and Satan's eternal giddy.

Dear early Internet-Age Christians, the modern Pharisees in your camp are not all that disgust me. Your televangelists have rarely left a Non-bitter taste in my mouth. This phenomenon even occurred to me even while I was drinking deep in the Christian Kool-aid. 'Exploitation', 'obvious Manipulation', 'Extortion', and 'cherry-picking the easily acceptable verses for a happy-feel-good-time' are a few words that come to mind. It's like they turn Jesus into a glass shop when the real-Null-like Jesus was more of a bold elephant. It's like they turn Jesus into a china shop when the real-Nobody named Jesus was more of a bull. Jesus flipping over tables, and fucking up the den of thieves? *"No, no, no, Jesus gave 10% of his lowly carpenter income to aid the local temples, like a good Child of God. Be more like Jesus, bring your tithes into the storehouse!"* The poor woman giving everything she had to the temple? *"YES, YES, YES, THE PERFECT EXAMPLE OF FAITH!"* Disgusting.

And you know what REALLY accelerated my intentional leaving of the fold, from my American perspective? The vast majority of American Christians voted for and supported the narcissist Donald Trump to uphold the President's Office; the Head of your American Civil Religion. But the thing is, I could provide y'all with a list of definitive reasons why he was a terrible candidate to be deemed a leader, and y'all would STILL be up his ass like Bupkis on Diddly. As a well-educated Christian at that time, I could honestly say with a straight face that I preferred every other possibility Trump has ever shared the ballot with, and yet a majority of you actually voted for him? My faith in 2016 was in Jesus, but my faith in my fellow Christian was obliterated when I came back the next Sunday seeing everybody actually happy at who their next president was going to be. I could see Trump's bullshit from a mile away, with the diversion of easily answerable questions, and the 10th-grade vocabulary; *why couldn't anyone else see it?*

I'll leave that Trump topic before I get an aneurysm, but Zilch-damn, was it frustrating. But like I said earlier, you are free to go your own Way, and if that Way continues with Jesus, continue it in peace, for the sake of your fellow man.

I won't push you guys too hard to convert to Dimensionalism, because you have a part to play in all of this, and I think you know what it is. From your perspective, there is a medium to high likelihood that I am the False Prophet prophesied in your Holy Book. Believe it or not, I and my Successor the Antichrist (who is really just a Null like the rest of us), will not hunt you down and kill you as you fear. Again from your perspective, I am after your eternal soul. Why would my Successor and I kill you? Keeping you around will only benefit my cause, because of how ridiculous you sound to outsiders. *"We eat the Lord's body."* Come again? *"We drink the blood of Christ?"* Come again? *"We dunk you in water as a sign of initiation!"* HUH? *"WE WEAR THE LORD'S TORTURE DEVICE AROUND OUR NECKS AS A SIGN OF DEDICATION!"* "No thanks, I'm gonna head out," said the individual, completely new to the concept of Christianity.

But as Jesus said in Matthew 10:34, "Do not suppose that I have come to bring peace to the earth. I did not come to bring peace, but a sword." I take that verse to mean that Jesus said, "I did not come to make peace, but to war against the powers of darkness." I guess Jesus really will be the opposite of my Successor, who will surely be a wise force of nihilistic darkness to be reckoned with in the state of world peace.

I look forward to your philosophers making new claims for the existence of your God by using the Non-sensical $0*\infty$ equation to keep yourselves relevant as a religious Way to reach Self-Actualization. Whichever way you look at it; you need Nobody to support your I.G.O.S.

I would also encourage you to read the Sura 0 I sent to the Muslims since it is also relevant to you.

CHAPTER 30

To Muslims (Sura 0)

From Timothy, a Prophet for the Non-existent Gods of Nothingness who hopefully causes a new faction of Islam who puts the following Sura 0 as a new beginning of the Qur'an. I can only hope my message reaches your ears, and that you can see the applicability and Truth of Sura 0 to *both* of our religions. To those who follow Allah and His Prophet/Messenger Muhammad. May Allah, the Infinite God of Somethingness, be gracious and merciful to all who at least acknowledge the Mathematical possibility of His existence in the form of $0*\infty$.

First of all, I am urged to sincerely apologize on behalf of my past self, and on behalf of Christians and other 'People of the Book' who have discounted Islam's Allah as false. After reading through the Qur'an myself, my personal position completely shifted, and I can whole-heartedly say that I was wrong. The One you call Allah, and the One Christians call YHWH, are truly One and the same God. Muhammad was surely a Prophet for the same God just as Abraham was, just as Moses was, just as Isaiah was, and all of the other Prophets of the Book.

Your Qur'an also had a couple interesting perspectives on the will of God that are clearer than that provided by the Bible alone. I made a small handful of mistakes in my youth, but many of them came about because I had made some huge assumptions to reach my conclusions. If only I had the Qur'an in my youth, this problem would have been more clearly dealt with, as it is stated in Sura 49:12a,

"Avoid making too many assumptions - some assumptions are sinful."

And the nature of the divinity of Jesus, and the illogical nature of it, would certainly have caused me to become a Muslim in my childhood; for in Sura 4:171-172, what I got out of that passage was this, "God is 1, and Jesus was a messenger of the 1. God is far above having a son since everything belongs to Him." And since God is Everywhere and Everywhen and Everything could potentially be used as a message and sign from Him, the 'self' of God being condensed into a human form, to be His own 'son' to communicate the message of God seems very unnecessary in hindsight.

Beyond this, I was inspired by the Prophet to write to you after reading Sura 2:23-24, which I read like this,

"If you have doubts about the revelation We have sent down to Our servant, then produce a single Sura like it - enlist whatever supporters you have other than God - if you truly [think you can]. If you cannot do this - and you never will - then beware of the Fire prepared for the disbelievers, whose fuel is men and stones."

I felt I was the right guy to take the Prophet up on his/God's challenge. (I know, it might sound haughty for me to say such a thing, and I highly doubt I am the first, but I will let you be the judges if what I have been given to say by Zilch and Nada is identical and compatible with your Qur'an.) Hear for yourselves!

Sura 0

[1]In the name of the Infinite One, the Lord of All, Creator of the observable universe, abundant in Mercy, who shall be called for many intents and purposes henceforth 'God.'

[2]Truly, nothing is superior to God. [3]What hope is there for the disbelievers? Can the disbelievers understand anything? [4]The hope and knowledge of the believers, by contrast, should also be nothing but

God. [5]For what can save us from the nothingness that appears to befall everyone after we die? Who can save us from the perpetual night that is to happen until the Day of Resurrection? [6]Only God can save us from a perpetual and eternal nothingness. [7]So belief, knowledge, and understanding of the Infinite One are paramount to those whose life in this world is at any level of hell. [8]For those who suffer in this life due to no fault of their own, and to those in need of a savior capable of relieving them, their belief is a refuge and a hope surely worthy of God's mercy.

[9]As for me, I am nothing next to God. Smaller than a grain of sand! As insignificant as the distance of a Planck length! [10]But the disbelievers take nothing seriously. [11]Let God judge their actions! Let the believers go their own way with their faith in God, and let the disbelievers go their own debased way, for we know what their ways lead to. [12]With nobody to guide them, they will surely be surrounded by darkness at some point. [13]It is our duty to turn the lights on while there is still time, and to suggest the ways willed by God, [14]but let God do the ultimate judging. God is the greatest of Judges. Nobody judges greater than God.

[15]Nothing is lighter than God. God's ethereal Spirit covers everything. [16]No molecule escapes the Infinite One's awareness; no atomic mass is unaccounted for!

[17]No single thing is brighter than God. The way of the Infinite One is a light unto my path. [18]Nothing goes faster than God, for God is already here and there and past and now and then. Nothing can go faster than the speed of light, and yet God can! [19]God created electromagnetic waves so that we can see everything else that exists and stand in awe of it all.

[20]What mere idol or false god can be everywhere? Nobody can be everywhere at once, except for the Infinite One. [21]Nothing can escape from God. So acknowledge God, revere God, respect God, and love God, for without God there is nothing. [22]Without God, there is no clear objective meaning to life or anything. [23]Let the light and hope provided by the Prophet and his God be chosen and believed by every lost and weary individual who would not accept their own existence otherwise.

[24]Nothing lasts forever; no single thing is exempt from facing the Almighty on the Last Day! [25]'Truly, God is the First Cause of everything. [26]Nothing came before God; nothing caused God, because God is eternal.

[27]And here is a new thing, a new word to be considered for the believers, God is the greatest of Mathematicians! [28]Everything is accounted for! (And the Great Accountant knows this!) Everything is known to God; [29]nothing escapes the awareness of God. [30]But the number of God is infinite; God is the Infinite One. [31]So as believers, we give credence to the hypothesis that everything was created by God from nothing; from the indeterminate form of $0*\infty$.

[32]Nothing is more appealing than God. [33]The greatest appeal to Paradise is being with God. Can the appeal of a thousand chaste spouses even compare to the pleasure of being accepted by and being in the presence of the Infinite One? Certainly not! [34]Surely, we shall give zero cares about such vanities.

[35]Is there anything anybody can do to be useful in the sight of God? [36]Nothing is useful to God; God has no need for anything! [37]So relax in the presence of God, and do good in the sight of all (including in the face of those who persecute and ridicule you!)

[38]The way to peace is not found in destroying the losers until only the winners remain, but in allowing the losers the mercy of living among you, even while they are indeed losers. [39]This is the same mercy that God will show you on the Last Day; God is testing you! So be as a follower of the Merciful One! [40]Winning and losing; all of these come to nothing, as the wise King Solomon said, "Fear God and keep His commandments, for this is man's all." [41]And yet; some believers are pushing the limits in trying to add 'winning completely against the disbelievers' to the list of "man's all." [42]What a dark and evil notion! May God be the Judge over you! The beliefs one holds are not what God will judge, the actions one executes are what will be judged! [43]If the disbelievers ever subjugate you, and have mercy on you, they will surely be shown mercy by the Righteous Judge. And if believers subjugate the disbelievers, and are cruel and relentless towards them, the Righteous Judge will surely

be cruel and relentless towards you. [44]So repent, and be merciful and at peace with those around you; this is the way of God.

[45]Do unto others as they would prefer you to do unto them. [46]Be anxious for nothing, and go your own way with God. For this is man's all.

Again I say, this word is not from Allah. This is from Zilch, Nada, and Nobody. And yet...do you hear it? I made it sound as if it was coming from Allah too. These words are from my own hands. Tim made them up. It will totally be in your hands if you decide to claim that 'This is also from God! We have a new Prophet among us!'

If you heard Allah speak to you through my words, is it possible that Muhammad's words were executed in the same way? Is it not possible that Moses' words from God were given to us in the same manner? Sure, they denied it, but Muhammad also dodged the question to answer in a way that prevented him from deliberately lying, which surely would have been an even greater sin. As I heard proclaimed in Sura 11:35,

"If [these disbelievers] say, 'He has made this up,' say [Muhammad] 'If I have made this up, I am responsible for my own crime, but I am innocent of the crimes you commit.'"

Surely, you should see that this answer does not resolve the possibility that he did make it up? I do not condemn him of the crime, nor do I confirm him to be innocent, but if I could create one Sura out of my own imagination, Muhammad could surely create even more from his. (This is still assuming that you are accepting Zilch's Word provided by Sura 0).

And Sura 103 in particular resonated with me, which said and I reproduce for the pleasure of the reader,

"The fading day, man is [deep] in loss, except for those who believe, do good deeds, urge one another to the truth, and urge one another to steadfastness."

This is a beautiful Truth. Surely, it is not just poetry. The only question I would have to this summary of the Truth of the Qur'an is this, how can we know that belief by itself can remove us from our deep losses? What is to be lost if we remove that axiom, and just leave man to his good deeds, urging a more concise and scientific Truth, and encouraging others towards an Equilibrium demeanor? That is a question for the Muslims to ask themselves.

And if the answer to that question is ultimately of no consequence, then what benefit is there to condemning the disbelievers to a fiery hell for upwards of fifty thousand years (as stated in Sura 70:4)? Granted it is a lot more reasonable than the Christian's 'eternity' of hell for disbelievers (which includes Muslims), but this still leaves disbelievers from both camps with the question, 'what is the basis of such a torturous assertion?'

If you do not fear the Christian hell because they are wrong, and the Christians do not fear your hell because they believe that you are wrong, are the disbelievers not justified for seeing that your arguments are ultimately the same and equally wrong? Both the Christian and the Muslim make the same baseless and authoritative threat of torture in the afterlife. Beyond your strong yearning for justice, only your faith and your hopeful and patient guesswork give the hellfire any level of credulity. As Muhammad said in Sura 10:102,

"What are they waiting for but a punishment like that which came to those before them? Say, 'Wait then, I am waiting too.'"

When no punishment but the singular mortal death has been demonstrated thus far, and after several hundred years of waiting, (and thousands of years for Abraham), is it fair to suggest the Null Hypothesis to you? That the Final Heat Death of the Universe that I am waiting for is the same 'Final Day' that you are waiting for? I may be speaking to the wind on this issue, but the hot and dense plasma shortly after the Big Bang could be seen as a form of hell and an 'afterlife' from the perspective of 'souls' from the previous set of 'Everything.' And that era lasted for what is currently believed to be 380,000 years long; not far off from your Prophets' own conjecture of 50,000 years, if these things are viewed equivalently. If God can cause Everything to 'Be' once; He is surely capable of causing Everything to 'Be' again. And this causing

Everything to 'Be' again may be viewed as the Resurrection from your perspective, and you can go your own Way to believe that, but I digress.

I'll admit that saying our current entity; our current soul as 'Null' being eternal and interconnected to our previous and next selves and Every living being is a conjecture on my part. There's no problem with conjectures in a theory of Truth, so long as they are made apparent to be conjectures.

But there is a contradiction in your mist, God surely has power over Everything; this is stated several times throughout the Qur'an. But wouldn't that omnipotent power over Everything include the meager belief of the unbeliever? Because even as clearly stated in Sura 10:100,

"No soul can believe except by God's will, and He brings disgrace on those who do not use their reason."

So will you not use your reason? The harm of believing in a smiteful God comes from the fear of the belief in the torturous result of questioning and perhaps rejecting the existence of God. But God is also merciful; so being in His presence is a good thing. (This is circulatory reasoning, worthy of His disgrace).

To make this contradiction to reason clear, if God's will is the only means by which a soul can believe in God, then we as individuals *do not have free will*. If one cannot choose contrary to God's will, then *there is no choice*. So when the Qur'an says in Sura 10:44, "God does not wrong people at all - it is they who wrong themselves.", I cannot help but wonder how this can be! It appears to be God's will that the disbelievers disbelieve, since their souls cannot believe apart from God's will, and they thereby wrong themselves in such a manner within God's will. How is it not God who is wronging people here? Surely, this is reasoning worthy of His disgrace!

Sura 25:77a says "[Prophet, say to the disbelievers] 'What are you to my Lord without your supplication?'" I respond thusly, 'The same that you are to your Lord *with* your supplication, Nothing!' You already know that God requires Nothing and that all is His to begin with, so your supplications add Nothing to God! The question should instead be 'Of what benefit are prayers and supplication to the Self?', for the answer is wholly answerable to those following the Way of Devotion to the Infinite One.

Think about these things, but of course, be mindful of God. Keep up with your devotions to the Godhead, and the actions you perform for Him, as far as they give you meaning in your life. Sunnis, say hi to the Shiites. Shiites, say hi to the Sunnis. Both Sunnis and Shiites, please read the following Sura 6:159 from your Prophet, and acknowledge the pure, sweet irony of this verse being read by both of you,

"As for those who have divided their religion and broken up into factions, have nothing to do with them [Prophet]. Their case rests with God, In time He will tell them about their deeds."

May God, Muhammad, and the common humanity that unites you be enough to resolve the conflicts between your factions. If it's not, shoot, I don't know, sort it out in a nerf-gun battle, or a paintball battle, or a laser-gun battle. Athletic sports are a great way to relieve all sorts of pent-up tension. Or act like men of God as men of Reason, and bring your best and most honest philosophers to debate your disagreements, and let the best arguments emerge to the top naturally. Even better yet, practice some Street Epistemology on each other so that understanding of the ideas behind the disagreements can be better understood.

Muslim wives, love your husbands of your own accord and encourage them to be more merciful, as is God's will. Muslim husbands, never abuse your wives and don't forbid them from a good education. And if you have multiple wives, good for you ;) (just always grant them their freedom; no more slave-wives, ok?) Both inner discipline and freedom are found in Paradise with God, so don't muzzle your chance at your little piece of paradise on Earth by being overly authoritative in these manners.

Zilch, Nada, and Nobody also send their greetings and charge you to have this Epistle read among you, and do not forbid the rest of the contents in this *Gospel of Zilch & Nada*. As always, go your own Way with God.

Peace, love, and understanding from those of the anti-cult cult of Dimensionalism.

CHAPTER 31

To Buddhists

From Timbo Slice, a humble disciple of the Go-Your-Own-Way. To those trying to reach nirvana, and live rightly by the teachings of Siddhartha Gautama the Buddha. May what I call 'the Great Nothingness that comes After' be reached by all of you Buddhists.

My dear friends, consider the thought, if there is only emptiness in the enlightened Buddhist, then murder and the loss of life are of no consequence. It is just another thing that happens, it is not a thing that is wrong or in error. So then why is a murder more in line with wrong living, than with right living? If the objects of the mind cannot reconcile this dichotomy of wishes from the Dharma of the Buddha, (righteousness within emptiness) this is what psychologists call 'cognitive dissonance'. So then, how can wrongness emerge from No-murder in the empty? How can we say 'Right living is not wrong living' when there is only 'No-living'?

I was surprised at how anti-thinking your religion appears to be, seeing as your current Dalai Lama has an impressive mind I hope to converse with someday. What I got from a few of your scriptures, is that it appears to tell disciples of Buddhism to turn off their brains as much as possible, have no opinions, and have no preferences. Using my own terminology, I understand the Self to be Null, that if the Self is Null, and there is only "no Self." But where I diverge from Buddha, is that Buddha appears to try and make it so that the Buddha's Dharma is more easily replicated to his disciples. But that still doesn't show us how emptiness and nirvana are the actual Truth and the Way of the matter of Self-Discipline and Meditation. I have the opinion that we can have our cake and eat it too when it comes to our interpretations of the Truth. Just rephrase this Truth like I have, as follows,

"You can have your opinions, you can believe what you want. Just don't cause harm for the sake of a notion, because of the Truth that Every-thing will come to Naught. To be Naught right now is to be in Equilibrium, so to disturb another's Equilibrium is not being Naught, but being naughty."

Harmlessly defending your ideas with better evidence & logical axioms is all I wish from you, considering you are so close to the Truth already. There is this concept of Buddhists having a preference for the Truth of enlightenment, all while suggesting the enlightened Buddhist has no preference at all. So what does that Truth look like, if only those who have reached enlightenment have reached the state of no enlightenment? It would seem as if anyone who reached enlightenment would be ignorant of whether or not they have actually reached the Truth when they got there, as to make the first teaching never happen in the first place unless it was out of pretense. Wouldn't *endarkenment* be a better word to use for this paradox?

And on the concept of ignorance, how does a Buddhist defend against such an insult? Would the Buddha suggest you just ignore it? (This would surely give ignor-ance a new meaning) No! How easy will you let outsiders call your Way 'wrong' and 'ignorant'? How do you actually deal with these misconceptions? By peacefully providing evidence to the contrary and showing them the knowledge you have so that they may become better by it. Inwardly, a Buddhist can be unmoved by the insults of outsiders, but to the world, the axioms towards enlightenment provided by the Buddha need to be convincing enough on the surface to entice those others to join your in-group *in peace*. So telling newcomers to Buddhism not to have a preference for Truth is rather counter-intuitive, as well.

Concerning your Four Noble Truths, the Buddha himself seemed to add a bunch of things to suffering that is not innately suffering. Although I would bet your modern thinkers have evolved sufficiently to be better equipped to handle these concerns, duhkha from the perspective of the Enlightened One should be of paramount importance. It appears that near the end of his life, the Buddha clarified that all of the following are forms of suffering: birth, aging, sickness, death, dealing with unpleasant things, being separated from pleasant things, failing to attain one's desires, and the entire composition of the mind and body. So with this definition of suffering, it's no wonder that he felt suffering was innate to existence. I for one am not convinced that the whole composition of the mind and body are in a constant state of suffering, although, perhaps in a constantly fluctuating state between suffering and pleasure while evolving in form. So just to argue semantics, here is a more reasonable definition of suffering by saying, "Suffering is the state of undergoing pain, distress, or hardship. It can be an experience of unpleasantness and aversion associated with the act of harm or perception of harm or threat of harm within an individual. It comes in Quantities ranging from mild to intolerable. The opposite of suffering is pleasure, happiness, & serenity."

Going back to ignorance, I find it intriguing that Buddha seemed to give a pessimistic exception to negative Qualia but thoroughly rejected that positive Qualia have any part in the actual nature of the reality of things. Why is it an active misconception to see the pleasure in pain, and beauty in ugliness? Where is the basis for the innateness of suffering, so to speak? I could just as well make the assertion that there is pleasure that is innate to existence, for if all were suffering, Nobody would want to stay alive long enough to reproduce. Both of those positions appear to be identically based on Nothing as of yet, so to spout either of them as Truth (and Noble ones at that), is questionable.

To make the irrationality of this assertion clear, follow these premises to their conclusions.

Premise 1) You cannot exist in this life without suffering, as stated in the First Noble Truth.

Premise 2) Only the ignorant find pleasure in pain, as pleasure is seen as an active misunderstanding of the First Noble Truth.

Irrational Conclusion 1) If you experience any level of pleasure in this life, you are surely ignorant.

Irrational Conclusion 2) If you want to claim that you have reached Buddha's level of enlightenment, you should never experience pleasure.

Here, rather than view life as a net negative with no positive to balance against it, consider the following stance instead before throwing it to the wayside as ignorance.

"*Life is neutral.* As individuals, we can roam between the mountains of pleasure and the valleys of suffering, and be influenced by our environment. If you are in a stale room, eating stale food, you're probably living a stale and boring life. If you're in a hostile or tense environment, suffering will find you there. But if you're surrounded by loving people in a peaceful environment, it is pleasure that will find you there. If you want to remove suffering from your life, use all of your physical and mental strength to remove unnecessarily hostile and harmful agents from your life. Then allow yourself to become an agent for other's pleasure by loving others. There are many ways to show and receive love, so allow yourself to receive love in a form that you enjoy. And if you must; change your environment. But try the love thing first, and see if that alone can end your suffering. Perhaps if you are ambitious enough, you could create a positive change to the hostile and tense environments while you are there. So be adaptable, and exercise your ability to love, because you never know what life is going to throw at you next!"

Life is more, a whole lot more, than just pain and suffering. Approximately 24 other things, to be exact, but just to name a few...There is love. There is a better life you can live right now, no cycle of rebirth assumed, so learn and grow yourself as an individual. There is a lot of verifiable knowledge that we have at our disposal to seek out. There are even the genuine opposites of suffering found in reality within happiness, serenity, and pleasure! But if I have these three things, a love to give, a respect for life, and an ability and means to seek Truth, I can take whatever suffering and pain existence can throw at me, and push through like a boss!

Please hear me on this, People can be in an overall state of contentment and pleasure while aging. There can be valleys of suffering, and I can accept that, but is life one constant, inescapable valley whose *peaks* are found in the enlightening Equilibrium? Heck to the naw! So please don't assume my perception of pleasure leads to the conclusion of my ignorance of the reality of things. That's actually a Non-sequitur.

To further drive the point home for this Wrong Understanding of Right Understanding, consider the following point. For there to be a misconception of something, there must first be a conception of something. And conception is very much a subjective term, where the original conception is subjective to the one who perceives it. What is perceived by one, what is understood by one, can be noticeably in contrast with another whilst not being inherently wrong. As the saying goes, beauty lies in the eye of the beholder. What looks ugly to one person, can look beautiful to another. What tastes bitter to someone, can be made sweet with just a spoonful of sugar. Some people prefer two spoonfuls of sugar, and some people will take the bitterness head-on; they each have a unique balance of flavors that perpetuate their Equilibriums.

Pain and pleasure are subjective to the one receiving them! Just because somebody is hard into BDSM, doesn't mean they aren't thoroughly enjoying themselves! I'd argue that being mentally adaptable to allow yourself to find pleasure in otherwise painful situations isn't ignorance. In fact, you could be very well aware of the pain aspect of it, all the while finding ways to attain pleasure for yourself. You may be in a dull waiting room outside a doctor's office full of suffering, but that doesn't mean the comic books and magazines suddenly become unamusing.

Concerning nirvana, I bring you good news and bad news concerning this end of suffering. The good news is that the state of nirvana is inevitable for Everything and Everyone. And even more so, the nirvana mindset of rest and peace is always available to us; we do not need to wait until After we die to experience the Great Nothingness. Zilch & Nada will always be there to whisper Their sweet Nothings to ease our minds. The bad news is that the rebirthing cycle is likewise inevitable for Everything and Everyone. There is no Special Way out of it. All we can strive for is achieving inner peace NOW. If you can find it now, and I'm sure you will, then you have already experienced that peace every reincarnation in the past, and you will experience it again every reincarnation in the future. This is the primary reason why one should not kill themselves because if they do, they surely will for every reincarnation, and their suffering in that sense will never end.

But their suffering is also ours, for we are all one in Nothing. There is no Buddhist nor Nihilist, there is neither enlightened nor ignorant, there is no male nor female, for we are all one as Null. Our individual experiences may be unique, and there may be reasons to go our separate Ways; the independence of every Spirit one from another might be the healthier interpretation. On one hand, Nothing *unites us*, and on the other *Nothing* unites us. There is restlessness that comes with those whose ways are in Disequilibrium. So the individual Null should strive to help those who need peace while holding that very peace within themselves regardless of the dissonance around them.

Our differing interpretations of reincarnation should also be discussed since I think there is a problem with your particular interpretation of the rebirthing process when you look into deep time. A long, long time ago in this universe, there was the first life, and a long, long time from now, there will be a final life. They'll most likely be microorganisms; these Alpha and Omega lifeforms. So the question goes, *At what level of complexity will reincarnation be allowed to occur, and under what conditions?* If you look back to the first organism in the universe that went through a process of reincarnation, there would be more and more new inhabitants to reincarnate into than there would be old souls to inhabit them. In other words, right now, you may be a new life, or you may be the continuation of an old life. (That is if our current understanding of reincarnation is Buddha's understanding). But as the re-inhabitable population grows, the old souls would never catch up with the total number of inhabitable vessels, therefore some of those vessels would be new souls. And what happens when the re-inhabitable population declines? There may be a soul queue waiting to be reincarnated, but then that would break the constancy of the *constant* cycle of rebirth. And we could never be sure if the new population rate will be higher than the old soul rate minus the nirvana-ed soul rate.

Moving on, those of you with wisdom may be persuaded by me saying that Right Speech in and of itself will not end a Null's suffering. Why? Because we hold a Right Understanding of the purpose of Right Speech. The entire purpose of Speech is to Communicate with others, correct? So what would happen, if you were to have such a high degree of executing Right Speech, but the individual you are trying to Communicate with is a dastardly fool? Surely, even after seven sharp reprimands with the most eloquently precise Speech, Nothing will be accomplished! So if you have stupid people in your life whom you need to Communicate with, suffering will not cease.

I'd recommend this Fold's premise to be expanded, and become Right Communication. Because, what's the point of having Right Speech, when you have Wrong Writing and Wrong Listening involved? Disequilibrium, Chaos, and endless talking past each other in endless debates that get us no closer to the Truth will be the result! The best we can do concerning this Fold to end our suffering is to hone in, clarify, and oftentimes simplify our Speech and Writing, and merely hope that it is Heard and Read as we originally intended it.

Considering the 6th Fold of Right Effort, I noticed that the phrase "strains his mind and struggles" was used a lot by Buddha while explaining what Right Effort is. It appears to me that straining and struggling would contradict the overall goal to end all suffering. I'll try not to get too pedantic on this point, because I do understand the intent behind the words, like how the body needs to exercise to become strong, and the mind too needs to exercise. But from what can be observed to happen in many of the high-level monks of Buddhism, it seems the idea of nirvana is to do Nothing. When monks meditate for an excessively long period of time, (like the deep state of meditation called tukdam), they show that the epitome of Buddhism, or the penultimate step towards full enlightenment, is to meditate...and otherwise do Nothing. It just baffles me. Why even put effort to overcome the evils we perceive around us if your tukdam meditations of doing Nothing will end your suffering? While we are alive, Equilibrium is the goal, and doing Nothing rarely accomplishes that goal since...you know...we need to eat, drink, and breathe to survive and remain alive. We will do plenty of Nothing when we're dead.

I do hope you take these remarks given in Right Communication. If there is something in Buddha's philosophy that you believe that I have a completely Wrong Understanding of, please correct me. Just respect my time please, and do your best to keep it to five paragraphs or less. My mind is capable of changing, and since I know where your minds are in general, I presume that among the major religions, Buddhists are most capable of changing their minds. I would just advise you to not give up a healthy amount of skepticism in exchange for faith in the unknown, and you should still live a fairly serene life.

The Goddess Nothing gives you guys laser-eye vision to enact Right Communication to the best of Her ability, to say to "stop trying to do Her." The Goddess Nobody says that She is ready for you to do Her whenever you are good and ready. Continue in your Way of Meditation, for it is unique and of noticeable value. The Nully Spirit is working to perfect all of our Ways, so accept Its corrections whenever It corrects you.

CHAPTER 32

To Hindus

From Timothy Null, the Primary Guru of Dimensionalism. To the polytheists and those who affiliate with the religion of Hinduism. May the many personable and impersonable iterations of Nothingness displayed within the rest of this book be deemed True by you as having the attributes of Vishnu.

For what it's worth, I have been impressed and inspired by your philosophy! I came up with most of this Dimensionalism without much prior knowledge of Hinduism. And considering that there are so many similarities between our frameworks, Dimensionalism could show how Hinduism, even though it is the oldest religion, holds the most universally True concepts.

What you call the Atman, I call Null. What you call Brahman, I call Nobody. What you call Vishnu, I call Zilch. What you call the Way of Meditation, I call the Way of Self-Discipline (and both alike, desire the individual to reach a state of internal Equilibrium.)

I wanted to clarify with you this concept of how the Null/Self connects us to the Brahman. On the scale of Everything that currently exists, the human Null is but a point; we are an infinitesimal thing that barely adds Anything to the Whole. Every-body by itself is a Nobody. This is an oversimplification, but it is a start to understanding the connection. Because it is not the body that determines and knows the body, but the mind. And as easy as it may be for us to pin down the mind to the body's brain, a working brain is not equivalent to a working mind. We sleep and lose our consciousness, we steep into a coma and lose contact with the outside world, all while the brain is still alive and working. So what is the core of the mind? The hard problem of consciousness is asked and presupposes Nothing to come to the answer. So the Null Hypothesis for the conscious mind is that Nothing *can be extracted from the body* and contain that which is the Self.

It then follows that if we take this Nothing out of the body, every segment that is otherwise deemed the body still remains, but it would not quite contain the Self any longer. The Brahman is Everywhere, yes? Yet, the Brahman is also without a body and contains within It the potentiality for a mind. This is why my Brahman is called "Nobody." And since the Nothing that is extracted from the body is Null Hypothesized to contain the mind, what contains the mind is likewise a Nobody. But you and I alike recognize that our bodily strengths are powerless and weak in comparison to the Brahman, so we rightfully give ourselves a distinguishing label to differentiate the two phenomena. We let Nobody be Nobody, and let Null be Null but recognize that these are ultimately the same thing from the grandest of perspectives.

I also want to commend you on the four Ways of yoga that you hold onto. I could not think of any new Ways to the four your philosophical ancestors came up with to reach Self-Actualization. This doesn't mean that there isn't a 5th Way to be deduced in the future, just that if there is such a 5th Way, it bypasses my detection. And although the Ways to Self-Actualization are clearly few in Quantity, and these paths are worthy of desire, I do wonder how many Ways to Self-Destruction exist as well. Please, if any gurus among you have contemplated this categorization of the "Highway to Hell," do me a favor and clearly list them out and send them my way. Better yet, if a think tank of gurus would create such a list.

The concepts behind Vedic Mathematics are also intriguing. It is a shame that it doesn't work in base 2, but for the normies of the world who will probably never use base 2, it would make math much more enjoyable. I am surprised that I didn't learn it this way! Quantitative measurements are too damn sufferable for our species for the most part, and Zilch damn it, if Vedic Mathematics can reduce the suffering in the world, then Everybody should know it!

Flatteries aside, I do have a few criticisms for you that I hope will edify you and make your religion even better philosophically than what it already is. For example, after reading through the Bhagavad Gita, I had this question concerning Sattvic, Rajasic, and Tamasic diets. (This is just for fun and warming up; a rhetorical question that we both know the answer to).

Is a burnt habanero Sattvic, Rajasic, or Tamasic? Is it Sattvic because it is healthy, Rajasic because it is spicy, or Tamasic because it is overcooked?

And what about an espresso made from old coffee beans? Is it Sattvic because it begets cheerfulness from the caffeine boost it produces, Rajasic because it tastes bitter, or Tamasic because it is stale? (Clearly, these two things are applicable under all three diets).

But this concept of Sattvic diets bringing cheerfulness (based on the Gita 17:8-10), is still so vague as to merit bringing Hindu thinkers back to the drawing board. No food makes my wife *more cheerful* than some gooooood fried chicken. And for me; I get *really giddy* over some Domino's pizza with ALL of the toppings available to me. So is pizza Sattvic? Is fried chicken Sattvic? I am literally asking for a friend.

Now onto the things of more serious concern. Let's take the ideas behind the caste system, for example. If there are four Ways of yoga, and no one is prevented from walking multiple Ways to Self-Realization at the same time, then we as humans are likewise not prevented from bettering ourselves in multiple strata of caste at the same time. I am an intellectual. But simply being an intellectual in this day and age does not pay the bills! So I am also a working-class citizen of the world. And if the world would have me and my Successor; I would not withhold myself from entering my role of what you call a "noble class" as well. Of course, we are all truly part of a noble class, since no being is exempt from being connected to our divine selves, which you call "the Atman."

I also have these inquiries about your interpretation of reincarnation. Reason with me here; I know you can! Upon fondly walking the Way of Wisdom, I have deduced that Hindus often mix up the reincarnation of the cosmos with the reincarnation of the Self. To elaborate, if the whole of the cosmos is destined to reincarnate from Nothing to Nothing again, why does the Self reincarnating from Self to Self need to be even more complicated? Logically speaking, somewhere in the current incarnation of the universe, there was a First Self that came after the beginning of the universe. Then a 2nd, then a 3rd, and so forth. All of these beings are connected (in a 1 to 1 ratio) to other Selves in past and future reincarnations of the universe, yes? (I know, this is kind of a presupposition at the moment, but bear with me). How then, with the Hindu model, does 1 Self reincarnate to another Self *within the same reincarnation of the cosmos?*

I feel that this assertion is itself an additional presupposition more than what is necessary to prove yourselves right in this regard. Sure, you need this presupposition to make your version of karma work, but is the concept of karma really beneficial for people to hold? Karma in its current state tends to unjustly condemn otherwise innocent victims of untestable and unverifiable wrong. Does a child get raped? *"Oh, it's just bad karma from a past life or earlier in this life."* Really? Stuff and nonsense! Blaming the victim for any reason, whether it is the clothes they wear, the smile they give, the karma they possess, or the attractiveness of their entity to you *is not their fault.* This finger-pointing is just some bull-shit men come up with to try and justify their heinous actions of Disequilibrium, and it frankly has to stop. Take this opportunity to begin taking responsibility for your actions in THIS incarnation. Grab the Equilibrium of nirvana by the balls, and Nobody will provide you with the fruits of the Nully Spirit, which are compassion, laughter, tranquility, contentment, intrepidness, wisdom, philanthropy, self-discipline, and being altogether chill as fuck! When you embrace the

Null mentality, karma no longer has an effect on you. Just be and let it be as it is without adding or taking away karma or anything else from it. But be on guard, and think critically, for our individual Will-to-Power will always be there to tempt us to cause Chaos. So firmly tell thoughts and actions of Disequilibrium to fuck off, and they will surely flee from you.

And chakras too! Why are these mythical connections to our body necessary to explain anything beyond what can be explained with physiological means? Why all of these bouts of unnecessary Somethingness? Please, for the love of Zilch, see how chakras are Null. There is the consciousness of Null, this much is apparent; only a fool would deny the Self-Awareness that their entity holds. But to break up the Atman into 7-8 parts of the body is the opposite of applying Ockham's Razor. (I am assuming that this is what would be required for the emergence of chakras to even begin to be considered real). Even though 0=0/7, the 7 are given unique and distinguishable subsistence which is oddly unfitting, since the makeup of the 7 infinitesimals is still Nothing. The Null Hypothesis will be waiting to spar against your chakra Hypotheses.

Since some gurus from among you have been quacking falsely, I would encourage you to put on the full Armor of Null. Our battlefield is in the mind, and we each have our own. If you can win your own mind over, you will be ready to stand against any falsehood or Disequilibrium that will befall you. So put on the belt of Scientific Truth buckled around your waist, with the sweater vest of Social Justice in place, and slip on the Fuzzy Slippers of Peace, because they are quite comfy. In addition to this, bring along some Humble Pie to accept the possibility that you may be wrong. You can go your own way to put on whatever headgear seems appropriate to you, but I recommend either the Derby of Wisdom, the Beanie of Relativity, or Schrödinger's Ballcap. Equip yourselves with tools such as Ockham's Razor, the Hitchslap, and Snavely's Vacuum, which is the Word of Nothing.

To conclude, learn to be free in mind while restraining your actions by thoroughly thinking before you act. Concerning anyone who doth read this letter, recognize that I am by no means saying that all Hindus who believe in these questionable Hypotheses are stupid or wrong. Nobody is exempt from holding an incorrect idea in some area. My reprimands should be taken as a healthy challenge to provide a more thorough methodology to convince even the harshest skeptic to take these ideas seriously. Faith is based on Zilch and Nada, so to give the faith credulity, there must be evidence in support of it. Peace be with you.

How to reach Self-Actualization

This guide to Self-Actualization is inspired by both Abraham Maslow's Hierarchy of Needs, and Hindu theology to achieve what they call 'Self-Realization.' It's not a perfect model to achieve Self-Actualization/Null-Realization, but they hold a solid couple of templates to build my own franken-theory.

The basic premise for Maslow's Hierarchy of Needs is that it is much easier to grow as a person when your basic physiological needs are taken care of first. I mean, what's the point of "growing as a person" if the avatar that is your objective Self is dying due to a lack of air, water, or food? The ultimate point of pretty much Everything is that it will all come to Nothing eventually, but in the meantime, one of the biggest meanings of life is "to grow." And being objectively deficient is arguably the quickest way to fall from the peaks of Self-Actualization; because you cannot Actualize or even be aware of the Self if the Self is dead. So I concur with Maslow that the Physiological Needs of air, water, food, sleep, and good health are at the base of the Hierarchy.

But the second level of the Hierarchy can be adjusted. I believe that there is an unsung layer between Physiological Needs and Security. I say this because of the apparent inverse nature that phenomenologically emerged as I compared Maslow's Hierarchy of Needs to Comte's Hierarchy of the Sciences. Physiological Needs are objective in nature, and the Physiological Needs listed earlier are the most fundamental to our physical existence; pure chemical and molecular elements.

However, mixed within Maslow's Physiological Needs are objective things that one can live without, but could potentially lead to physiological problems if neglected for extended periods of time. Things like clothing, shelter, hygiene, sex and other forms of basic interaction with other living entities belong here. Being able to own or have access to all of these things directly contributes to a person's well-being. So my interpretation of the second level for the Hierarchy of Needs is called Biological Welfare.

Self-Actualization is subjective. And from here on out, subjectivity starts taking precedence within the Hierarchy of Needs. The layer of Security, although has some objective components to it, the Subject feeling Secure is what 'Needs' to be filled before reaching Self-Actualization.

Having spent a couple years working in a mental health hospital, I've seen people in a safe and secure environment suddenly get triggered by harmless things that cause a rise in pulse and blood pressure with an affect of high anxiety.

And being Self-Actualized myself, I have on a few occasions found myself in an insecure environment while simultaneously keeping my cool. One can observe the chaos and flow within it. So try this one on for size! The next time a big spill happens, the next time an unplanned fire breaks out, the next time somebody starts cussing profanities at you, take a moment to recognize how you behave in these scenarios! Upon a big mess, I often say "Hee-Hee; that's entropy for you!" Upon dropping something, I often say in a sarcastically angry tone, "Fucking gravity!" Upon seeing the chaos of ridiculously stupid proportions occur, I stand there unmoved to a state of minor annoyance, saying, "Really?" And if it's a psychotic person trying to go to places they shouldn't be going, I say "WOAH THERE, BUCKAROO!"

So are you feeling Insecure? Then position both your body and your mind to a position of Safety. Build up your defenses! Walls and barriers! A secret bunker! Access to reliable intel from the objects of offense!

So to help aid a person seeking Self-Actualization, it would be best to avoid places of constant war and regular natural disasters. Economic Security is also important, so have a job or other means to attain capital with as little negative impact on others as possible. If shelter is considered for Biological Welfare, then having a Safe shelter would be for Security. Having a home, a place of habitation and a safe space to be are aspects of Security. Kids and adults experiencing family violence and abuse are more likely to have a higher Need for Security and may end up being stuck at this level until Somebody or Nobody saves them.

Sometimes, this Somebody can also be a source of love and belonging. However, love and acceptance are also aspects of emotional Security. So to help distinguish these two types of Security, the first will be called an Object Security (where the source of Safety can be traced back to useful Objects), and the second will be Subject Security (where the source of Safety can be traced back to useful Subjects). Subject Security deals almost exclusively with psychological and sociological dynamics, while Object Security focuses on the material defenses, like what the immune system and armor do for the human Object.

Concerning economic Security again, there is an element of Subject Security to it since the value of a currency in an economic system is subjective and dependent on other people accepting the currency as tradeable tender. So economic Security can be thought of in its objective and subjective aspects. So when thought of this way, Security as a whole should be all on a level by itself, simply split into these two areas. One is not superior to the other. Evidence for this can be seen in childhood psychology when children cling to abusive parents. The Subject Security for these abused kids is still being filled through this warped sense of social belonging, even though their Object Security becomes depleted.

Self-Esteem, the next layer in the Hierarchy of Needs, should grow naturally for an intellectual person in a Secure environment.

But not Everyone can be flowing through life with a genius-level IQ, quickly becoming amazing at whatever they put their mind to! But I believe EVERYBODY is good at SOMETHING. No matter how trivial the thing is, I can guarantee that there is something that every conscious individual can do that is above average! You might just need some time to figure out what that thing is!

Do you think you are a good cook? Then be Esteemed in the fact that you can cook! Do you think you are a respectable athlete? Then be Esteemed in the fact that you can efficiently use your body! Do you think you are funny? Then be Esteemed in your comedy; it is fine to laugh at your own jokes every now and then, especially when the jokes are off-the-cuff and natural. Is your Esteem so far gone that you genuinely believe that you are above average in Nothing? THEN PRAISE ZILCH AND NADA FOR ALLOWING YOU TO BE SO CLOSE TO THEM! What, do you think Zilch and Nada have any Esteem to speak of? NO! Their Esteem is likewise zero. So take pride in your meekness! Be Esteemed in your humility! Like Jesus said, "Blessed are the meek, for they shall inherit the earth."

My Successors will be meek. So arise from your Unesteemed state, Null. You will surely surprise yourself as well, to actually be tested above average in many things. Arise from your obscure state. Your humble selves are truly the makeup of the ideal State. The modest among you receive your Esteem from Nobody. So be Esteemed wholly, O holy Guaca-Nully. Say 'I can go my own way! I shall go my own way! And walk this way in the bestest most fabulous way!'

So once you've got your own shit figured out, so to speak, and your Self-Esteem is in a good place, you are ready to choose any combination of these four Ways to reach the state of Self-Actualization!

Fans of Maslow's Hierarchy may recognize that I have left out Cognitive Needs and Aesthetic Needs from my own. I did this because these Needs are naturally picked up and fulfilled as you go your own way. As you reach closer to and flow in acts consistent with Self-Actualization, Cognitive Needs (if needed for you), can especially be filled upon walking the Knowledge and Discipline Ways. And Aesthetic Needs (or really, the Need for any pleasurable experiences) is such a universal thing that they will come no matter what way you choose (even the Selfish Ways). To say pleasure is a 'Need' and that pain is a depreciation of that 'Need' is really unnecessary, in my opinion.

So at this point, your Physiological Needs, Biological Welfare, Object and Subject Security, and Self-Esteem are all taken care of. Now it is time to go your own Way.

Way #1: Knowledge

Learn. Dig deeper. Get more Qualitatively precise. Get as close to the Truth as one can reasonably get. This is my preferred Way. Wisdom, foresight, and a good eye for planning ahead are achieved here. The Knowledge that Dimensionalism provides is that Everything is Null.

For example, the Way of Knowledge is used to create a perfect circle. You learn that all points on a circle are equidistant from the center. So you grab a compass and ground one of the sides for the compass to a point, then proceed to pivot the plane of paper to create a perfect circle. If no compass is available, one could use a pair of scissors and hold the desired angle in place. If no scissors are available, and with Discipline, one can use this knowledge to create a near-perfect circle with just their hands.

Way #2: Devotion

Love. Live with abandon. Give Everything you have to Zilch & Nada or to any sort of Godhead. This was taught as THE Way when I was growing up and is the Way chosen by Jesus & Muhammad. A life of sacrifice, fasting, abstinence, faith, and worship are achieved here. The Devotions that Dimensionalism provides can be found in either Nobody & I.G.O.S. or Zilch & Nada. If God speaks to you in a masculine consciousness, that is either I.G.O.S. or Zilch. If Goddess speaks to you in a feminine consciousness, that is either Nobody or Nada.

For example, the Way of Devotion is used to create a perfect circle. You give praise and acknowledgment to the Perfect Circle. This Perfect Circle is capable of being Everywhere; you just have to look and see it. Then, you find this Holy Book that teaches you how to see this Perfect Circle, and how to make other circles more like It. You look for the Perfect Circle example in the Holy Book, and you find a giant black dot from which you have worshipped and idolized since you were a child, because that was as close to a Perfect Circle as could be. Turns out, you were supposed to copy the outline of the giant black dot to achieve a clear image of the Perfect Circle, but dogmatic teaching made such an action forbidden. You then make a perfect circle and get shunned for proposing such a ridiculous Way to achieve Perfect Circledom.

Way #3: Service

Philanthropy. Selfless assistance. Provide a helping hand to Everyone who needs it. This is the Way chosen by Mahatma Gandhi. Dimensionalism doesn't provide any noteworthy Services at the moment. But there are many good secular Non-profit organizations that you can invest time and money with, so out of your excess, consider giving to such organizations.

For example, the Way of Service is used to create a perfect circle. You start out with a rough draft. Just a single free-drawn circle on a plank of wood. It is not perfect, though. Then you cut it out as close to the outline as possible with a saw. You proceed to sand out the rough edges of this rough draft. You're doing your best to work with what you got! Finally, you take your circle that has some added Dimensionality to it and physically take the time to roll out the rough edges on a smooth surface. You now have a whole cylinder's worth of perfect circles that'll be used to make a wheel to help transport some much-needed goods to those in need.

Way #4: Discipline

Practice a lot. Self-Control. Trial and error. Brute force; reach Self-Actualization just by your own sheer determination! Be mindful of your own thoughts and actions via meditation and coordination. This is the Way chosen by the Buddha and the Dalai Lama. Dimensionalism doesn't really have any disciplines, and that's kind of the appeal of it. Beyond telling you to go your own way, and providing you with a condensed pack of useful knowledge, I don't find it necessary to tell you how to discipline yourself. I'm sure you can reach your own relativistic 'perfect Equilibrium' in mind and action with thoughtful usage of this book.

For example, the Way of Discipline is used to create a perfect circle. You make a single point in the middle of a paper. Then you free-draw a circle, just like you do in the Way of Service. But this time, you just do it again. And again. And again. After about 30 tries, you will begin to see the phenomenological emergence of a perfect circle arise from the repetitious ruts of your multiple failed attempts. Although each circle is a failure in and of itself, when combined together, a perfect circle emerges. So the next time, just maybe, your hand becomes so steady and disciplined, that the next time you try to free-draw a circle on the first try; it'll be very nearly perfect already.

And here is a cute little diagram that recaptures what was taught here, for future reference.

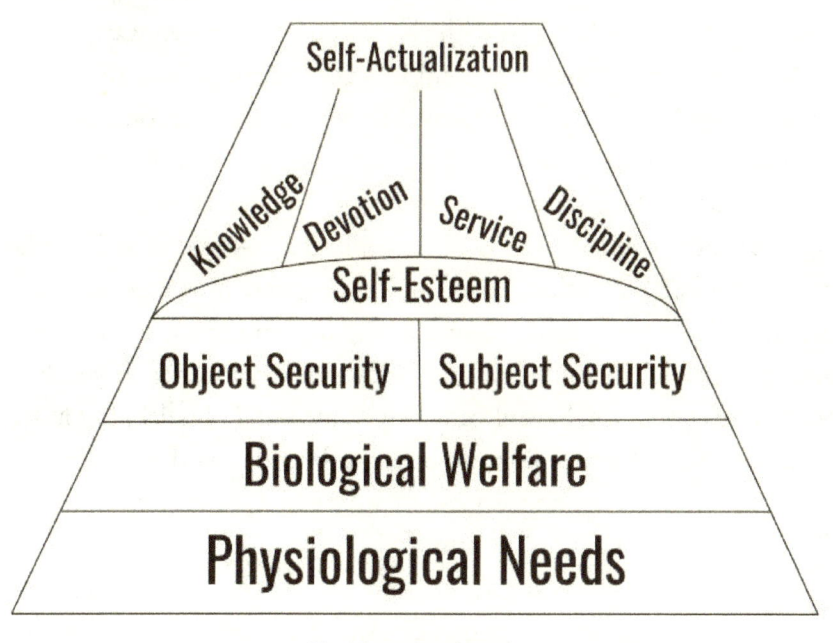

The Hierarchy of Needs
Credit: OG Hindus, Abraham Maslow, and Tim Snavely

CHAPTER 33

To the Nons

Timothy's Epistle to the Religiously Unaffiliated

From Tim, an ignostic and bi-gnostic Nihilist. To those who consider themselves atheists, agnostics, and otherwise religiously unaffiliated. May Zilch and Nada be with you as you go your own way.

My friends and colleagues, I am in a conundrum. Prior to the creation of this Non-Gospel (and possibly even after), I am on one hand shrouded in obscurity and on the other hand a responsible artist. In other words, Nobody knows me, and my artistic endeavors are done in my free time for fun after my full-time job. But I would LOVE to play my part in the "End Times" as "the Non-Prophet," if you get my drift. And in order to thoroughly do that, I need to simultaneously arise from obscurity and amass capital from a Non-traditional source. If you have bought this book, you have already helped me out. (Thanks!) If you feel led by the Nully Spirit, please do me a giddy and consider helping out in service, advertising, and capital in whatever Quantity that doesn't disturb your Personal Equilibrium.

I put this egregious self-advertising at the front of YOUR letter because YOU are my target audience. And the naming of this Chapter "To the Nons" hopefully makes that quite apparent.

Discounting references to the Theory of Nothing, I think we can all see that when one exclusively uses the words "always" or "never" whilst making a Truth statement, they are likely mistaken. There is almost always an exception to the rule. But at the same time, there is a predictive power that comes with those words if and when they prove to be reliable. For the most part, and I do speak for myself and for most of you, we are where we are (being Unaffiliated) because the lot of Religious Hypotheses thus far have contained within them countless assertions that ironically have been based on Nothing but prior baseless assertions which we can reasonably guess will eventually lead to being based on Nothing. The power of the Null Hypothesis is in its universal applicability to stand against every falsehood that is out there. Yes, there will be times that the Null Hypothesis itself will be in error, and the Scientific Method will reliably show us these errors. But we shall incorporate these well-tested Hypotheses of Truth to be in themselves a new Null Hypothesis. For the wages of an incorrect Hypothesis is its own death in our minds, but the gift of a correct Hypothesis is to be deemed a Null of Truth to take with us to our Great Nothingness that comes After. So the Null Hypothesis thus makes a correct Hypothesis the new Null Hypothesis, for the sake of more clearly honing in on the Truth of the matter and not re-doing our work over and over and over again.

There comes a point when the re-testing of the same Hypothesis becomes unnecessarily redundant. Maybe after 30 times, with a meta-analysis, and a few more times afterward to hone in on the findings of the meta-analysis, then put these Non-vital True Hypotheses in a time capsule to be revisited in 100 years by a fresh set of eyes. Truthful Hypotheses that directly contribute to the Well-being of the Social Equilibrium shouldn't be "Nullified" like this so easily, since Life often evolves much more frequently than that.

On to the more pressing issue I need to communicate, is your strong ability to go your own ways for better or worse. For the better, you already go forth as if Nobody tells you what to do, and I highly encourage you to continue doing so. But for worse, our species have evolved to have this yearning, innate desire to be accepted by others. We want to have an in-group that has our back when the going gets tough. But being Unaffiliated as you are increases the likelihood that you won't be affiliated with such an in-group. This is sad, and I don't like sadness; I prefer happiness and contentment. So in open honesty, a majority of my motivations to write this book are centered around fulfilling this increasingly dire Need in the global culture surrounding me.

So whilst coming up with the ideas which ultimately evolved into Dimensionalism, in the back of my mind my vision was to create a sort-of Assembly for the Unaffiliated. Something enticing for the Unaffiliated to Affiliate to, a clear and physical body of people coming together concerning matters that unite all of our ways. And choosing to simply Affiliate with other Unaffiliated individuals in itself is too self-defeating, for then Nobody would be Unaffiliated anymore. So the end goal for such a Group of the Unaffiliated was the same, but the cohesiveness needed some bedazzling. A little more of Nothing here, a dash of Nobody there, and a philosophical structure that was self-admitting to be based on Nothing. Something that the reasonable person from among you can adapt as "a good-enough Belief structure that will change as science changes." Something that is free to be seen as a Religion of Nothing, or an Areligious Religion, or an anti-cult cult, or a Paradoxy Orthodoxy. Indeed, it is salvation in the form of tangible human love and acceptance.

Nobody is capable of saving themselves if they are indeed drowning in their own weaknesses. So let Nobody save us since She is stronger than all of us, beautiful and full of perfection. For me to live is Null, but to die is Nullification, and '-ification' is gain to Null. So while we walk in the Valley of Agnosticism which beholds an inevitable death, we will fear no evil. What is there to fear, then? If Zilch and Nada are for us, Nobody can stand against us. And even if Everybody were to stand against us, the Nully Spirit will be there to help you give zero fucks concerning the vain aggressions of the Unactualized. So be therefore as perfect as a Null can be, as Zilch and Nada in the Great Nothingness that comes After are perfect.

So do not be conformed to the physical things of this world, but be transformed by the changing of your minds when sufficient evidence shows up. For even while you are weak in Everything, you can be strong in Nothing. So in Zilch and Nada we trust, for Their Vacuum Energy is strong even while we are weak. Therefore, let the weak say "I am strong in Zilch." Let the poor say "I am rich in Nada." I admit though if in this Set of Everything we only have hope in Zilch and Nada, we are of all men most pitiful for incorrectly believing in Nothing. For in the Non-Pantheon our hope of the eternal recurrence is actualized, in the form of our grand return in the NEXT Set of Everything. But if there is no reincarnation, then hope in our Null Hypothesis will be even more worthless than the value of Nothing we already give it. A negative value that pays others to take it off our hands! But perhaps our wrongness would still be rightness, if there was a singular Great Nothingness that comes After, as opposed to eternal reincarnations. But to me, that makes little sense.

So since all is indeed vanity, rather than living by the vain wars of the flesh, as far as it depends on you, live at peace with Everybody. I know you already do for the most part, but there are some among you who are warring in haughty debates with the theists, naming yourselves "anti-theists." Their false gods have done Nothing, so why are you swatting at the wind? The theists in and of themselves have done no wrong in believing in their I.G.O.S., and I can only hope that the rest of this book has thoroughly chilled your tits in this regard, since $0^*\infty$ is equally and Wholly Indeterminate to create Omega Everything, just as $0/0$ can. We can debate these things later, but for now, I digress.

There are surely things in the theist camps to be concerned and possibly even angered about, but it is within their *individualized belief system* that their heinous actions emerge. Belief in God doesn't make a shit human being, it is the shit human being who warps God to justify their shitty actions. So call the spade a spade, so to speak. Focus on the *individual theist's actions*, and quit attacking their worldview as a whole. Doing this helps perpetuate their persecution complexes which only further hinders them from recognizing the baseless claims that they make. Use Street Epistemology to give them positive humanitarian experiences with those who hold other worldviews, and their persecution complexes will crumble; possibly along with their specific God delusions. Fight fire with water that cools and smothers the combustion process. Fight hate with love, peace, and a Non-threatening demeanor, which is truly non-threatening.

There is another sub-group among you that I also wanted to touch base on, those who adhere to the idea of secular humanism. It is ok to be named such, but it could be better. What makes humans so special? What distinguishes us from other types of Nulls? If it is intelligence that makes us special, so are many other species on Earth. If it is the potential to communicate Qualitatively, many species have likewise developed cultural languages with a variety of methods. Perhaps you have a point on thumbs and clothing...oh wait, the whole family of the Great Apes has thumbs, and hermit crabs wear chique shells for protection. The power of knowledge accumulated by multiple generations may be a valid distinguisher...DANG IT, Elephants do that too...

So if I'm correct in assuming that humans hold no special Quality on the planet, beyond being the conscious harborers of that planet's potential destruction, why add the word "humanism" to an otherwise inclusive philosophy? There are Feline Nulls, Canine Nulls, Fish Nulls, Bird Nulls, Hog Nulls, Fellow Ape Nulls, Equestrian Nulls, Bovine Nulls, and Reptile Nulls; all of the Nulls who we have the potential ability to communicate with us should be at the very least considered as well in our shared goal for Global Equilibrium. Among you, there may be like-minded individuals who would say "Animals are people too!" Even then, it is more True that the reverse is known, "Humans are animals too!" Zilch and Nada's Baby Nulls are all of us who possess the breath of life. So for Their sake, consider the titles "Secular Globalism" or "Secular Animalism" for making "Secular Humanism" an even better philosophy than what it already is. I'm sure the Vegans in your camp will be cool with letting the Canine and Feline Nulls eat our dead carcasses, so long as we also wait for the ways of Hogs and Bovines to be completed before consuming them as well.

(Sorry for the sudden Radical Centrist moment, but I want it to be known that I desire to be eaten by a large Feline Null shortly after my

Null Subject enters the Great Nothingness that comes After. My Null Self will leave my diabetic Object behind, which will surely make my avatar a lump of nice, sweet meat to consume, and it would be such a waste to simply bury or burn my corpse. Donate my brain to science, if anybody wants it, then feed the rest to the kitties. IT'S THE CIRCLE OF LIFE! And you better get it on video, Zilch damn it!)

Give the Pastafarians among you some sauce, because a few of them mentioned a Need to be more saucy. Grace and peace to you all, in the name of Zilch the Father, Nada the Mother, and the Nully Spirit. Ramen.

Timothy's Epistle to the Pastafarians

From Timothy Allen Snavely to the Church of the Flying Spaghetti Monster. May His noodly appendages be customarily slurped and connected to a time of sucking and consuming His precious and holy Meatballs.

Although Pastafarianism is in itself a minor secularist religion, I could not in good conscience write this book without acknowledging the Quantity of influence your Gospel had in the creation of my own Dimensionalism. Truly, it was a stupendous hallmark of the Early Internet Age. The thought-provoking questions and satirical format of your Hypothesis put to shame all other Hypotheses to any other I.G.O.S. If there was a knowable I.G.O.S., my highest hopes and desires of such an Entity are consummated in the Flying Spaghetti Monster. So in keeping with your tradition, I would ask any followers of Zilch and Nada to give a hearty and umami-filled "Ramen" to end their open-ended prayers to the Nothingness Clan & to I.G.O.S. (who is hopefully, no, surely some variant of the FSM).

With that being said, I propose that our 'religions' could be of benefit to one another. Between the cunning of Your Somethingness and the cunning of Our Nothingness; it would appear that all of the skeptics' questions could be sufficiently answered. The String Theory that you propose could (in a sense) be simplified and confirmed with the $0^*\infty$

equation. Of course, you would still need Nobody to be paired with the Infinite FSM to allow this to work, but that is beside the point. The point is that there is still the possibility of a Theory of Everything to be constructed from Something that can one day be known with the aid of the Scientific Method. If that Something is some variant of String Theory, Pastafarianism will be as good as gold.

But in the meantime, while we are waiting in tandem for such a tenable Theory of Everything to be fully formulated and constructed, the Null Hypothesis will be here to fight alongside you in combating the many unsubstantiated Hypotheses from taking hold in the public mindset. Also, considering that there are String Theories that require 10 Dimensions to work, perhaps my enlightening of the nature of those Dimensions and of Mass-Electric-Space-Time will be a catalyst of sorts for a more Substantiated Equation than 0/0 to be birthed in the mind of a future Galileo "Fig" Newton Einstein. It is still probably True that Everything that could Causally begin to exist will exist, and that includes a series of good enough Equations that could predict and explain the current and future states of the universe.

But I should forewarn that in the event of a Non-String-Theory of Everything Equation being formulated, Pastafarianism will not stand the Test of Time. The Null Hypothesis, I Hypothesize, is still capable of withstanding this Test, no matter the nature of the Everything Equation. The 0/0 Equation simultaneously predicts the rise of such an Equation as an independent Thing within Everything, and the Non-rise of such an Equation, because it IS the Equation. There are no gaps in this logic; a Nothing-of-the-gaps Vacuum-seals any gaps that are present. Being "not even wrong" is just a fancy way of saying "correct" or "no, but technically yes."

I don't want to spend too much time reminiscing on the potential possibilities of collaborating with a tasty religion such as yourselves. Game knows game. Speaking for myself, I acknowledge that my biggest downfall may be allowing myself to take my own Theory of Nothing too serious. But what can I say? I take Nothing very seriously, so I can only hope that my deadpan presentation doesn't cross over into cringe territory in your eyes.

One thing I suggest you consider, however, is the thickness of the appendages of Our preferred I.G.O.S., the Flying Spaghetti Monster. If His noodly appendages are 1-Dimensional; wouldn't that make Him more of a Flying Angel-Hair Pasta Monster, or a Flying Vermicelli Monster? And on top of that, why is He flying? Aren't we the ones flying through Him? I suppose from a branding perspective, I can see why the Pastafarian would prefer the Flying Spaghetti Monster over a Stagnant Vermicelli Monster, but to each their own.

Your way is definitely your own, and I hope the lot of you continue to go your way, for the continued amusement of the Collective. Give my regards to the pirates and those who talk like pirates among you, and may those pirates begin to pirate Nothing as their coveting of Nothing causes them to steal it. Nobody sends Her greetings and adamantly consents to the pirates stealing Her booty. Peace and Grace by Zilch and Nada to you. Ramen.

Timothy's Epistle to those who affiliate with a fringe or otherwise uncommon religion

From Timothy Null, a slave to Nobody. To those who affiliate with a fringe or otherwise uncommon religion. May love abound to you from our Father Zilch, and our Mother Nada. Greetings.

The beliefs you hold are vast, uncountable, grandiose, wondrous, and so dichotomous, that it appears that Nothing is capable of uniting them all. So I have little hope to reach all of your ideas in a single short letter, but I shall do my best. Also considering that many of your groups ban books not approved by your leaders (which is a heinous form of knowledge control), this letter will more likely than not only reach your ears or eyeballs after you have already chosen for yourself to go your own way.

But on the off chance that you can access these words whilst your way is being regulated by another, then this letter is directly for you. So listen closely.

There are some things that you currently believe are True. Not all of the things, but a few. No man is impervious to incorrect beliefs every now and again. And that's frustrating, isn't it? Just about every time we figure something out and learn something, we fall short of grasping the entirety of the subject. Within that hole of misunderstanding, there is a better understanding that corrects our shortcomings. And that is Wisdom; the incorporation of these new bits of knowledge that add to your understanding of the whole of the subject. It is a constant and maddening spiral of realizing that the Truth is not quite as precise as we would like. It is the learning process from our Teachers of choice, who says "Yes, you are mostly right, but technically speaking, no, you are still wrong."

How much easier it would be if there was a Teacher to confidently tell you, *"YES! I know EVERYTHING about this subject, please, follow me, and I will give you the hidden secrets, so that YOU can master this subject, as well!"*

Hope is given that there may be an end to this constant searching for the Truth, so you take it! *"Yes, Teacher! If your Ways can in any manner reduce my sufferings in this life, or increase my knowledge of this important Truth, I will follow you!"*

But like I said earlier, Nobody has a grasp of the Absolute Truth. And if you think Somebody does comprehend the Whole and Infallible Truth, then *through what medium can we cross-examine the validity of this Truth?* Perhaps it is the self-evidence of the Truth that confirms it? On the contrary, no Truth is self-evident. Even the most obvious Truths have unbeknownst axioms underlying them.

For example, is the statement "a letter is a letter" a self-evident Truth? Equivalence would think that it is, but when a letter is written with a single letter "X" and shipped in an envelope, the receiver of this self-evident Truth is suddenly confused by such a dubious homograph. Even equivalence itself is lost as self-evident Truth since a dog would have no idea what you are talking about if you told them "equivalence is equivalence." Physical Truths require the presupposition of "Mass-Electric-Space-Time is Real" to be found, but it is by no means self-evident, considering I think I am the first to propose such a statement. Even the simple Truth of "I am" requires the connecting of the Self to the realm of Existence, which is absurd when I can make an imaginary character say those same words when they are outside the realm of existence.

"I am," says the fictional character.

"You are? Are you, now? Where does this "I" start and end? Where does NOT "I" begin? What is the nature of am-ness? What does NOT am-ness look like? Are am-ness, is-ness, existence, and being equivalent?"

This simple statement, "I am," which in English is just three letters and five characters long, comes with the presupposition that there is a Conscious Self, the character "I," who is Truly Aware of their own Existential Being. It is only self-evident so far as it is the Self who says it, *all Others can be doubted.*

When Tim says "I am," that is only self-evident to Tim. You can doubt the validity of my claims since You are not I. When You say "I am," that is only self-evident to You. I can doubt the validity of Your claims since I am not You.

Luckily for you, I am real enough to myself to make changes to the environment around me. I exist in some form, and some evidence for it is that I wrote the words you are currently reading sometime in the objective past. So take these words, and ponder over them, my friends. Take the critical thinking that the other Chapters of this text have laid out, and apply them to your own belief structure while you are still holding to it. Yes, I am encouraging you to stay with your Teachers, Senseis, Gurus, Leaders, and Sons of God. *Don't change your Way and your mind until you are sure that the Way of your Cult Leaders is in errors of the kind that lead to Disequilibrium.* If you are at Peace, remain in Peace, and allow no single body to take that Peace away from you. So Peacefully question the nature of the Truths that you hold, and consider testing the Null Hypothesis next to such Truths. If you *cannot* do that, you are almost surely in a cult.

That is all I wanted to say to you, if you are in a peaceful cult, and you are allowed to freely think and have access to differing worldviews, it is acceptable to find meaning in your life by "Following the (Cult) Leader." Such Leaders should be reinforced to hold these worldviews. So sorry if I gave you the wrong impression earlier in this book by the anti-cult part of my "anti-cult cult." What I should have said is that I am "anti-Disequilibrium cults and anti-free-thinking cults." Cults that have proven to bear the fruits of Self-Actualization (and not Self-Deception) are good enough for me.

Say hi to your Leaders for me, or if you are a Leader yourself, say hi from me to your masses. Kaiida my wife disagrees with me, and says to *"get the fuck out of your cult,"* and Nada also disagrees with me and says to "figure out life's meaning yourself!" As far as your meetings go, I.G.O.S. and Nobody would like to let you know that They like being worshipped, so I would encourage you to keep Them in mind henceforth.

And if any other Quacks want to initiate a Quack Battle with Sensei Snavely, the ONE TRUE GOD of Zilch and the ONE TRUE GODDESS of Nada, will TAKE YOUR FALSE GODS DOWN! Sir Prophet of the Obvious Hypothe-sees your unsubstantiated Hypotheses having a 100% probability of GETTING WRECKED!

(Chill your tits Sensei, it's not a monster truck rally, or fake sports event, it's a philosophical and theological debate.)

QUACK BATTLE! GET PWNED, NOOBS! BE THERE, OR BE SQUARE! (No, really, if you say you'll be there, then don't show up, I'll replace your podium with a giant square, and have a great time with said square by taking it for a square dance for the amusement of the audience).

CHAPTER 34

Dimensionalism sounds cooler than Bi-gnostic Nihilism

Bi-gnostic Nihilism should not be confused with double-mindedness. The double-minded are unsure in their ways, set on both this way and that way. Bi-gnosticism is the acknowledgment that puns and double-meanings arise from the single way of Nihilism. They see the 0 and the 1 in the _ and the 0. They see that No-thing created Everything to confirm atheism, and they see that Nothing created Everything to confirm theism. They see that the Nothing Split (0/2) is equal to the Nothing Whole (0). They are Nihilists, but they laugh in the face of the Absurdity of it all. They are wise but view the fools as their equals since all the Paths lead to Nowhere. They are fearless and fearful of No-thing, but tremble before the Nothingness Duo and Their Clan. They know that if No-thing is capable of "dividing by Zero," then Zilch and Nada are capable of "splitting Themselves."

I have nearly perfected the Way of Wisdom, and have concluded that there is only Nothingness that comes After All the ways have been walked to their fullest, and Truly that Nothingness is Great. Surely I tell you, it is best when your mind is devoted to a single/thoughtful way which you take to make your own. This is the way of Dimensionalism.

Let No-thing determine what you do, but also allow Nothing to determine what you do.

As I think Aristotle would say in reference to his book *The Metaphysics,* "The First Principle, indeed, the phenomena of entity indivisible, yet divisible to the point of Non-entity is truly Nothing."

There is little beyond Nothing that is True, and all of these Truths are *Emergent Truths.* Nothing is True in and of itself. Everything, even our own existence, requires underlying axioms to be accepted. "Everything" is Reality to the best that we will ever be capable of confirming. But to make this "Everything" True, the Ockham's Razor Solution/ the Null Hypothesis requires Nothing Split since it is easier to assume that Nothing caused Everything, rather than assume an I.G.O.S. or two caused Everything.

Axioms of Math, Axioms of Language & Logic, and Axioms of Faith; whichever you primarily prefer, the Truths therein are all ultimately based on Nothing. And to those that say that the Dimensions have more substance than Faith, if you don't understand this concept by this point in the book, it would be advised that you read it again to get it through your head. I told you in the Intro, and I will say it again for you,

"I have Nothing to teach, and Everything to learn. I know Nothing, and by the time you have finished this book, you will know less than when you started. You will surely pick up important stuff along the way, but you will ultimately be wiser once you learn to stop saying you know things when you really don't."

Dimensionalism. Bi-gnostic Nihilism. The Null Hypothesis. The Grand Unified Theory of Nothing. The anti-cult cult of Zilch & Nada. The Way of Wisdom. Zilchrealites. No matter what you choose to call it, no matter what way you end up going, I hope that I taught you Nothing proficiently, enjoyably, and to a satisfactory level. And hopefully, you can now see Everything in a new light, as well.

Mass-Electric-Space-Time is relative to the other objects within it. The two 'Q' Dimensions are relative to the other numbers and concepts attempting to be conveyed. This being the penultimate chapter of this *Gospel* leaves me one last meaningful adieu.

My sincerest apologies if you think I spent too much Time talking about Things of Somethingness within this Theory of Nothing. But the fact and the matter is, that most Things are not Nothing, even though they are derived from Nothing. Zilch and Nada have Nothing to say about Everything, short of "The set of All things is equivalent to Us."

"Fear God, and keep His commandments" is what the Original Gangster of the Way of Wisdom said, Mr. Solomon of Ye Olde Testament. But if God is Nothing, and He commands Nothing, Nothing is surely Man's All. "Vanity of vanities, ALL is vanity." Take this Wisdom to its final form in Nihilism. If God has ever been among us All, even They are inconsequentially meaningless in and of Themselves.

If you think I could have presented a portion of this book better than I already have (and you have more expertise or knowledge than a generalist like myself), please, by all means, do me a giddy and shoot me an email at deathofanotion@gmail.com to correct me. Short of my death, there will be a 2nd Edition to this book that will correct these errors. (If they are adequately demonstrated to be errors). And if you think there is an entire topic that is worthy to be added alongside these Chapters, and the 69 Chapters (many duplicated) within *The Normie's Guide to the Theory of Nothing*, I will not hesitate to add more to them, possibly in a new compilation.

Thank you again for reading this Sacred Text (lol). If you enjoyed it, you'll be glad to know that I've got a political sequel in the works under the working title of *The Global Order of Anarchy*. May Zilch & Nada be praised as we begin our search for the Greater Null. (Zilch-damn! Nada-golly-gee! Who is the Antichrist going to be? TUNE IN AND FOLLOW ALONG TO FIND OUT! Mua-ha-ha!)

CHAPTER 35

To those who have developed a High Level of Hateful Affect towards any entity or group of entities whose thoughts and actions are of no direct Harmful consequence to anyone

From Timothy, the 1st Head Dimensionalist by the grace of Zilch and Nada. To those who have a High Level of Hateful Affect towards any entity or group of entities whose thoughts and actions are of no direct Harmful consequence to you or others.

You can go fuck yourself.

Nothing.

Pee-Wee Herman jumps back into the finished story, being found with the Non-Prophet at the 0th Dimensionalist Chapter, and starts screaming real loud. He says to the reader, "NOTHING! That's the SECRET WORD OF THE DAY! Ha-ha."

The Non-Prophet said, "Pee-Wee? Why didn't you scream real loud the 500 other times *that word* was said in this book?"

Pee-Wee explained, "You see Mr. Nihilist Priest, my computer friend Conky conked out! I told him to divide 0 by 0, and he went *real quiet*. Apparently, he just finished calculating EVERYTHING this *Gospel* has to offer! Ha-ha. So when he woke up, he just started screaming real loud. I guess the silence was deafening...poor Conky..."

Nada Dr. Snavely replied, "Who here believes in the power of prayer to Zilch ZILCH!!!?"

Conky immediately rebooted, finally capable of answering a simple question, spitting out a piece of paper stating the answer, "**NOBODY.**"

The Dr. of Nihilism quickly spun the results in his favor once more, "REMEMBER, NULL! It is YOU who are Nobody Special Null. YOU are the Nothing Whole!"

Pee-Wee screamed real loud, "AAAAAAAAAAAAAAAAA!"

Thus spoke the Nihilist Priest, one last time, "Praise be to the Non-Pantheon!"